Dissolving Classroom

Junji Ito

Table of Contents

Dissolving Classroom ·············· 003

Dissolving Beauty ··············· 043

Dissolving Apartment ··············· 059

Chizumi in Love ··············· 089

Interview with the Devil ············ 121

The Return ··············· 163

Children of the Earth ············· 169

Afterword ··············· 177

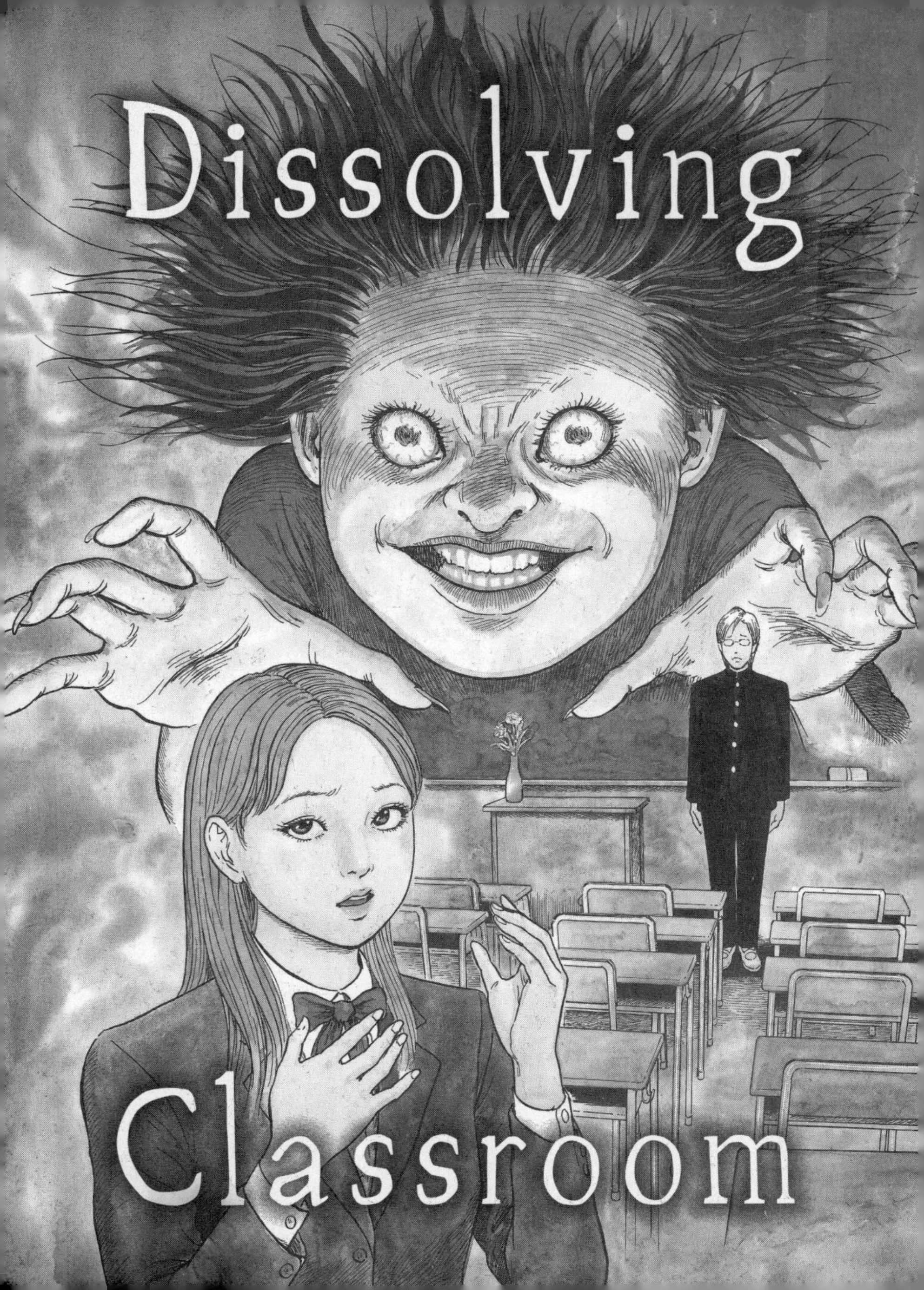
Dissolving
Classroom

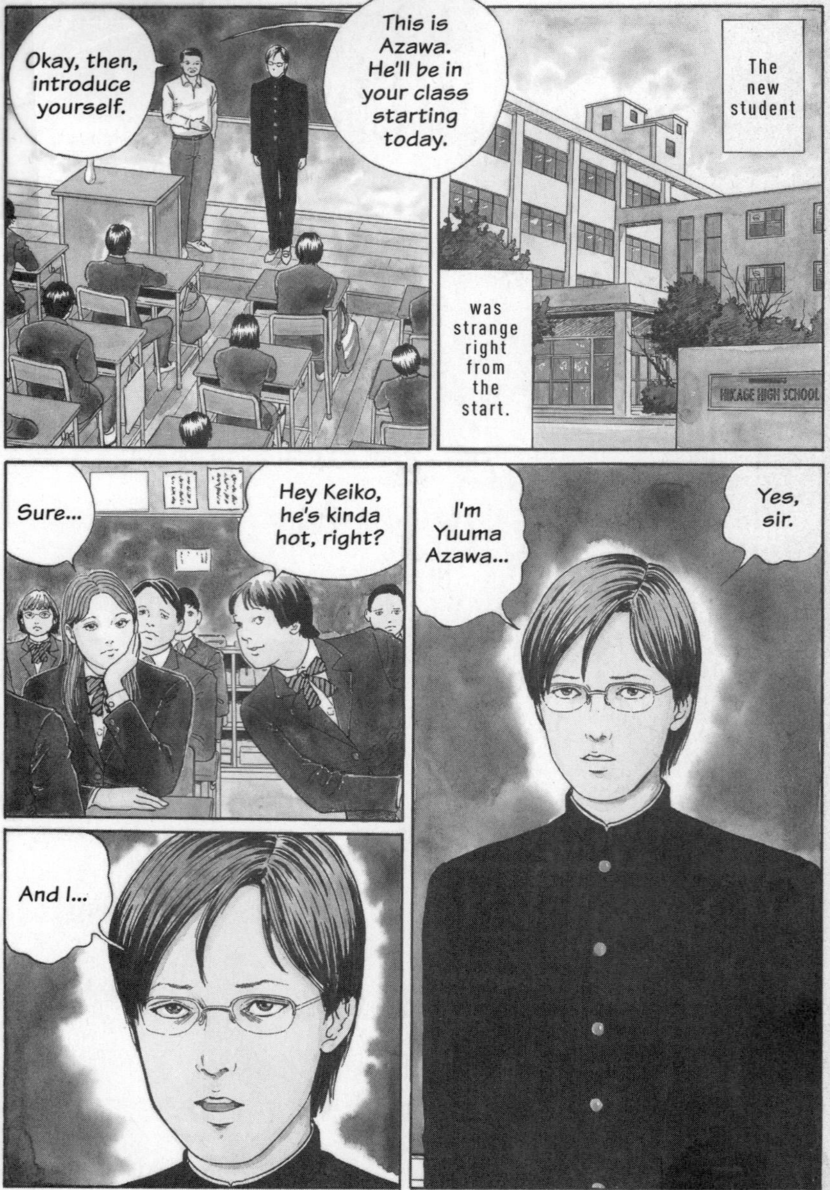
The new student
was strange right from the start.
HIKAGE HIGH SCHOOL
This is Azawa. He'll be in your class starting today.
Okay, then, introduce yourself.
Yes, sir.
I'm Yuuma Azawa...
Hey Keiko, he's kinda hot, right?
Sure...
And I...

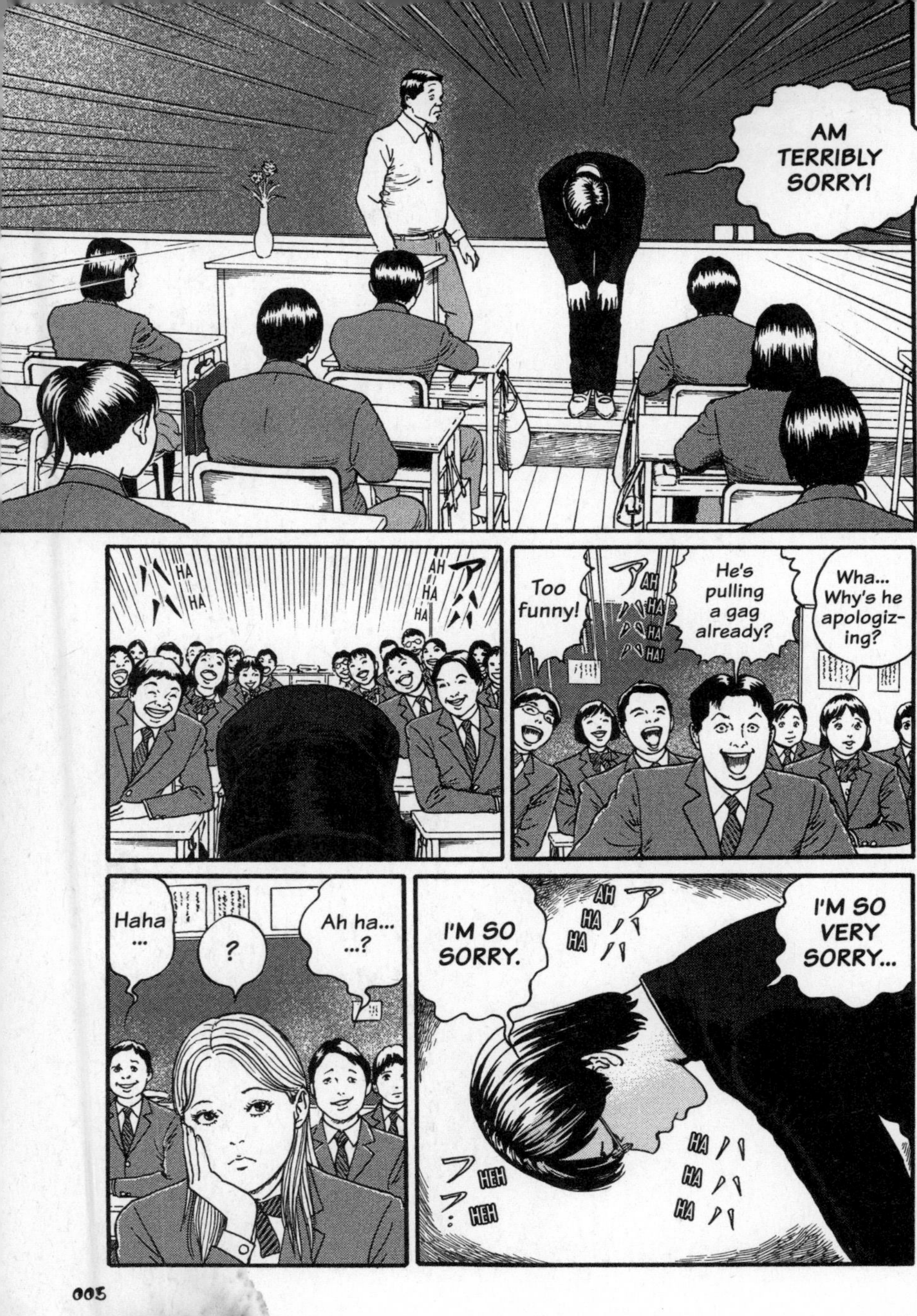
AM TERRIBLY SORRY!
Wha... Why's he apologizing?
He's pulling a gag already?
AH HA HA HA HA!
Too funny!
AH HA HA
HA HA
I'M SO VERY SORRY...
AH HA HA
I'M SO SORRY.
HA HA HA
HEH HEH
Ah ha... ...?
?
Haha ...

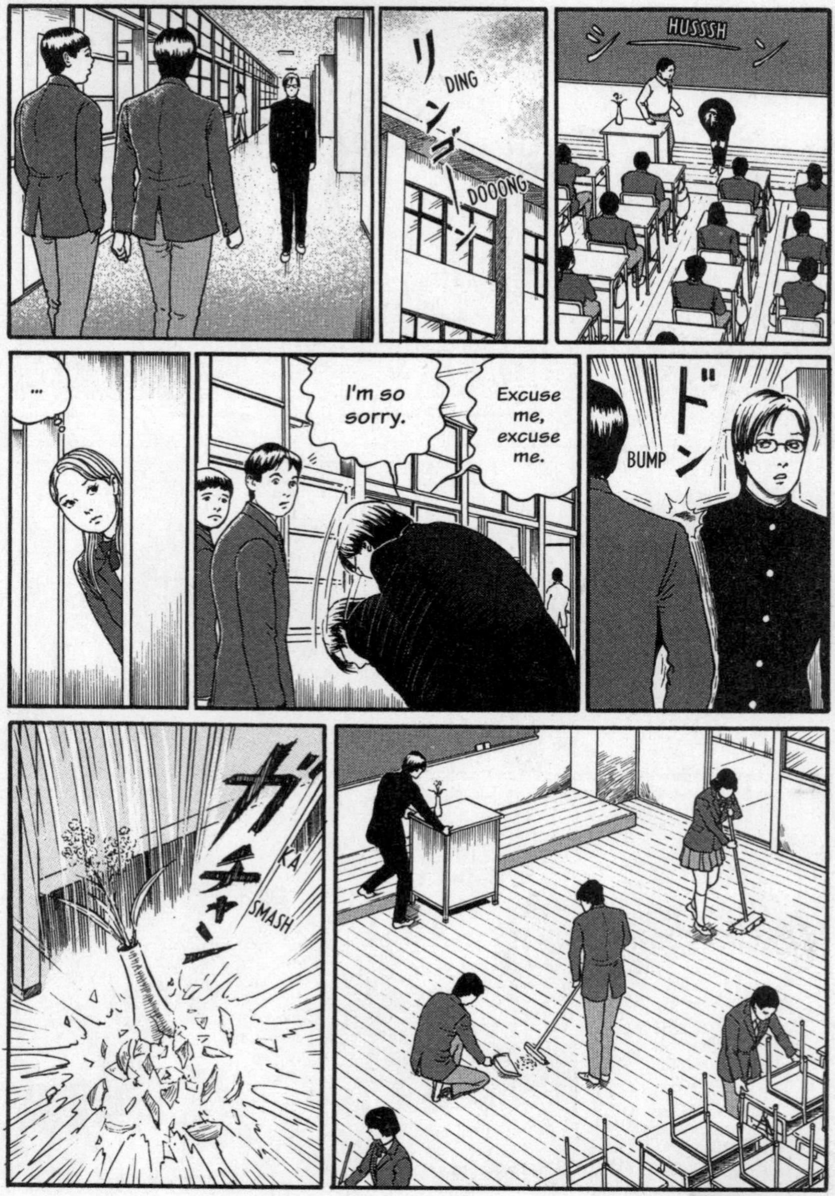
シーン
HUSSSH
リンゴーン
DING
DOOONG
ドン
BUMP
Excuse me, excuse me.
I'm so sorry.
...
ガチャーン
KA
SMASH

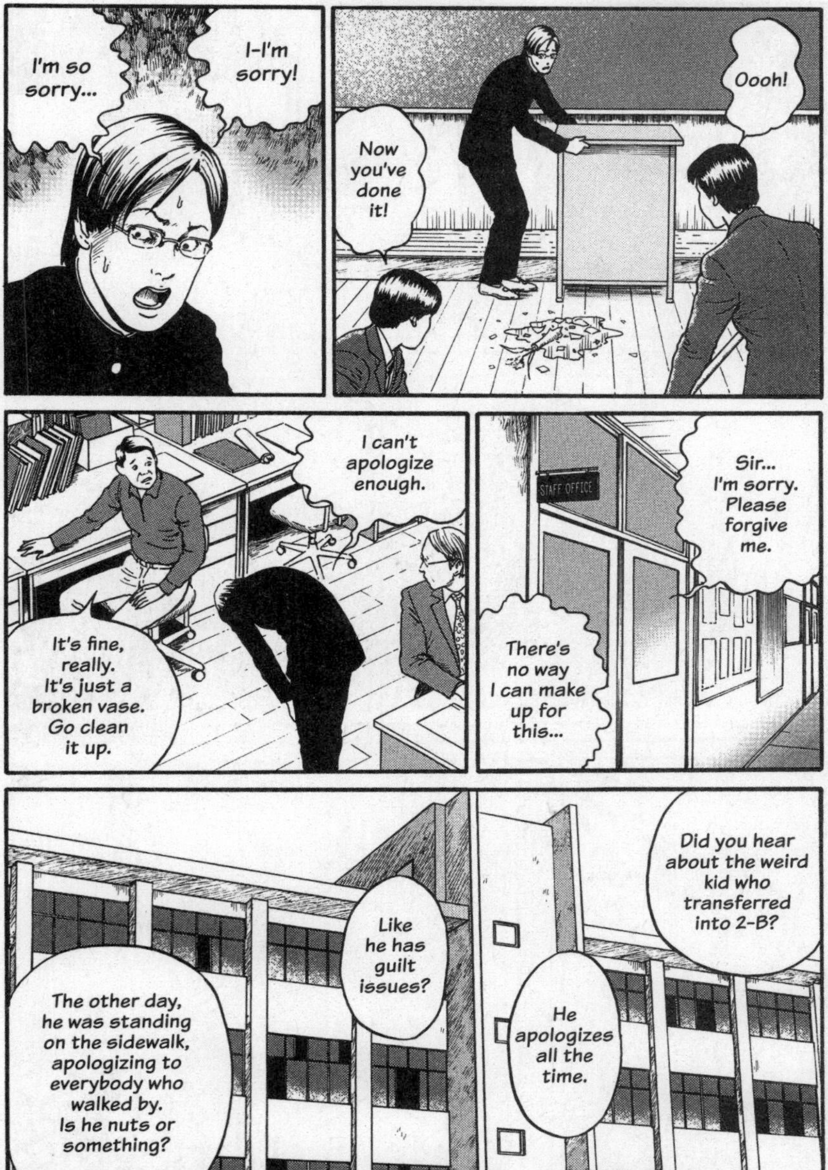
Oooh!
Now you've done it!
I-I'm sorry!
I'm so sorry...
Sir... I'm sorry. Please forgive me.
STAFF OFFICE
There's no way I can make up for this...
I can't apologize enough.
It's fine, really. It's just a broken vase. Go clean it up.
Did you hear about the weird kid who transferred into 2-B?
Like he has guilt issues?
He apologizes all the time.
The other day, he was standing on the sidewalk, apologizing to everybody who walked by. Is he nuts or something?

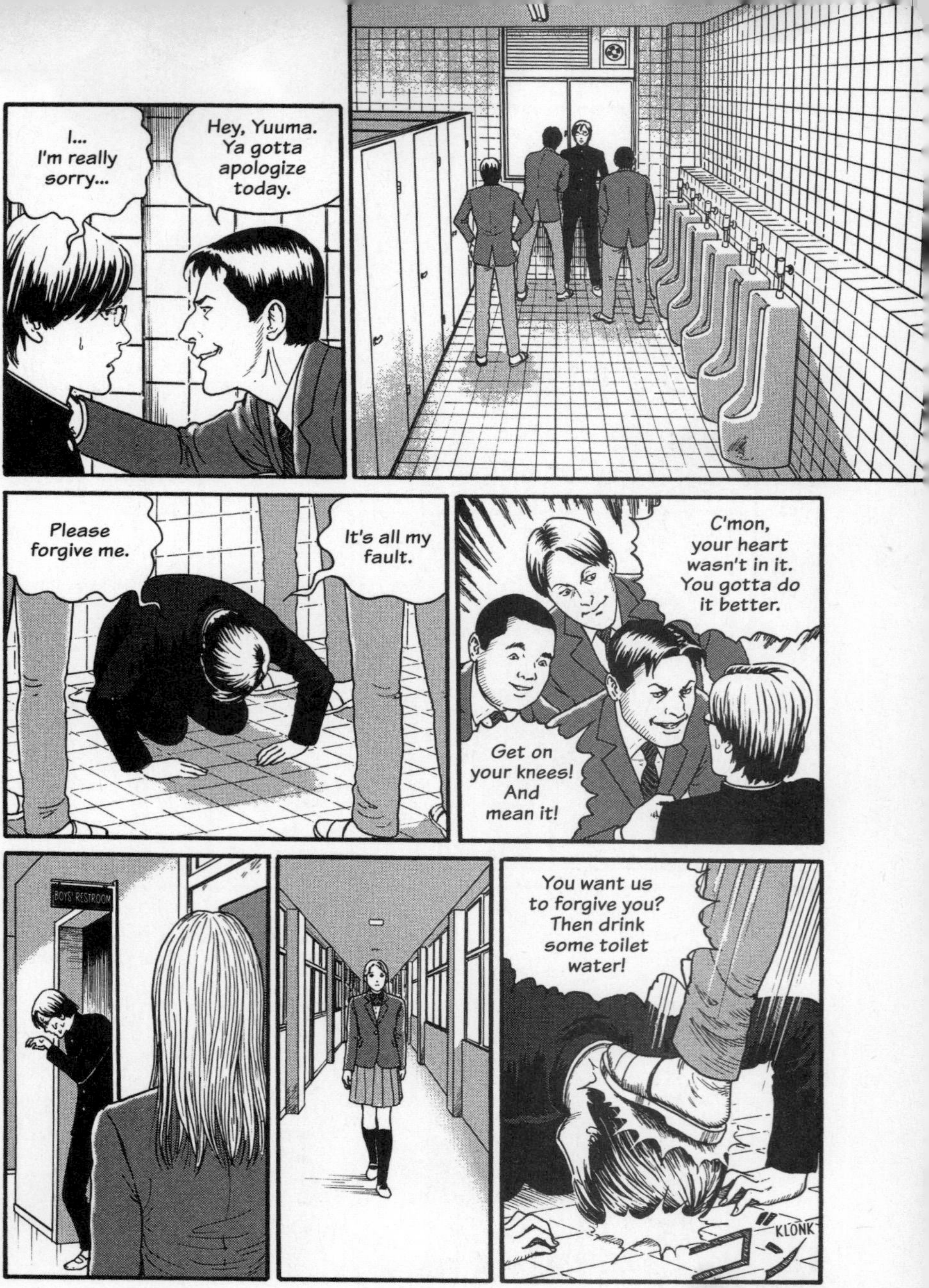
Hey, Yuuma. Ya gotta apologize today.
I... I'm really sorry...
C'mon, your heart wasn't in it. You gotta do it better.
Get on your knees! And mean it!
It's all my fault.
Please forgive me.
You want us to forgive you? Then drink some toilet water!
KLONK
BOYS' RESTROOM

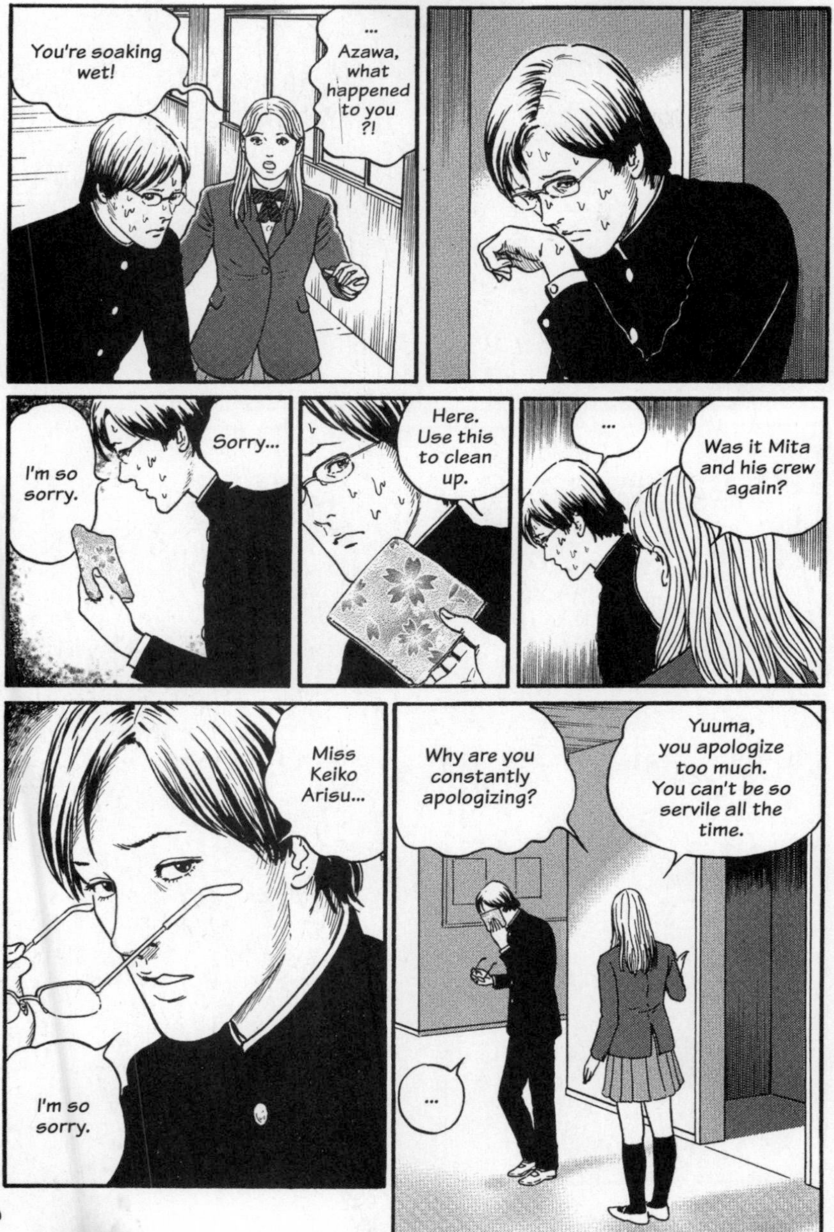

... Azawa, what happened to you ?!
You're soaking wet!
Was it Mita and his crew again?
...
Here. Use this to clean up.
Sorry...
I'm so sorry.
Yuuma, you apologize too much. You can't be so servile all the time.
Why are you constantly apologizing?
...
Miss Keiko Arisu...
I'm so sorry.

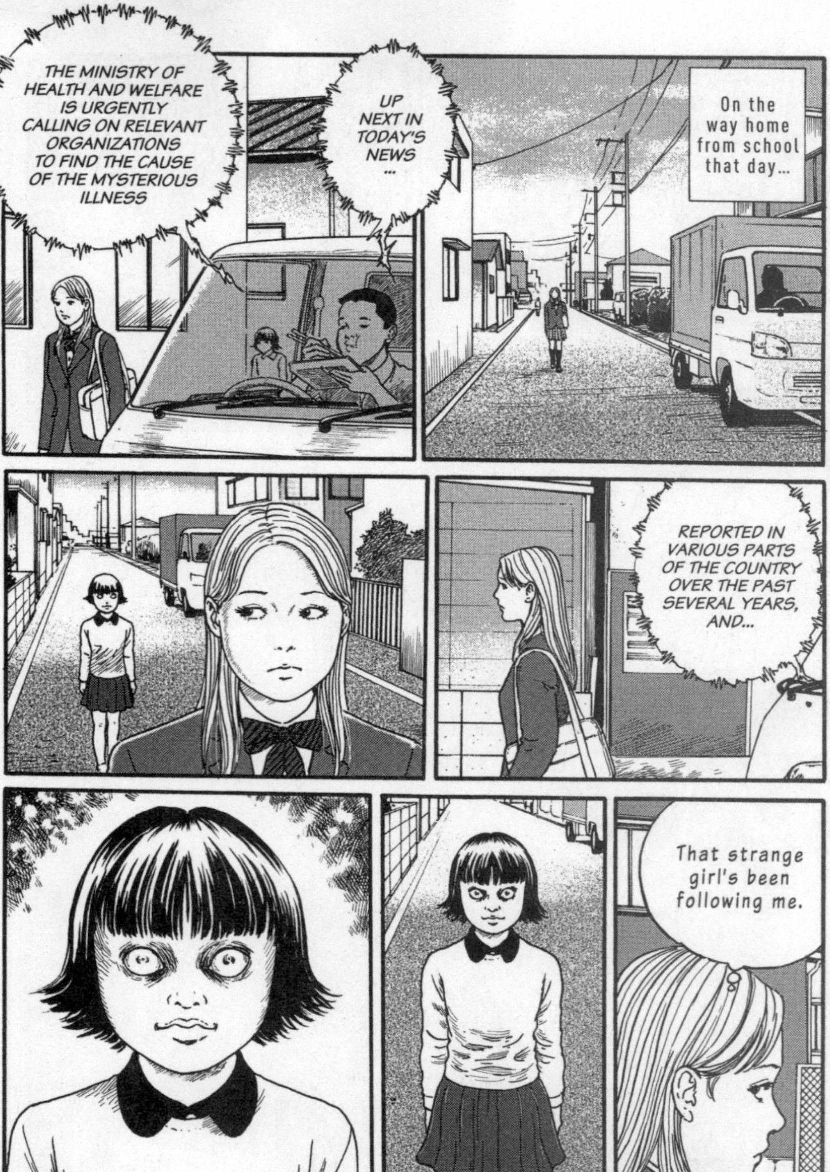
On the way home from school that day...
UP NEXT IN TODAY'S NEWS ...
THE MINISTRY OF HEALTH AND WELFARE IS URGENTLY CALLING ON RELEVANT ORGANIZATIONS TO FIND THE CAUSE OF THE MYSTERIOUS ILLNESS
REPORTED IN VARIOUS PARTS OF THE COUNTRY OVER THE PAST SEVERAL YEARS, AND...
That strange girl's been following me.

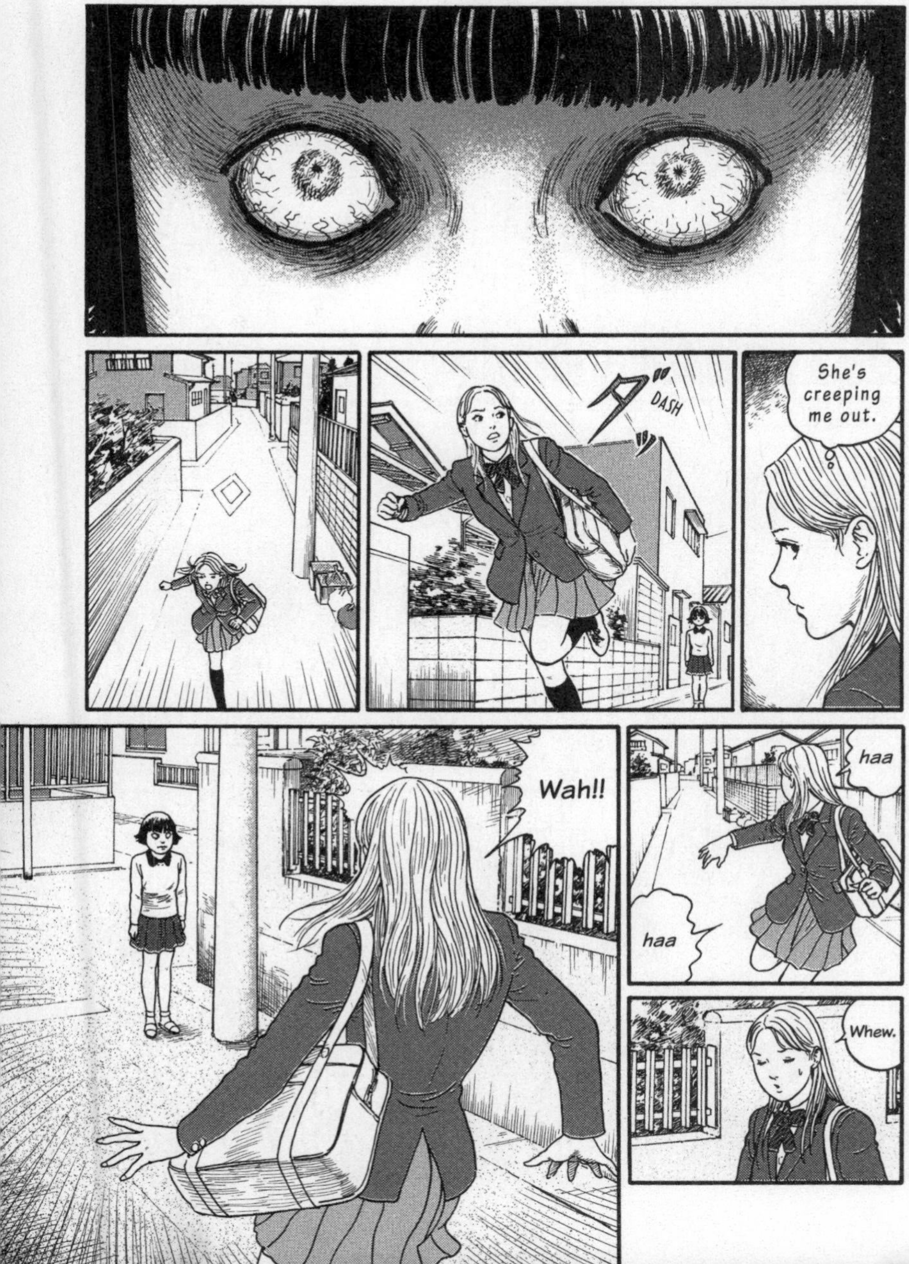
She's creeping me out.
DASH
haa
haa
Whew.
Wah!!

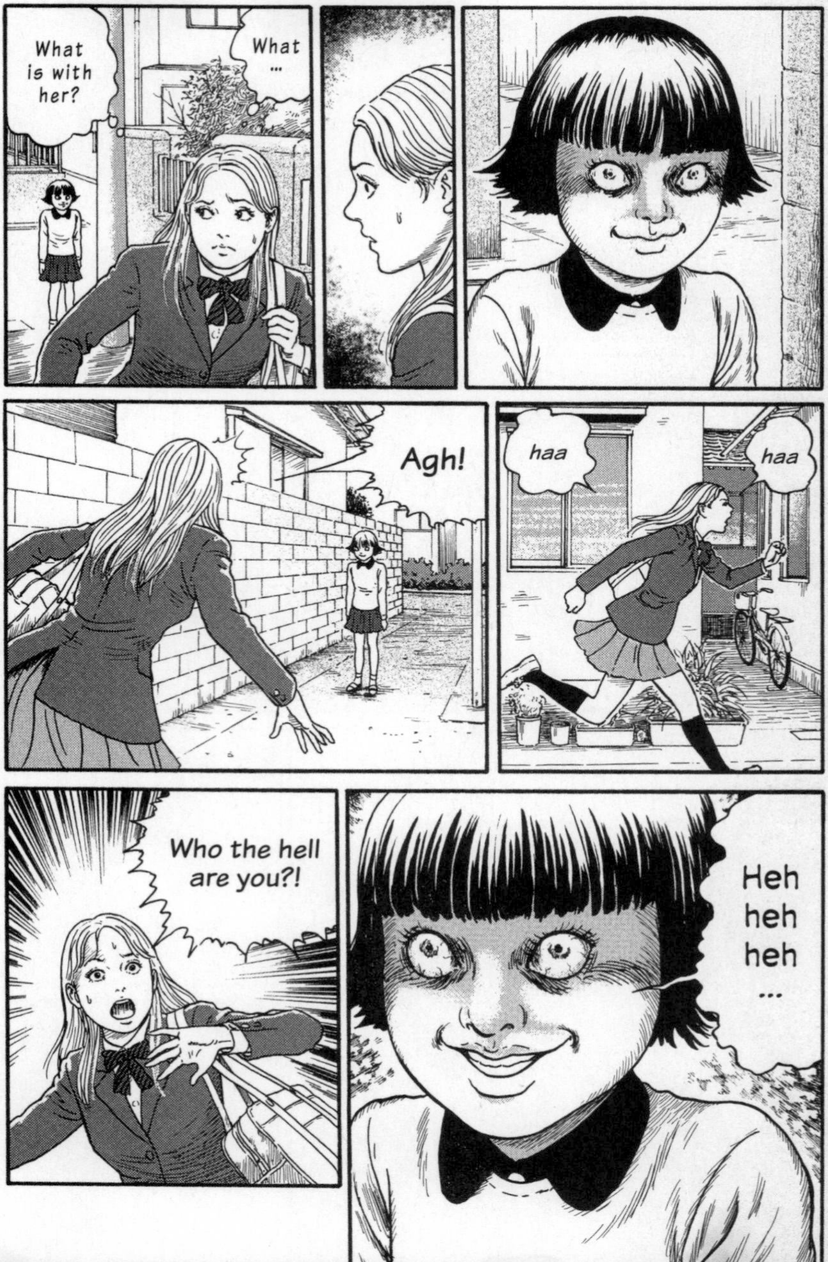
What ...
What is with her?
haa
haa
Agh!
Heh heh heh ...
Who the hell are you?!

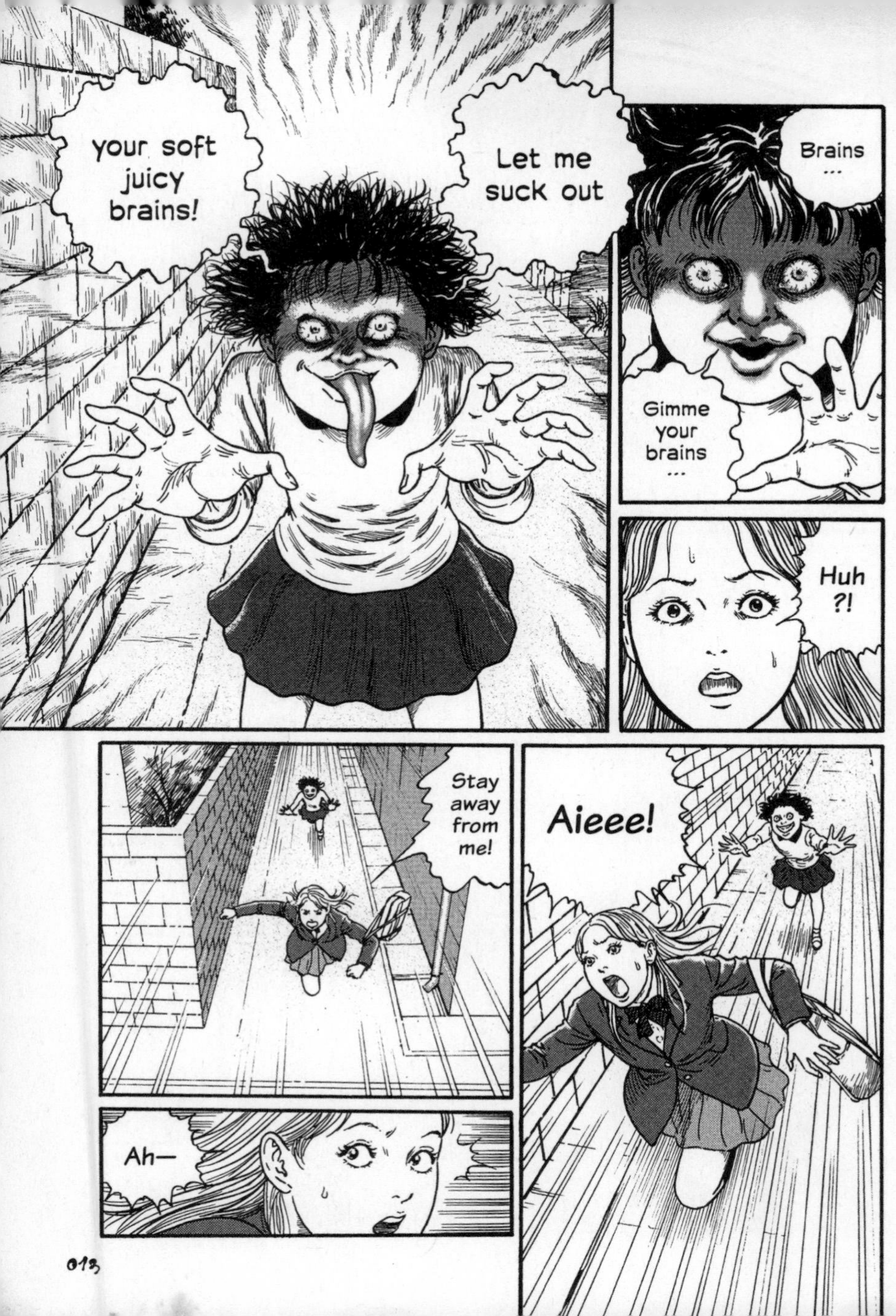
Brains ...
Gimme your brains ...
Huh ?!
Let me suck out
your soft juicy brains!
Aieee!
Stay away from me!
Ah—

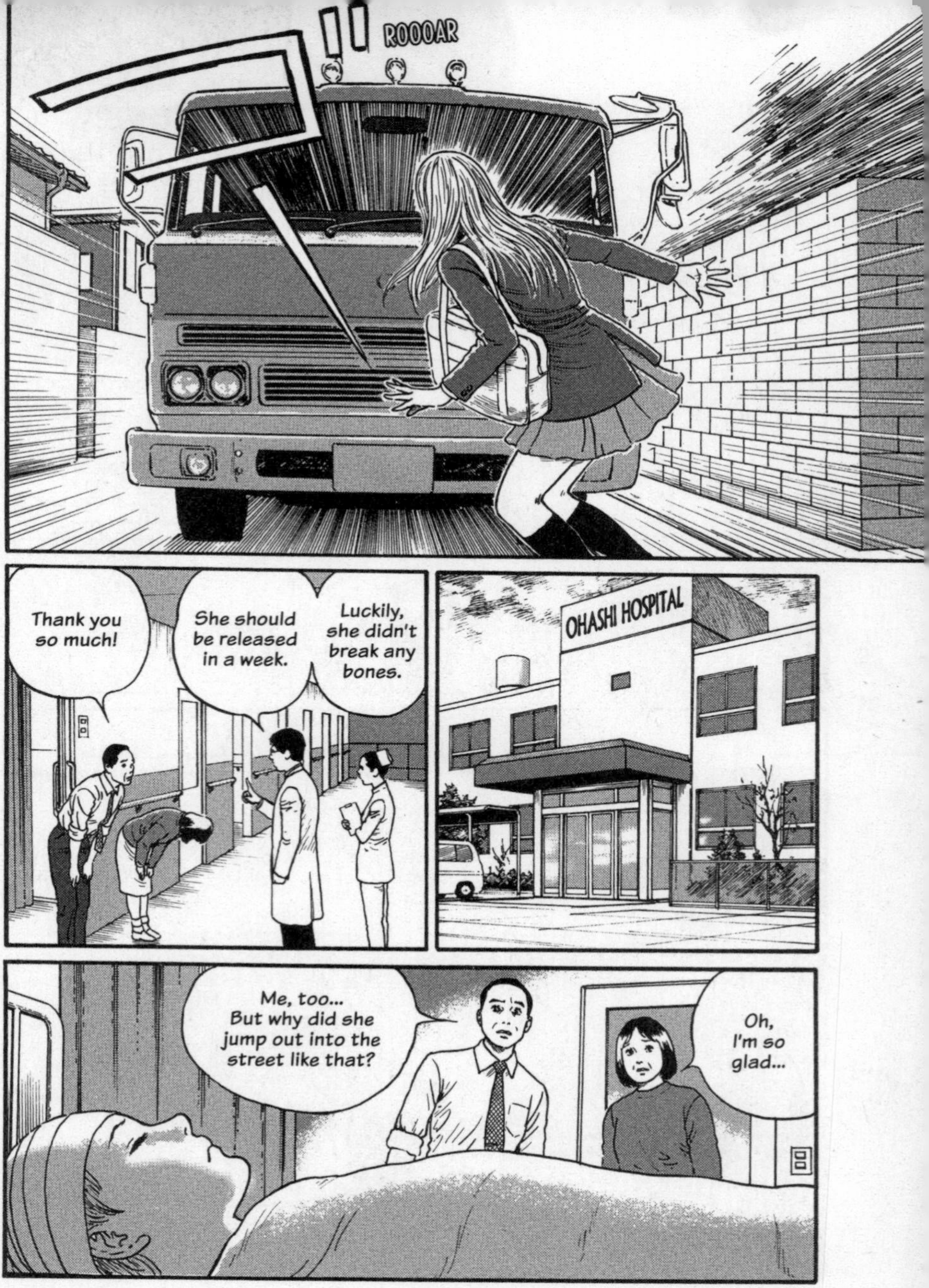
ROOOAR
OHASHI HOSPITAL
Luckily, she didn't break any bones.
She should be released in a week.
Thank you so much!
Oh, I'm so glad...
Me, too... But why did she jump out into the street like that?

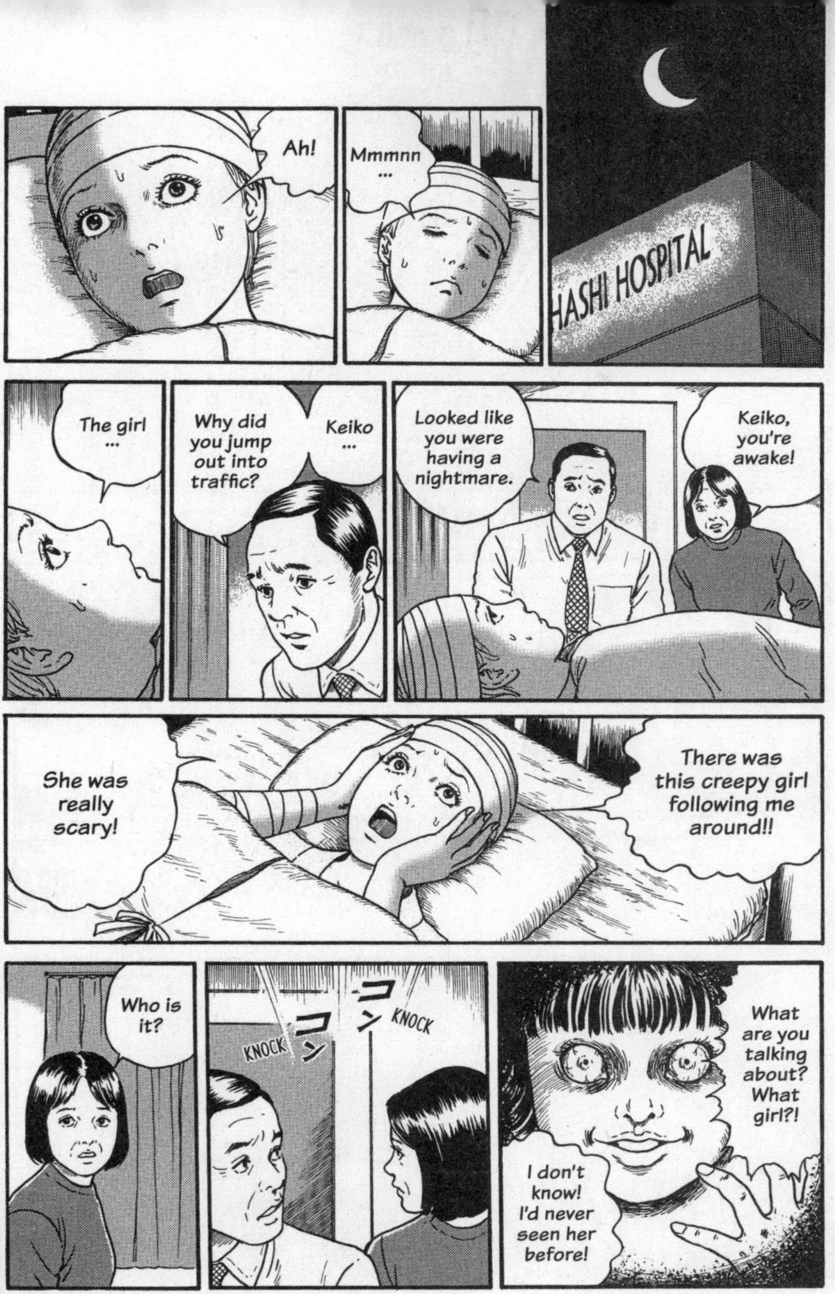
HASHI HOSPITAL
Mmmnn ...
Ah!
Keiko, you're awake!
Looked like you were having a nightmare.
Keiko ...
Why did you jump out into traffic?
The girl ...
There was this creepy girl following me around!!
She was really scary!
What are you talking about? What girl?!
I don't know! I'd never seen her before!
コン KNOCK
コン KNOCK
Who is it?

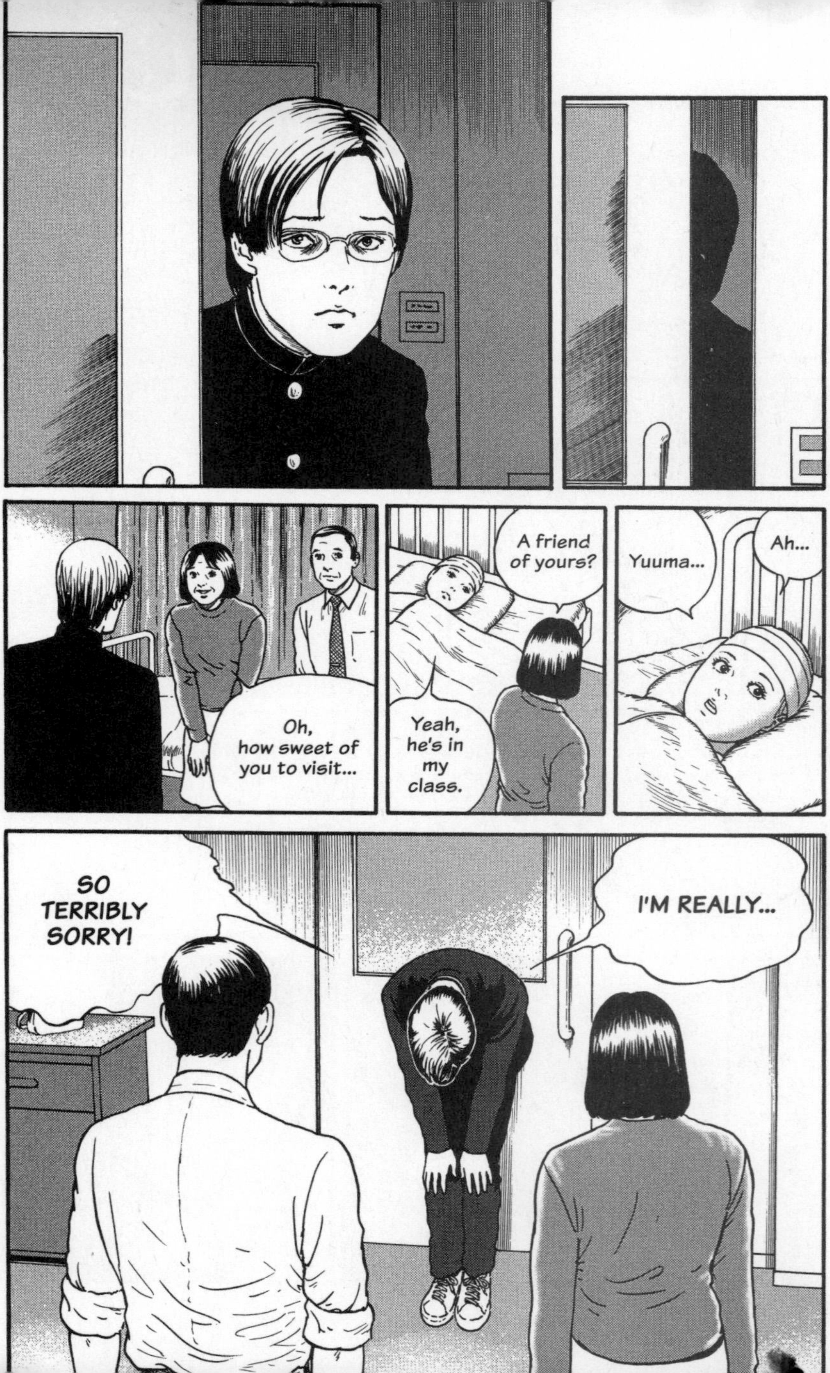
Ah...
Yuuma...
A friend of yours?
Yeah, he's in my class.
Oh, how sweet of you to visit...
I'M REALLY...
SO TERRIBLY SORRY!

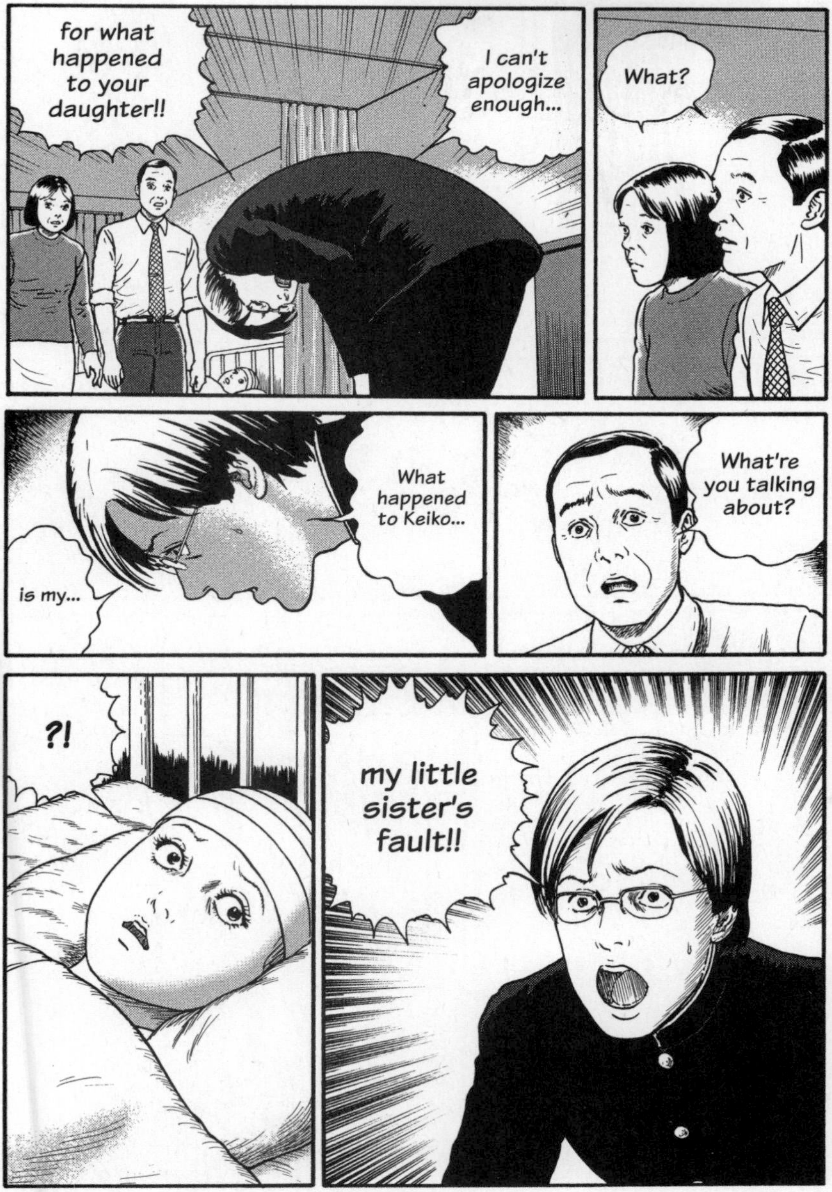
What?
I can't apologize enough...
for what happened to your daughter!!
What're you talking about?
What happened to Keiko...
is my...
my little sister's fault!!
?!

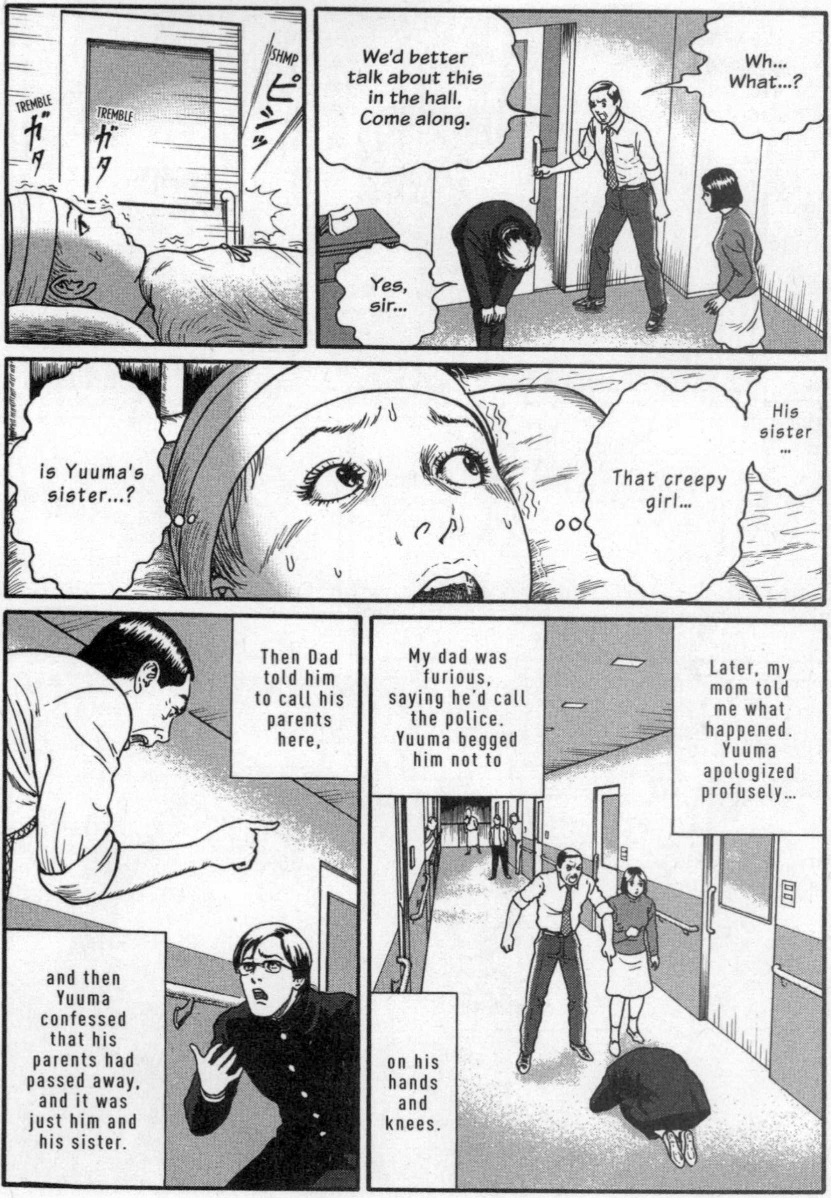
Wh... What...?
We'd better talk about this in the hall. Come along.
Yes, sir...
SHMP
ピシッ
TREMBLE
ガタ
TREMBLE
ガタ
His sister ...
That creepy girl...
is Yuuma's sister...?
Later, my mom told me what happened. Yuuma apologized profusely...
My dad was furious, saying he'd call the police. Yuuma begged him not to
on his hands and knees.
Then Dad told him to call his parents here,
and then Yuuma confessed that his parents had passed away, and it was just him and his sister.

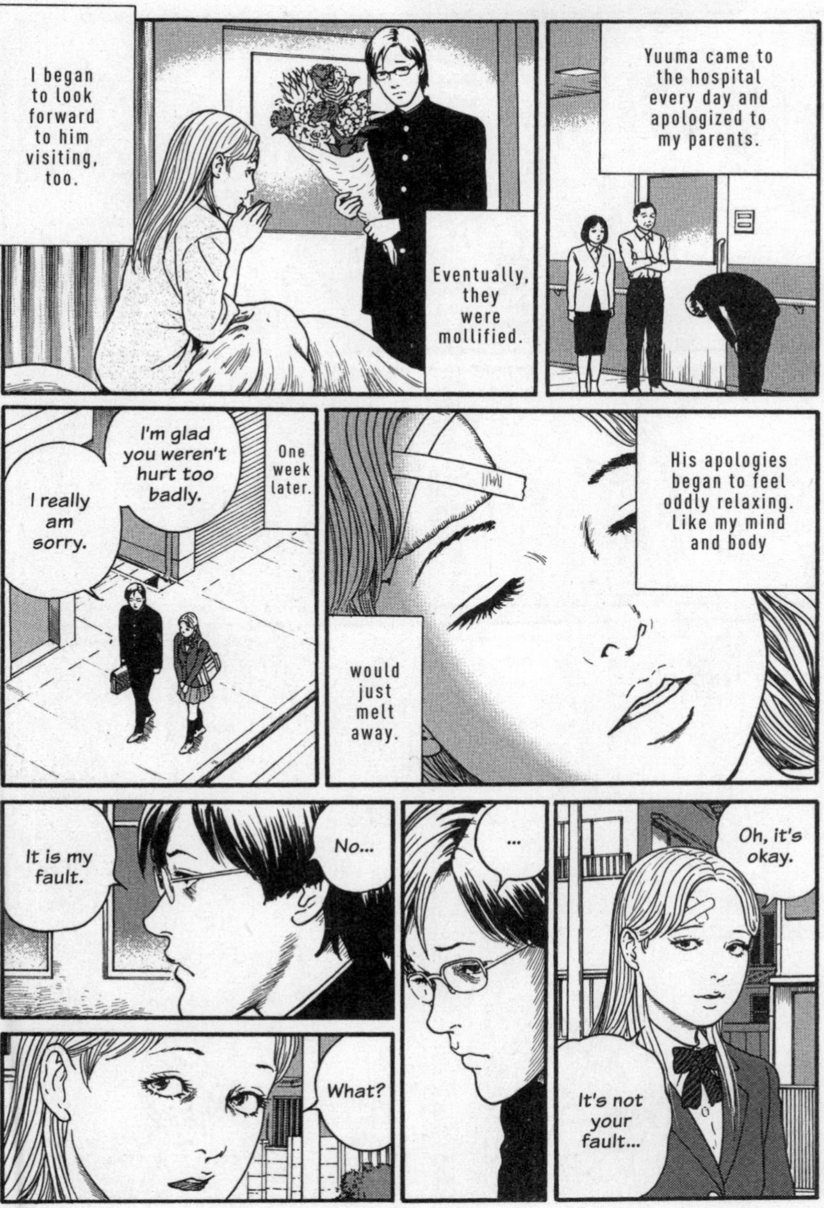
Yuuma came to the hospital every day and apologized to my parents.
Eventually, they were mollified.
I began to look forward to him visiting, too.
His apologies began to feel oddly relaxing. Like my mind and body
would just melt away.
One week later.
I'm glad you weren't hurt too badly.
I really am sorry.
Oh, it's okay.
It's not your fault...
...
No...
It is my fault.
What?

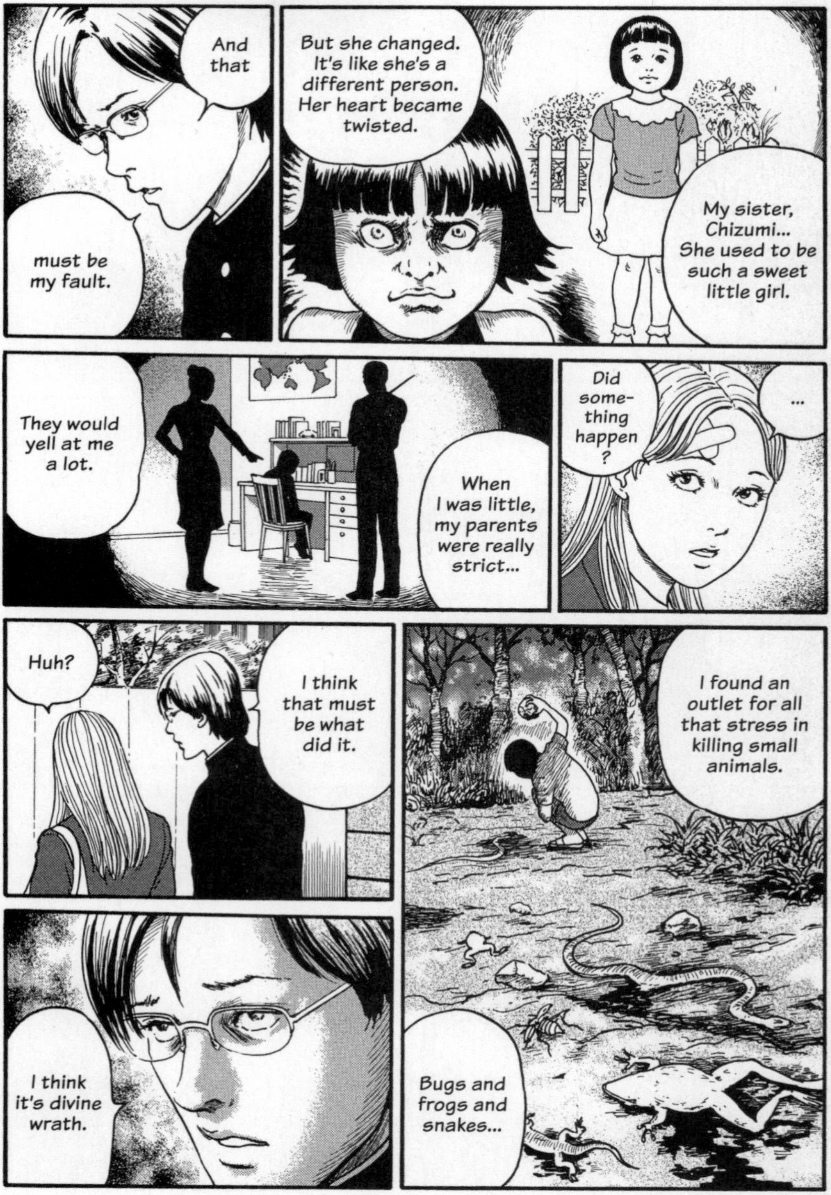
My sister, Chizumi... She used to be such a sweet little girl.
But she changed. It's like she's a different person. Her heart became twisted.
And that
must be my fault.
Did something happen?
...
When I was little, my parents were really strict...
They would yell at me a lot.
I found an outlet for all that stress in killing small animals.
Bugs and frogs and snakes...
I think that must be what did it.
Huh?
I think it's divine wrath.

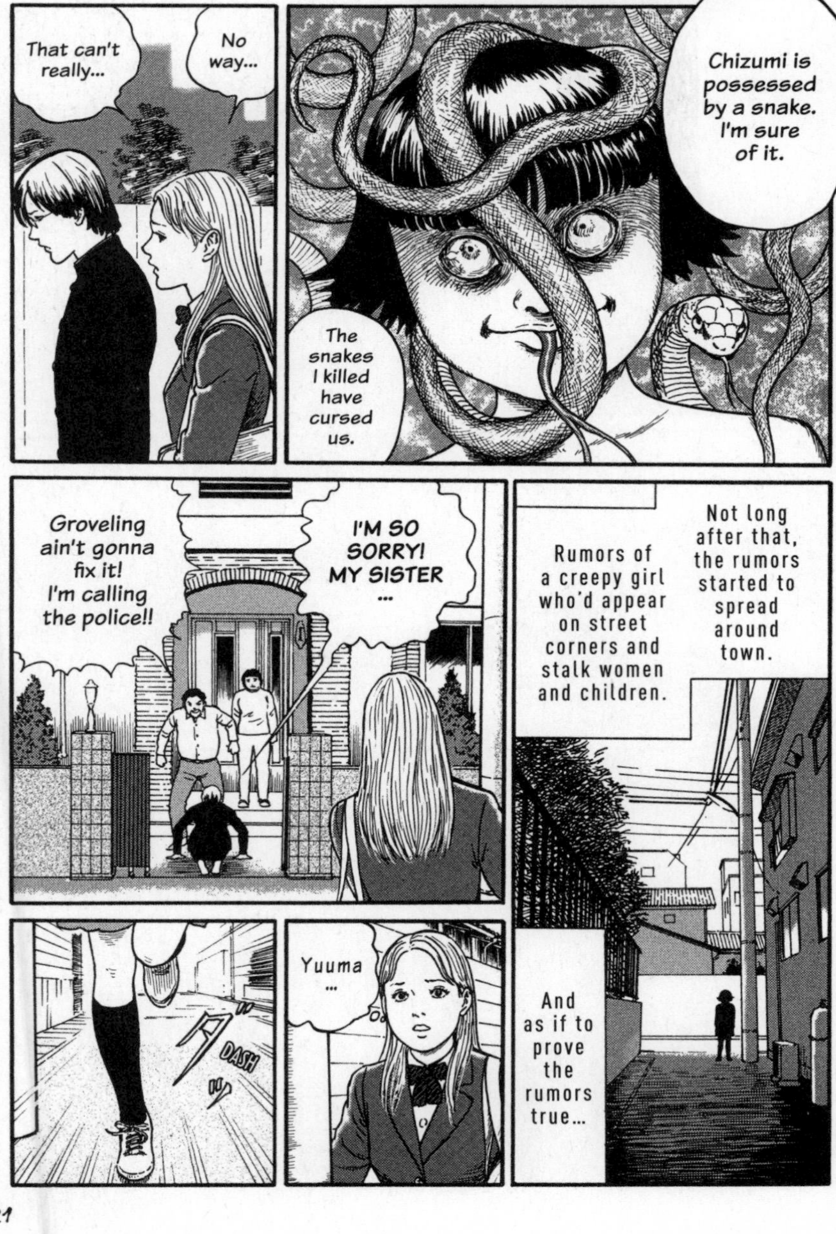

Chizumi is possessed by a snake. I'm sure of it.
The snakes I killed have cursed us.
No way...
That can't really...
Not long after that, the rumors started to spread around town.
Rumors of a creepy girl who'd appear on street corners and stalk women and children.
And as if to prove the rumors true...
I'M SO SORRY! MY SISTER ...
Groveling ain't gonna fix it! I'm calling the police!!
Yuuma ...
DASH

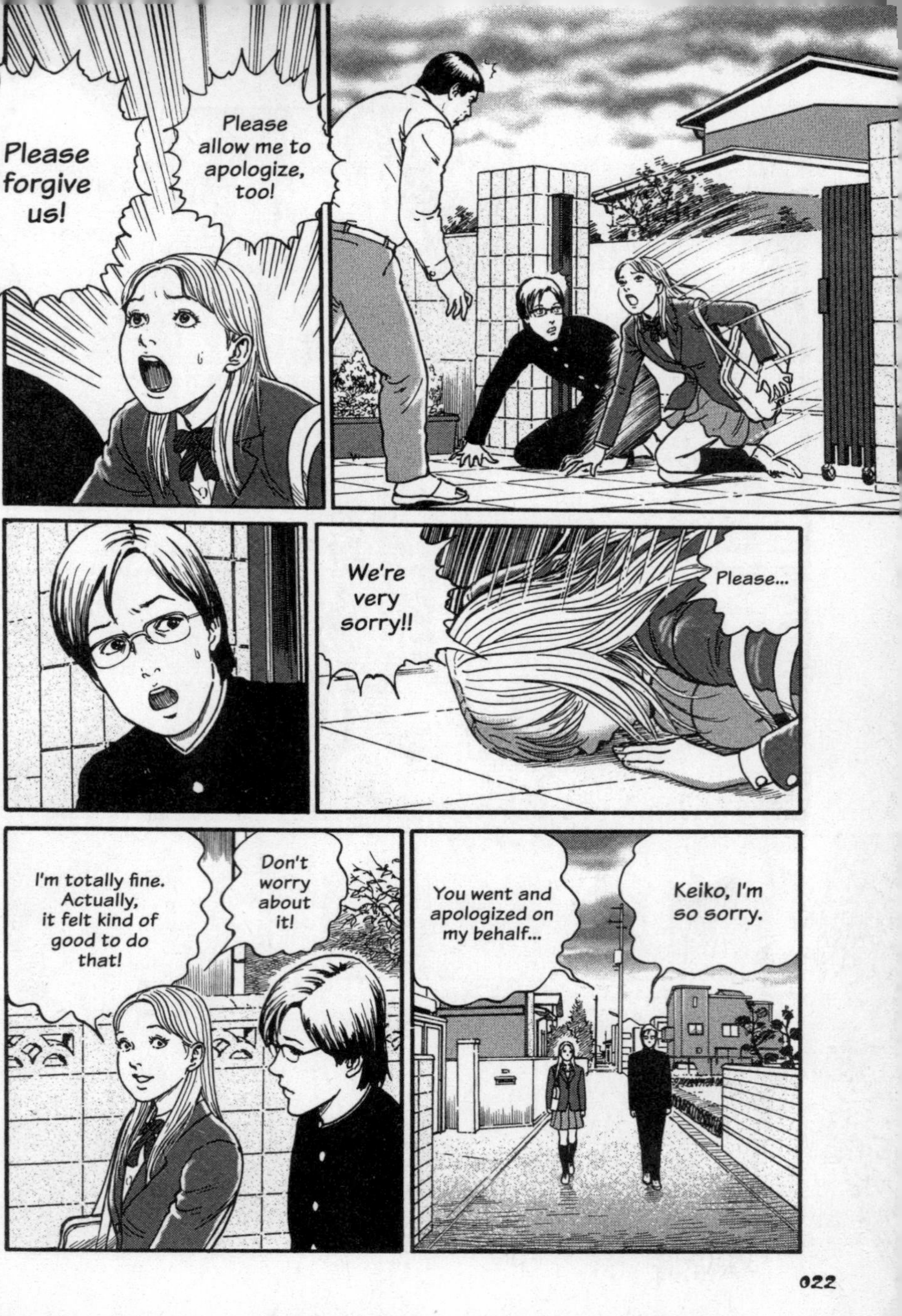
Please allow me to apologize, too!
Please forgive us!
Please...
We're very sorry!!
Keiko, I'm so sorry.
You went and apologized on my behalf...
Don't worry about it!
I'm totally fine. Actually, it felt kind of good to do that!

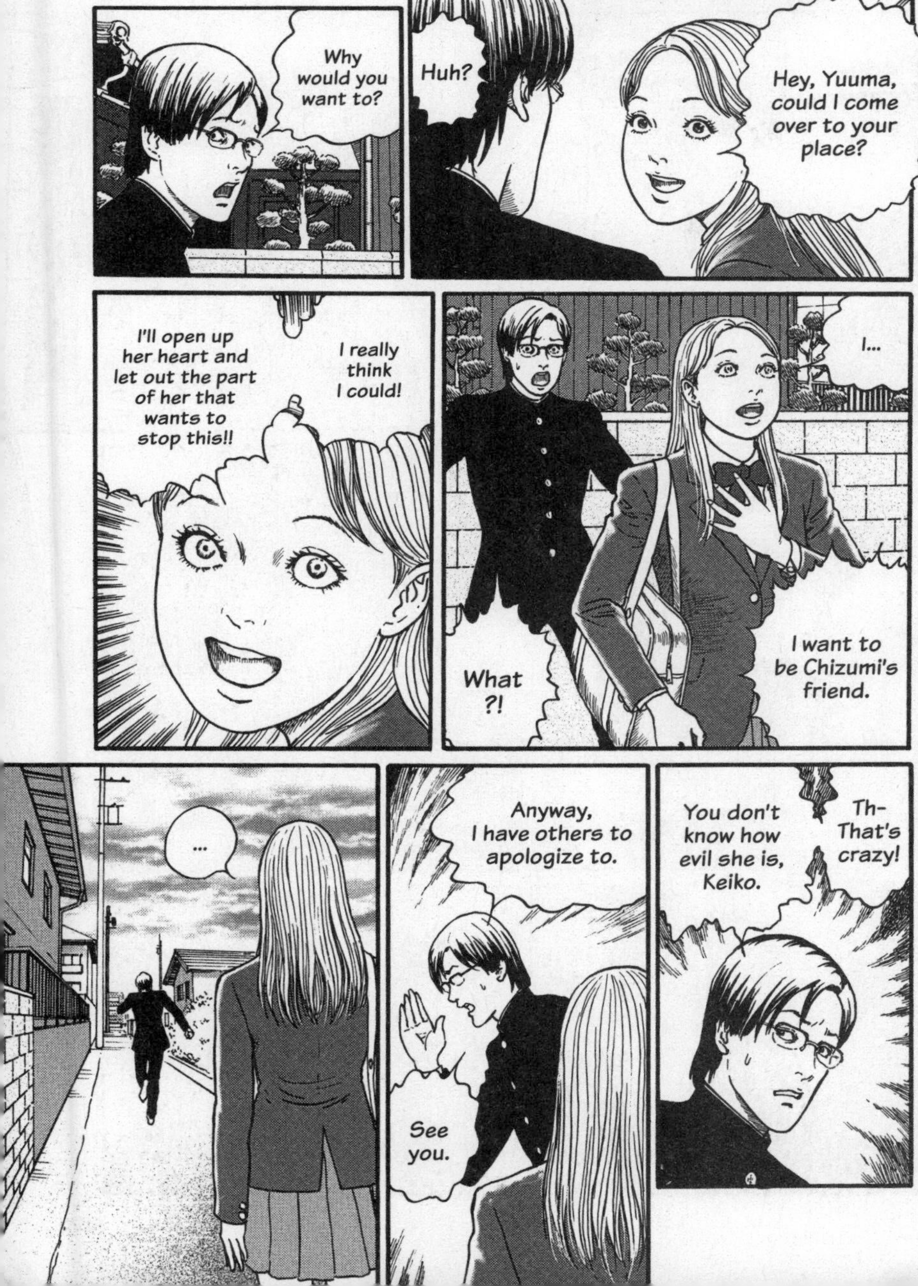
Hey, Yuuma, could I come over to your place?
Huh?
Why would you want to?
I...
I want to be Chizumi's friend.
What ?!
I really think I could!
I'll open up her heart and let out the part of her that wants to stop this!!
Th- That's crazy!
You don't know how evil she is, Keiko.
Anyway, I have others to apologize to.
See you.
...

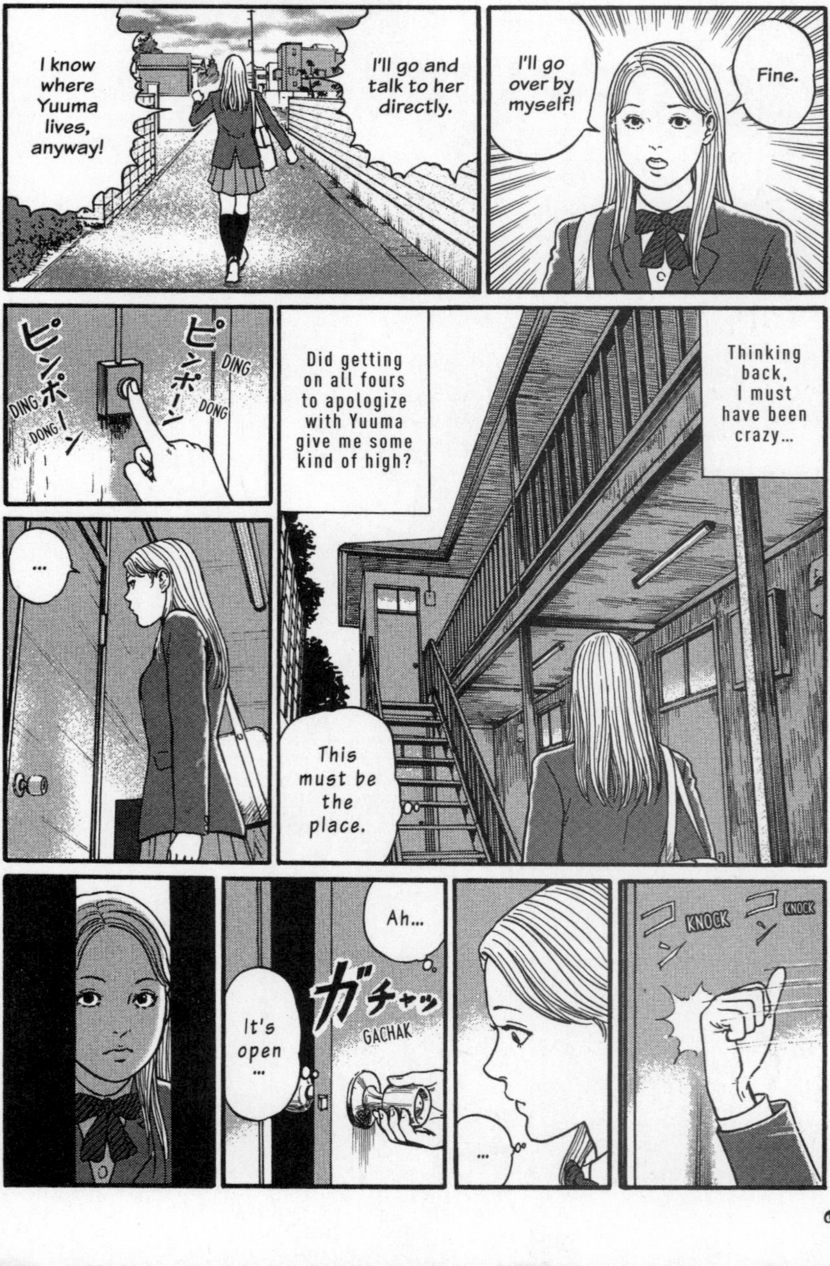
Fine.
I'll go over by myself!
I'll go and talk to her directly.
I know where Yuuma lives, anyway!
Thinking back, I must have been crazy...
Did getting on all fours to apologize with Yuuma give me some kind of high?
This must be the place.
ピンポーン
DING DONG
ピンポーン
DING DONG
...
コンコン
KNOCK KNOCK
...
Ah...
ガチャッ
GACHAK
It's open...

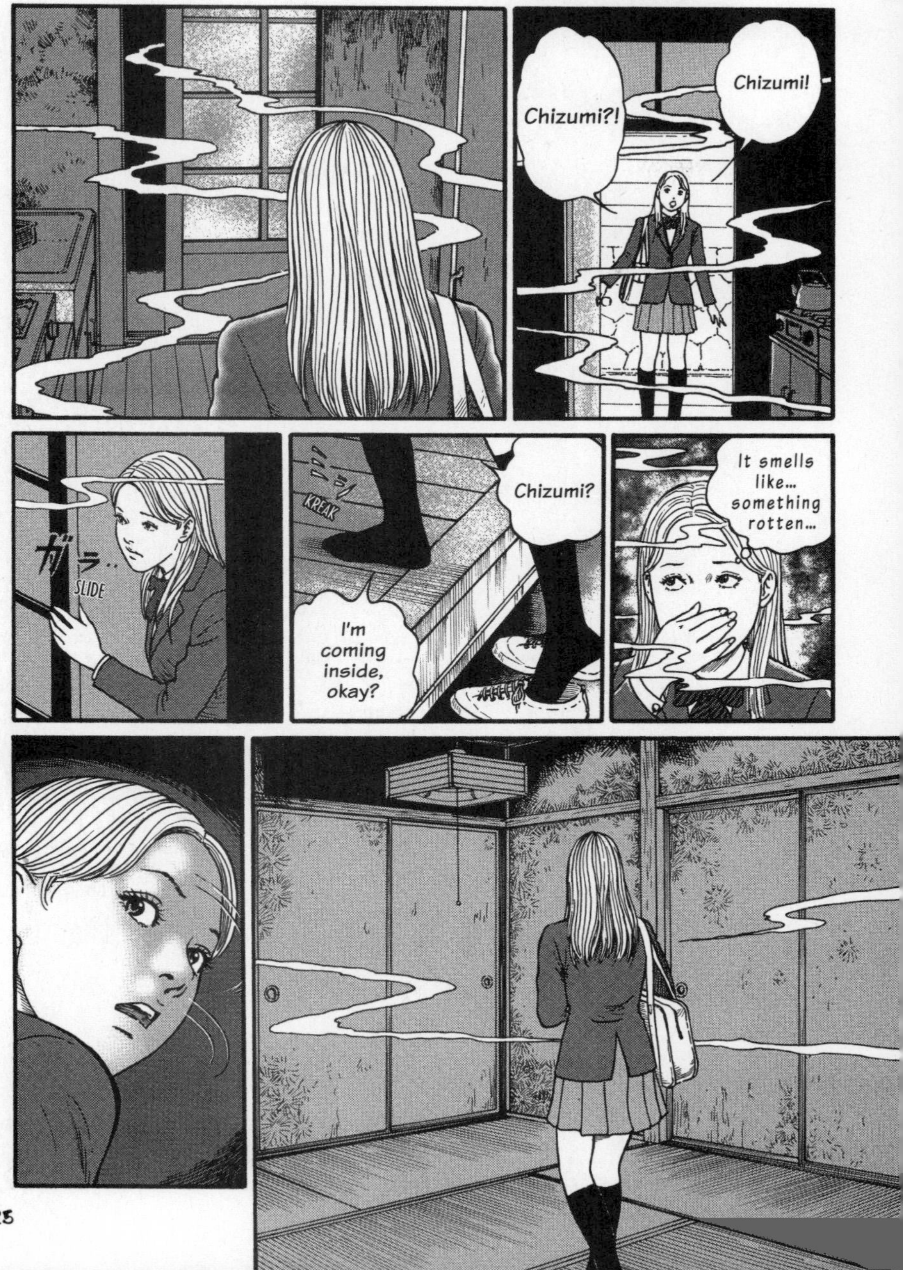
Chizumi!
Chizumi?!
It smells like... something rotten...
Chizumi?
KREAK
I'm coming inside, okay?
ガラ..
SLIDE

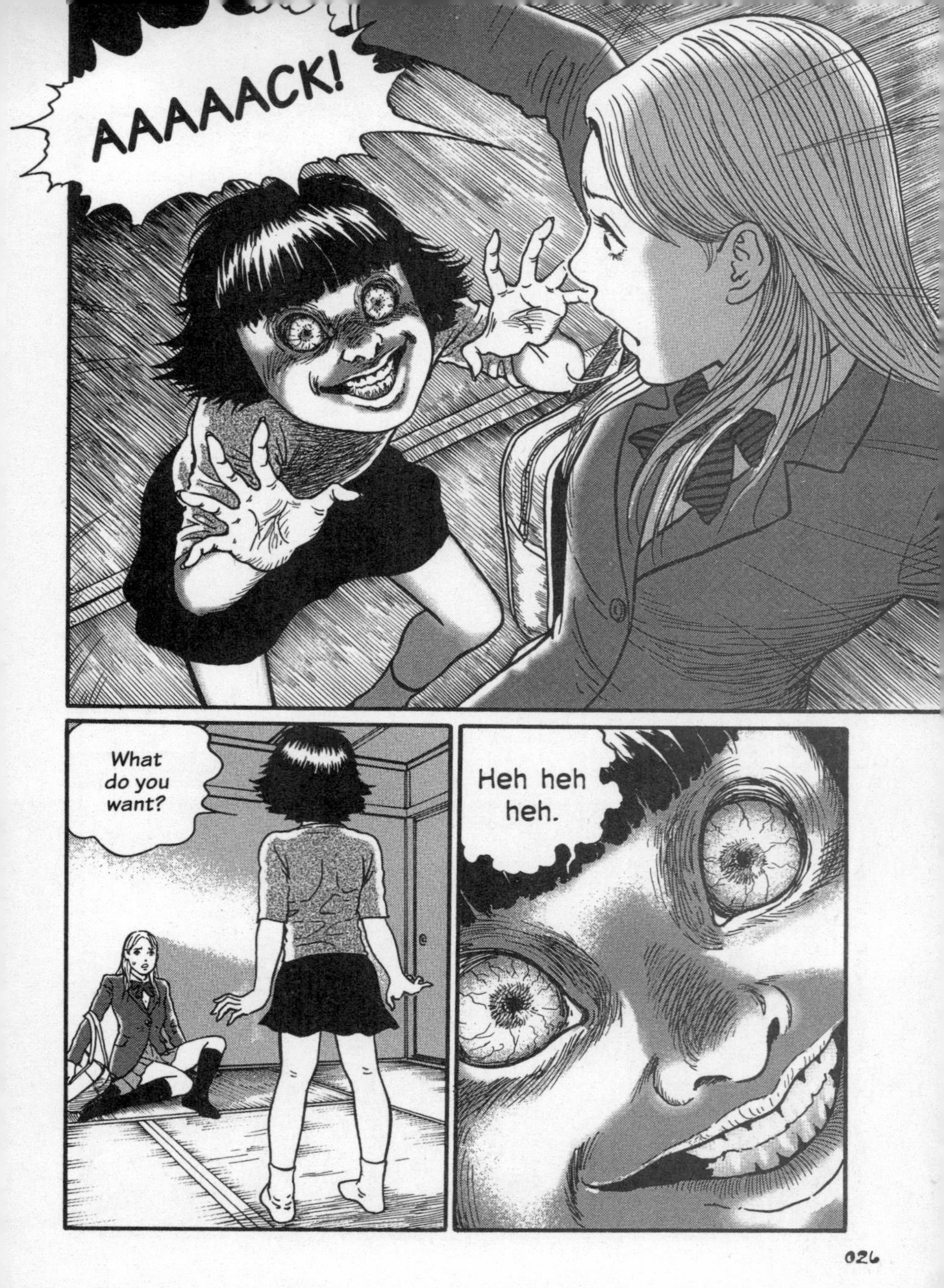
AAAAACK!
Heh heh heh.
What do you want?

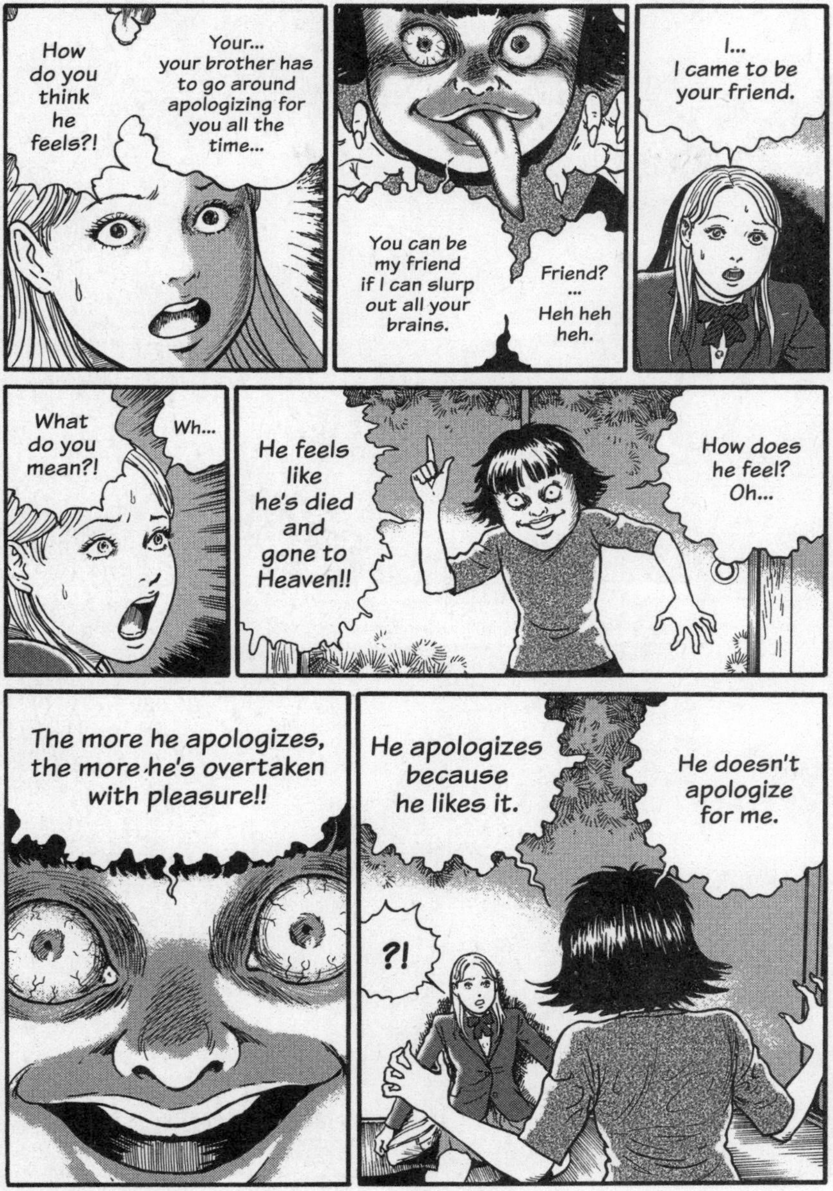
I... I came to be your friend.
Friend? ... Heh heh heh.
You can be my friend if I can slurp out all your brains.
Your... your brother has to go around apologizing for you all the time...
How do you think he feels?!
How does he feel? Oh...
He feels like he's died and gone to Heaven!!
Wh...
What do you mean?!
He doesn't apologize for me.
He apologizes because he likes it.
?!
The more he apologizes, the more he's overtaken with pleasure!!

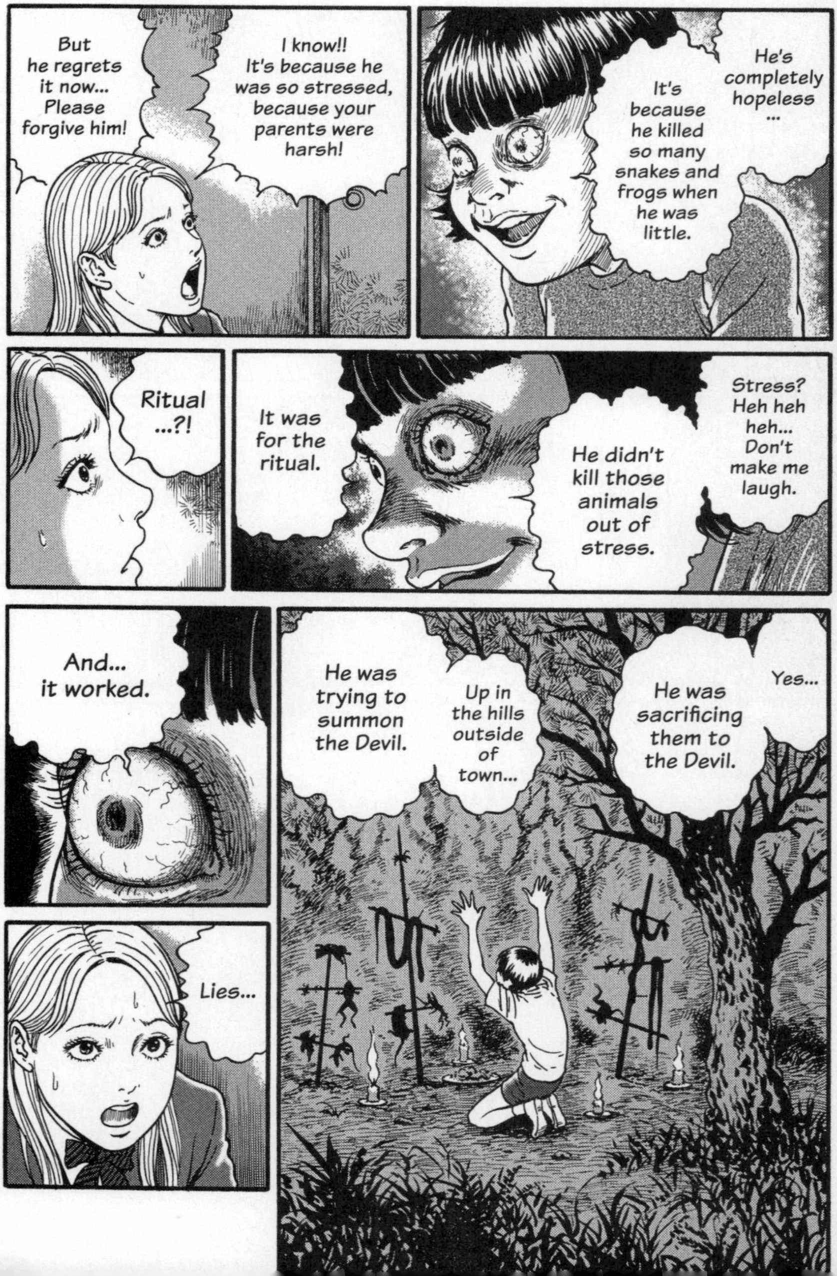
He's completely hopeless ...
It's because he killed so many snakes and frogs when he was little.
I know!! It's because he was so stressed, because your parents were harsh!
But he regrets it now... Please forgive him!
Stress? Heh heh heh... Don't make me laugh.
He didn't kill those animals out of stress.
It was for the ritual.
Ritual ...?!
Yes...
He was sacrificing them to the Devil.
Up in the hills outside of town...
He was trying to summon the Devil.
And... it worked.
Lies...

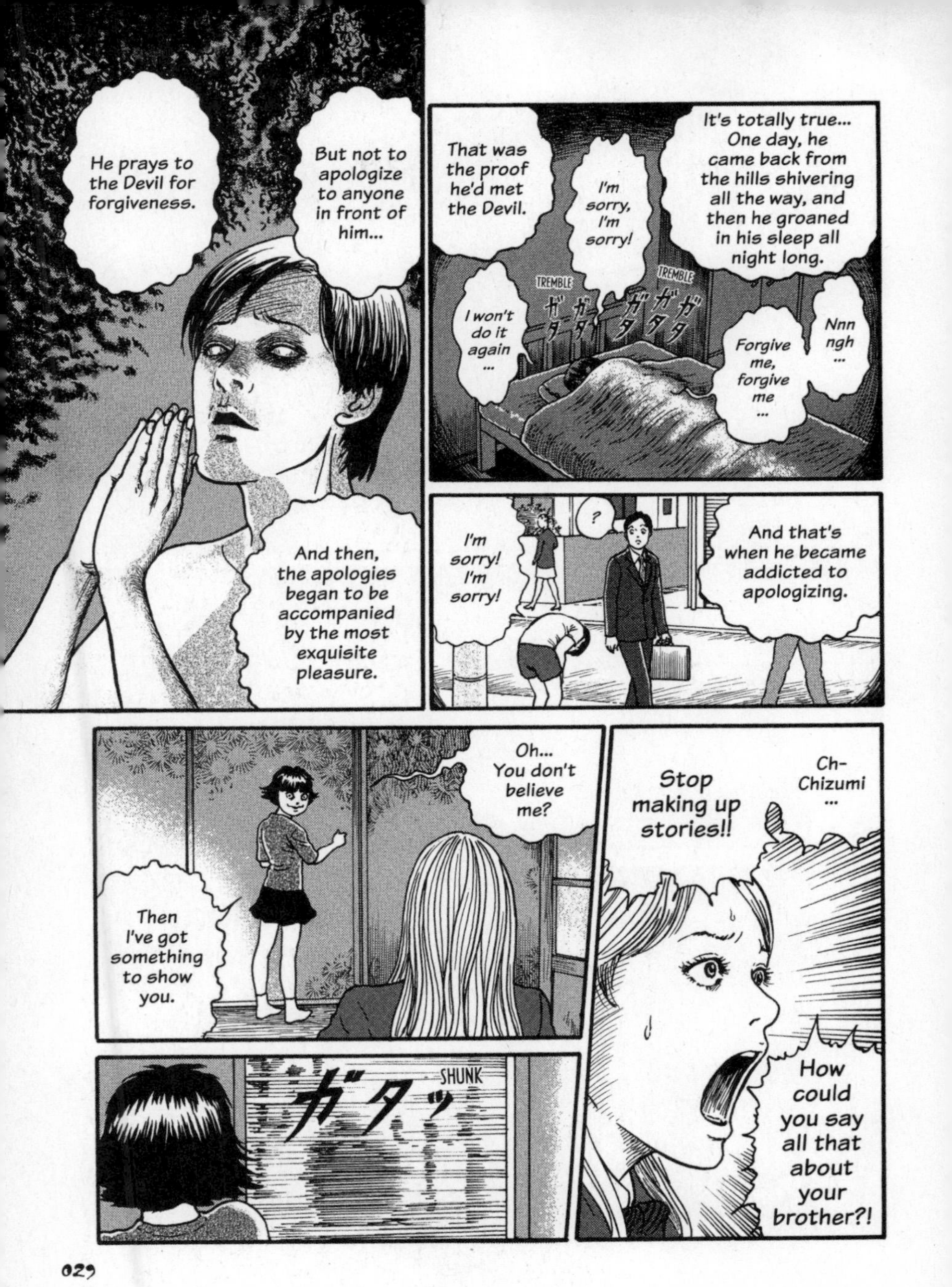
It's totally true... One day, he came back from the hills shivering all the way, and then he groaned in his sleep all night long.
I'm sorry, I'm sorry!
That was the proof he'd met the Devil.
TREMBLE
ガタガタ
TREMBLE
ガタガタ
Nnn ngh ...
Forgive me, forgive me ...
I won't do it again ...
And that's when he became addicted to apologizing.
?
I'm sorry! I'm sorry!
But not to apologize to anyone in front of him...
He prays to the Devil for forgiveness.
And then, the apologies began to be accompanied by the most exquisite pleasure.
Ch- Chizumi ...
Stop making up stories!!
How could you say all that about your brother?!
Oh... You don't believe me?
Then I've got something to show you.
SHUNK
ガタッ

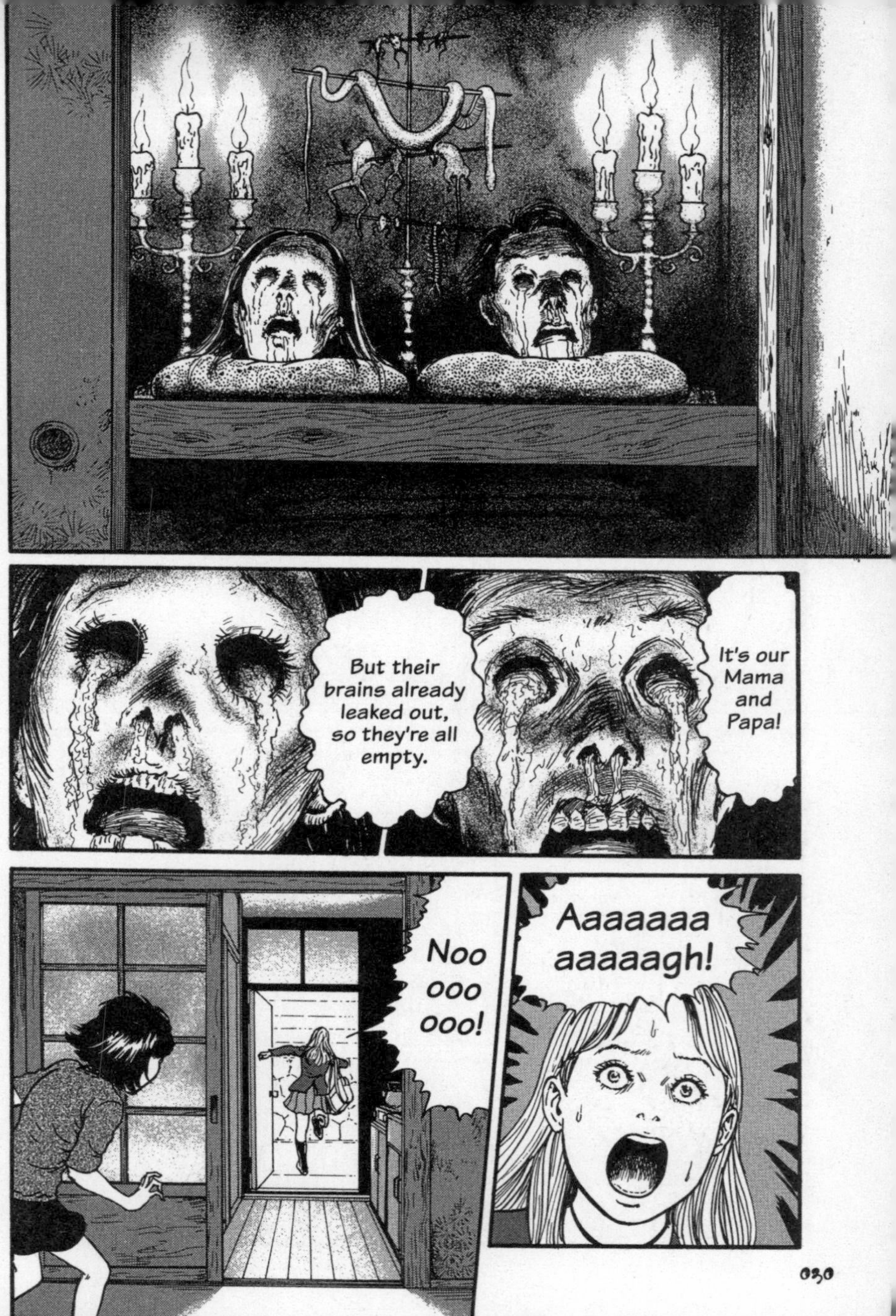
It's our Mama and Papa!
But their brains already leaked out, so they're all empty.
Aaaaaaa aaaaagh!
Noo ooo ooo!

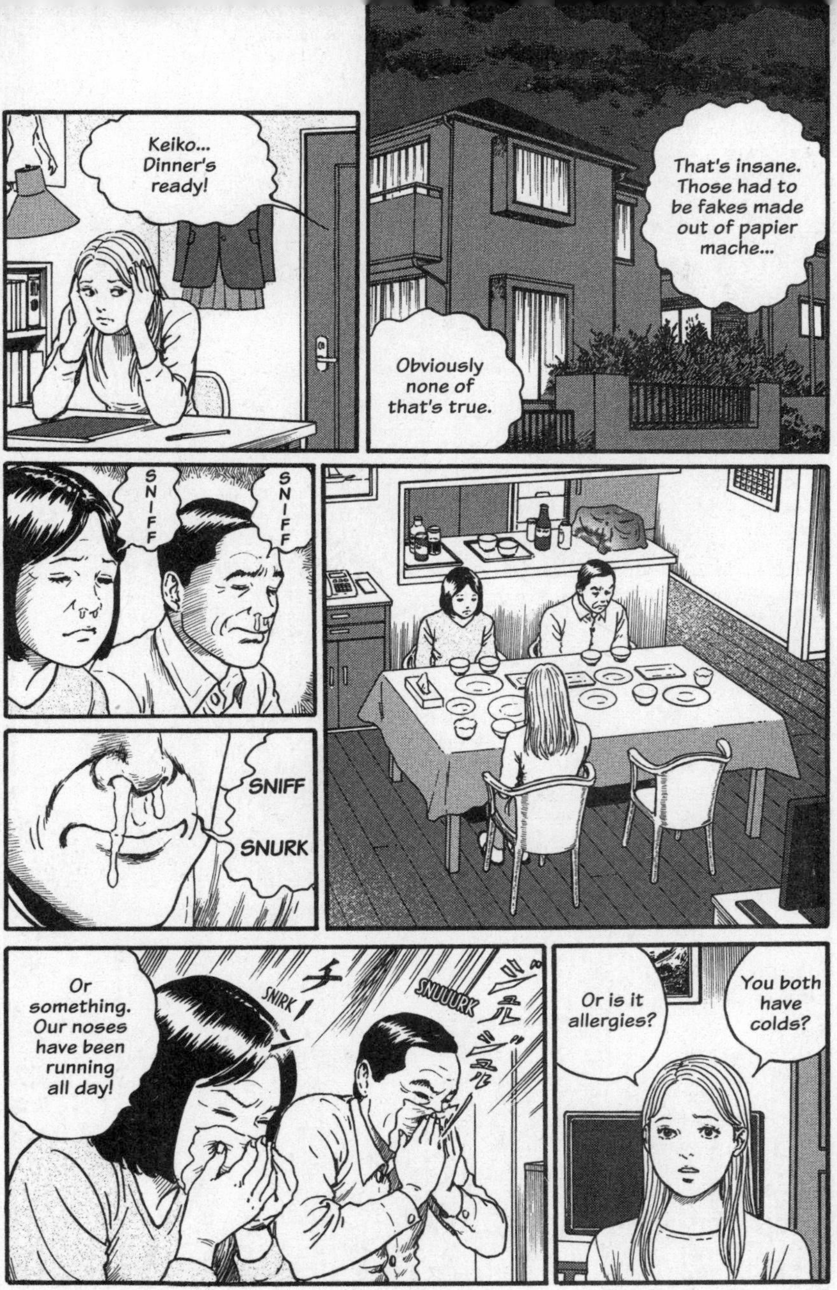
That's insane. Those had to be fakes made out of papier mache...
Obviously none of that's true.
Keiko... Dinner's ready!
SNIFF
SNIFF
SNIFF
SNURK
You both have colds?
Or is it allergies?
SNUUURK
SNIRK
Or something. Our noses have been running all day!

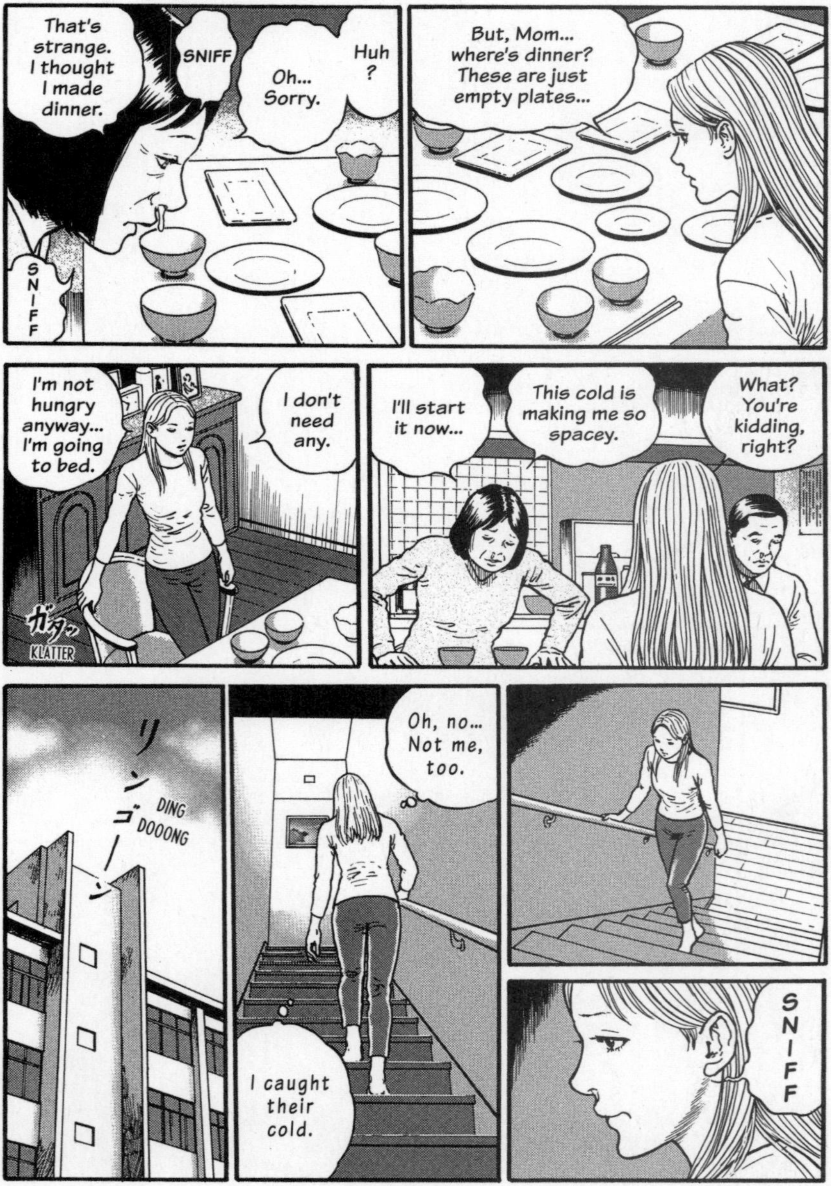
But, Mom... where's dinner? These are just empty plates...
Huh?
Oh... Sorry.
SNIFF
That's strange. I thought I made dinner.
SNIFF
What? You're kidding, right?
This cold is making me so spacey.
I'll start it now...
I don't need any.
I'm not hungry anyway... I'm going to bed.
ガタッ
KLATTER
SNIFF
Oh, no... Not me, too.
I caught their cold.
リンゴーン
DING DOOONG

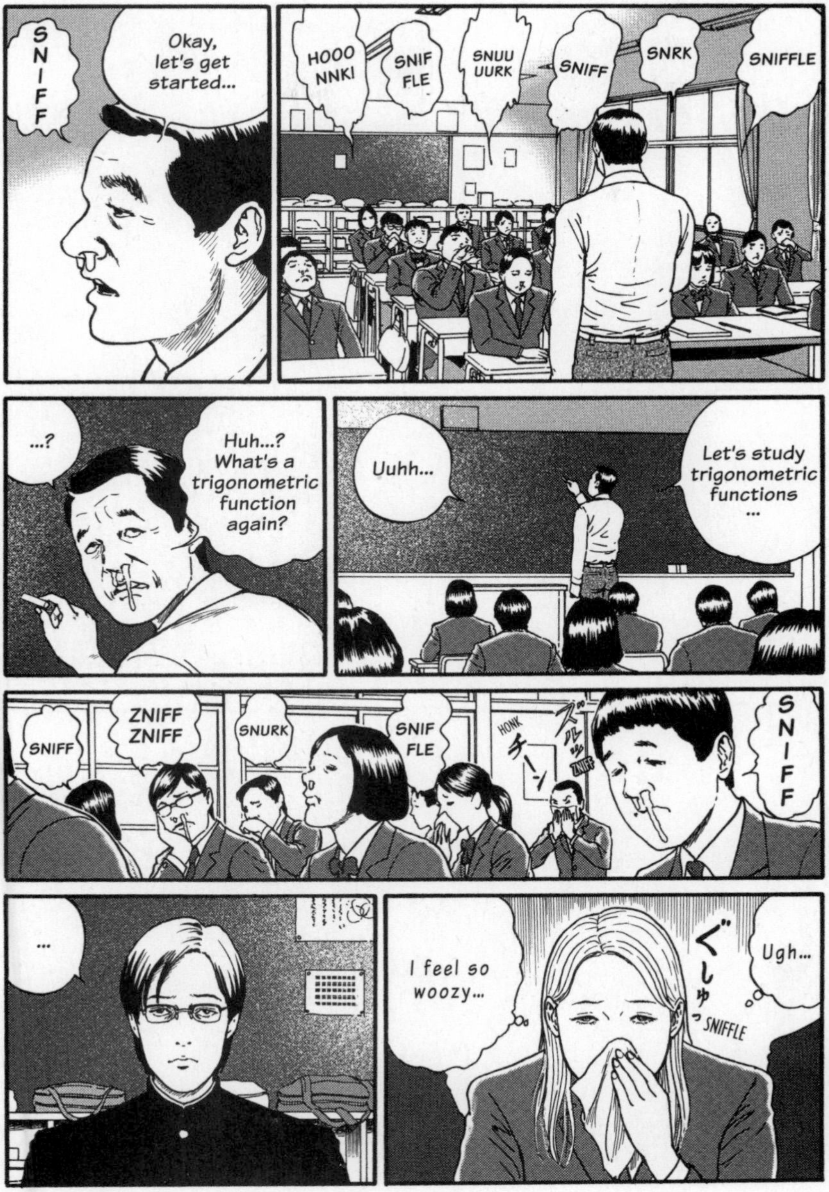
SNIFFLE
SNRK
SNIFF
SNUU UURK
SNIF FLE
HOOO NNK!
Okay, let's get started...
SNIFF
Let's study trigonometric functions ...
Uuhh...
Huh...? What's a trigonometric function again?
...?
SNIFF
ZNIFF
HONK
SNIF FLE
SNURK
ZNIFF ZNIFF
SNIFF
Ugh...
ぐしゅっ SNIFFLE
I feel so woozy...
...

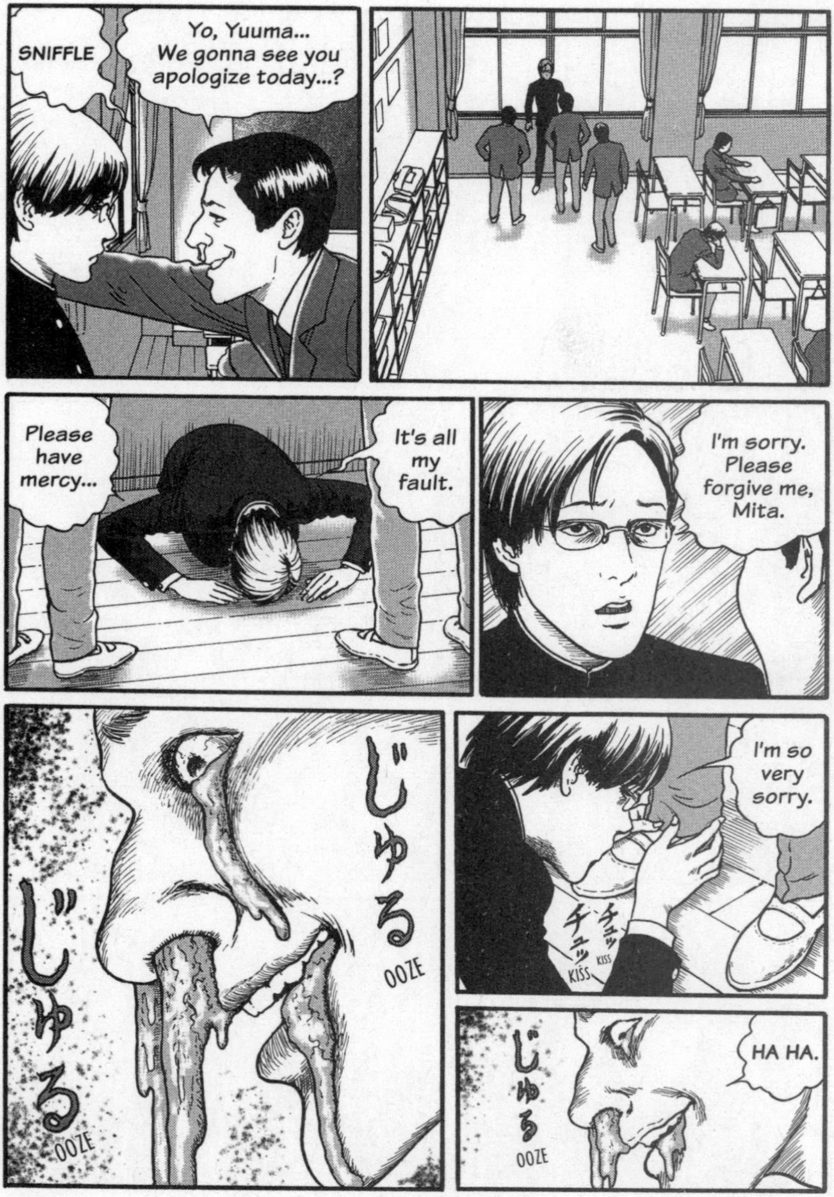
Yo, Yuuma... We gonna see you apologize today...?
SNIFFLE
I'm sorry. Please forgive me, Mita.
It's all my fault.
Please have mercy...
I'm so very sorry.
チュッ KISS
チュッ KISS
HA HA.
じゅる OOZE
じゅる OOZE
じゅる OOZE

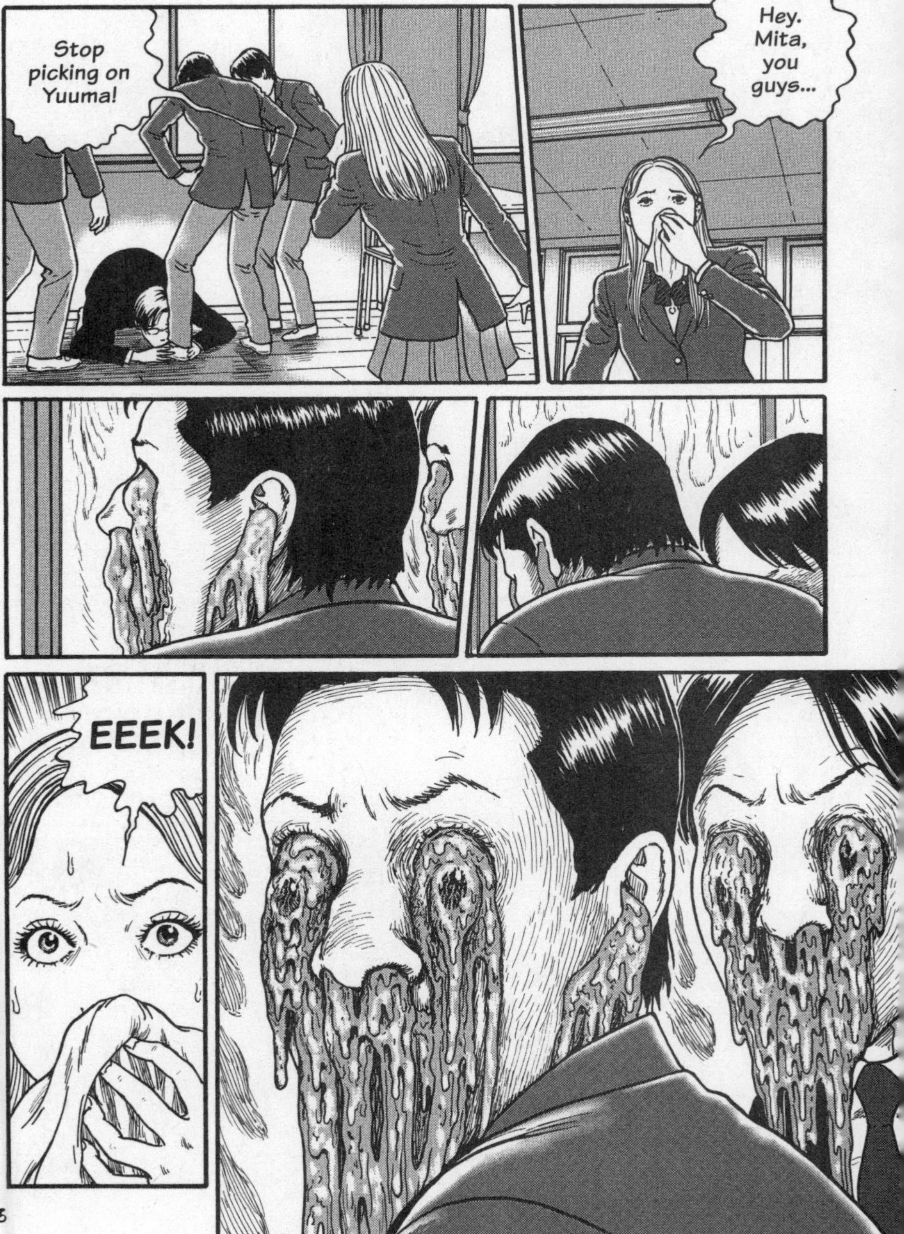
Hey. Mita, you guys...
Stop picking on Yuuma!
EEEK!

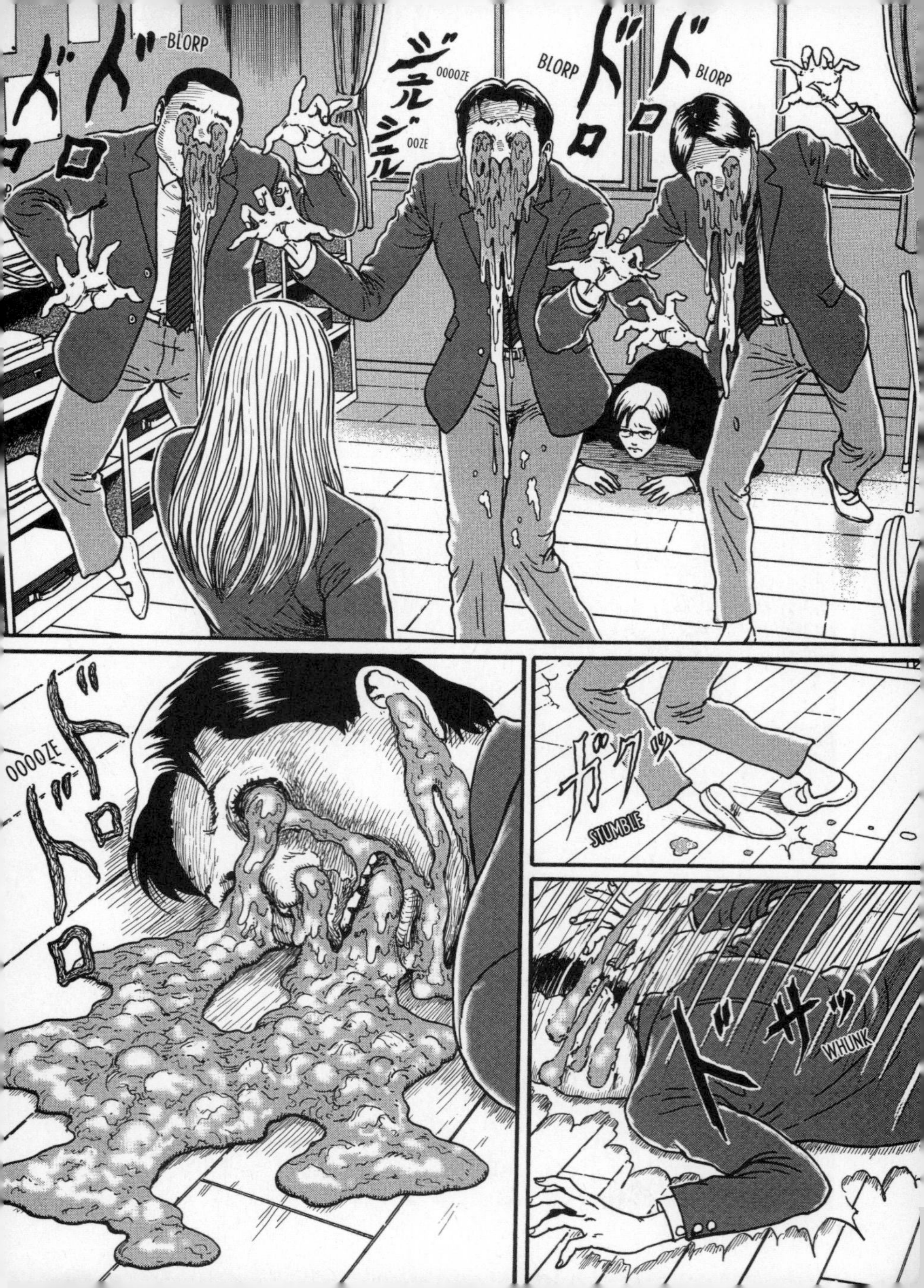

BLORP
BLORP
ジュルジュル
OOOOZE
OOZE
BLORP
ガクッ
STUMBLE
ドザッ
WHUNK
OOOOZE

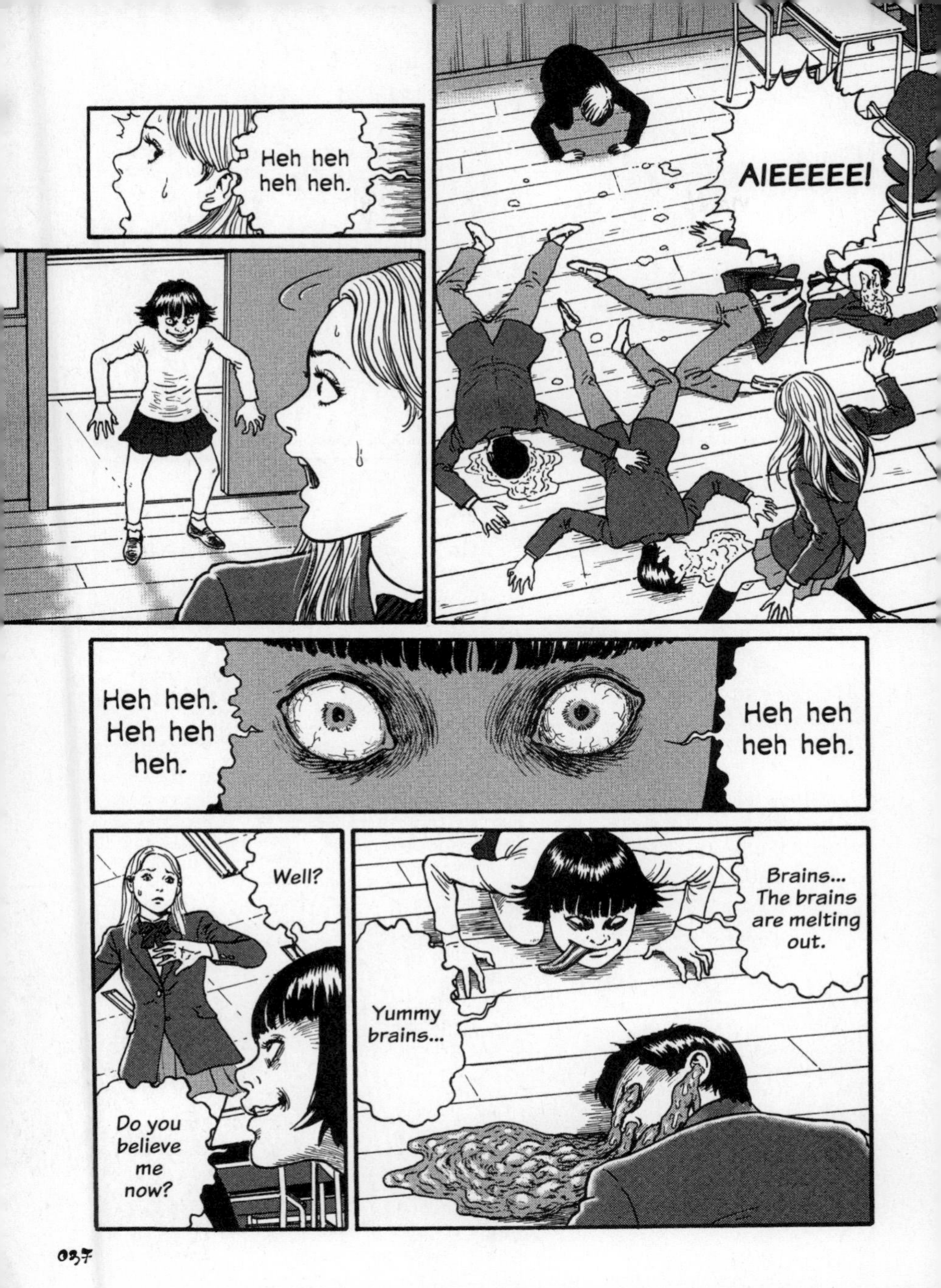
AIEEEEE!
Heh heh heh heh.
Heh heh heh heh.
Heh heh. Heh heh heh.
Brains... The brains are melting out.
Yummy brains...
Well?
Do you believe me now?

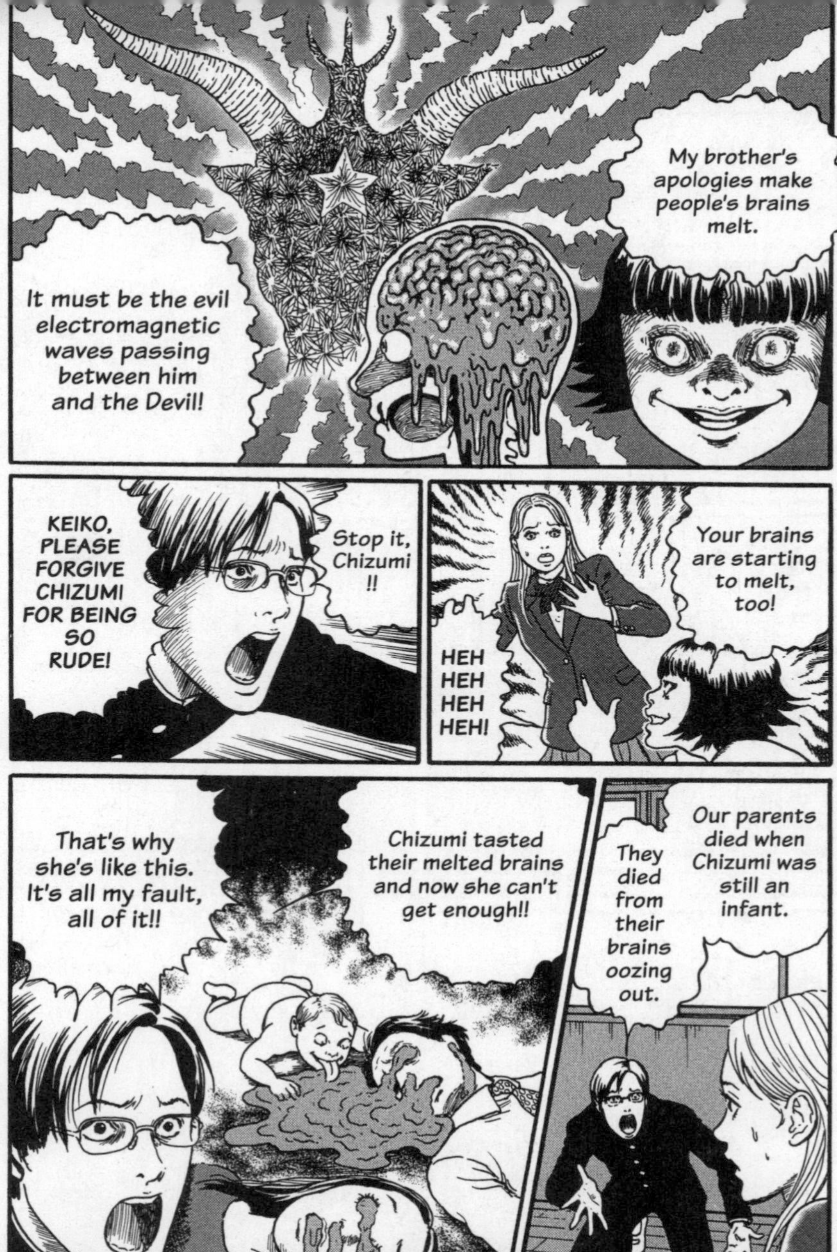
My brother's apologies make people's brains melt.
It must be the evil electromagnetic waves passing between him and the Devil!
Your brains are starting to melt, too!
HEH HEH HEH HEH HEH!
Stop it, Chizumi !!
KEIKO, PLEASE FORGIVE CHIZUMI FOR BEING SO RUDE!
Our parents died when Chizumi was still an infant.
They died from their brains oozing out.
Chizumi tasted their melted brains and now she can't get enough!!
That's why she's like this. It's all my fault, all of it!!

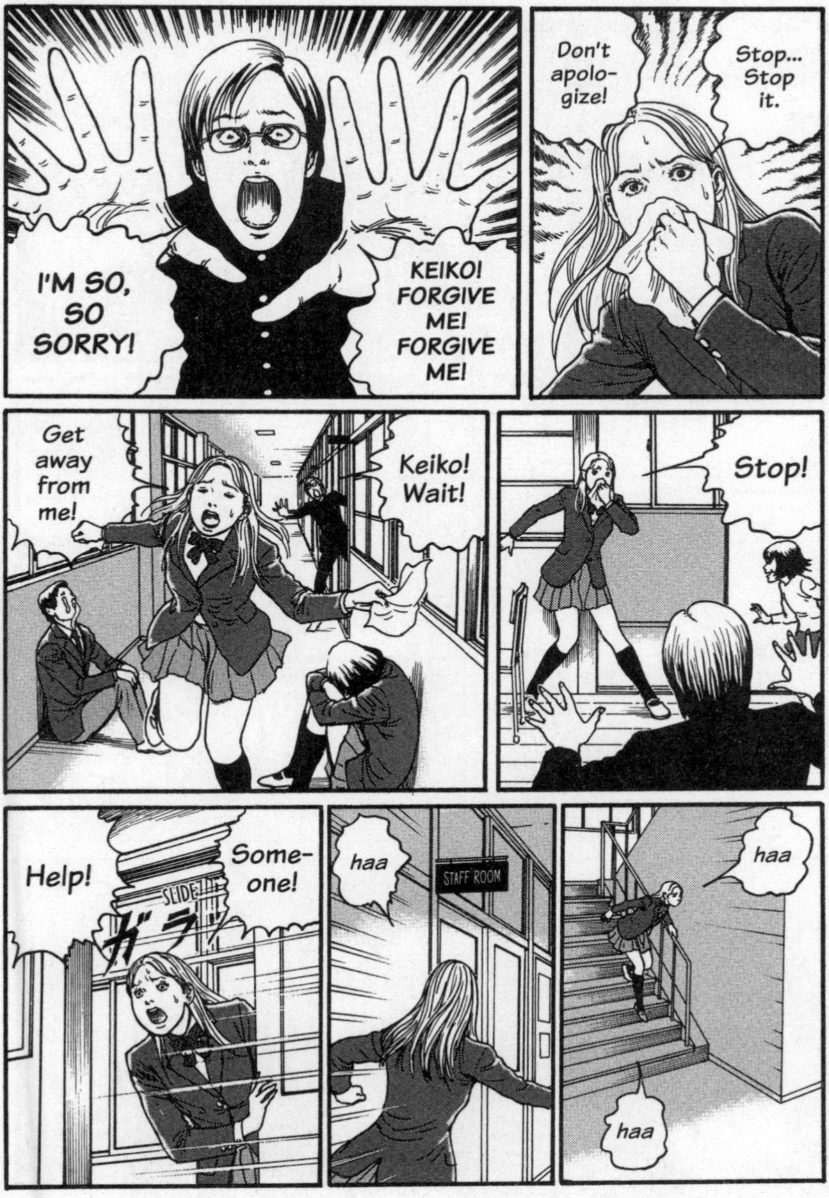
Stop... Stop it.
Don't apolo-gize!
KEIKO! FORGIVE ME! FORGIVE ME!
I'M SO, SO SORRY!
Stop!
Keiko! Wait!
Get away from me!
haa
haa
STAFF ROOM
haa
Some-one!
Help!
SLIDE!!!
ガラ

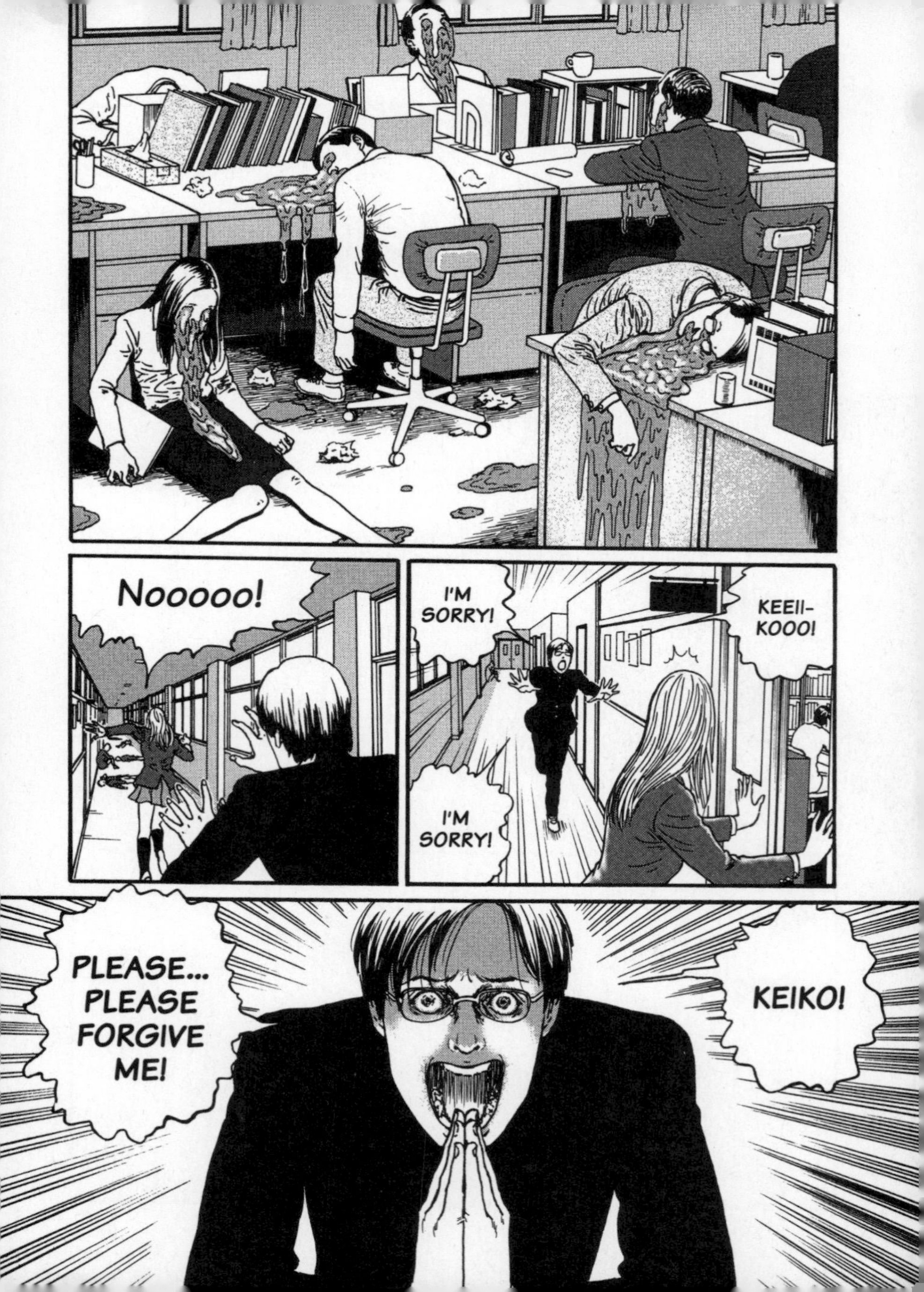
KEEII-KOOO!
I'M SORRY!
I'M SORRY!
Nooooo!
KEIKO!
PLEASE... PLEASE FORGIVE ME!

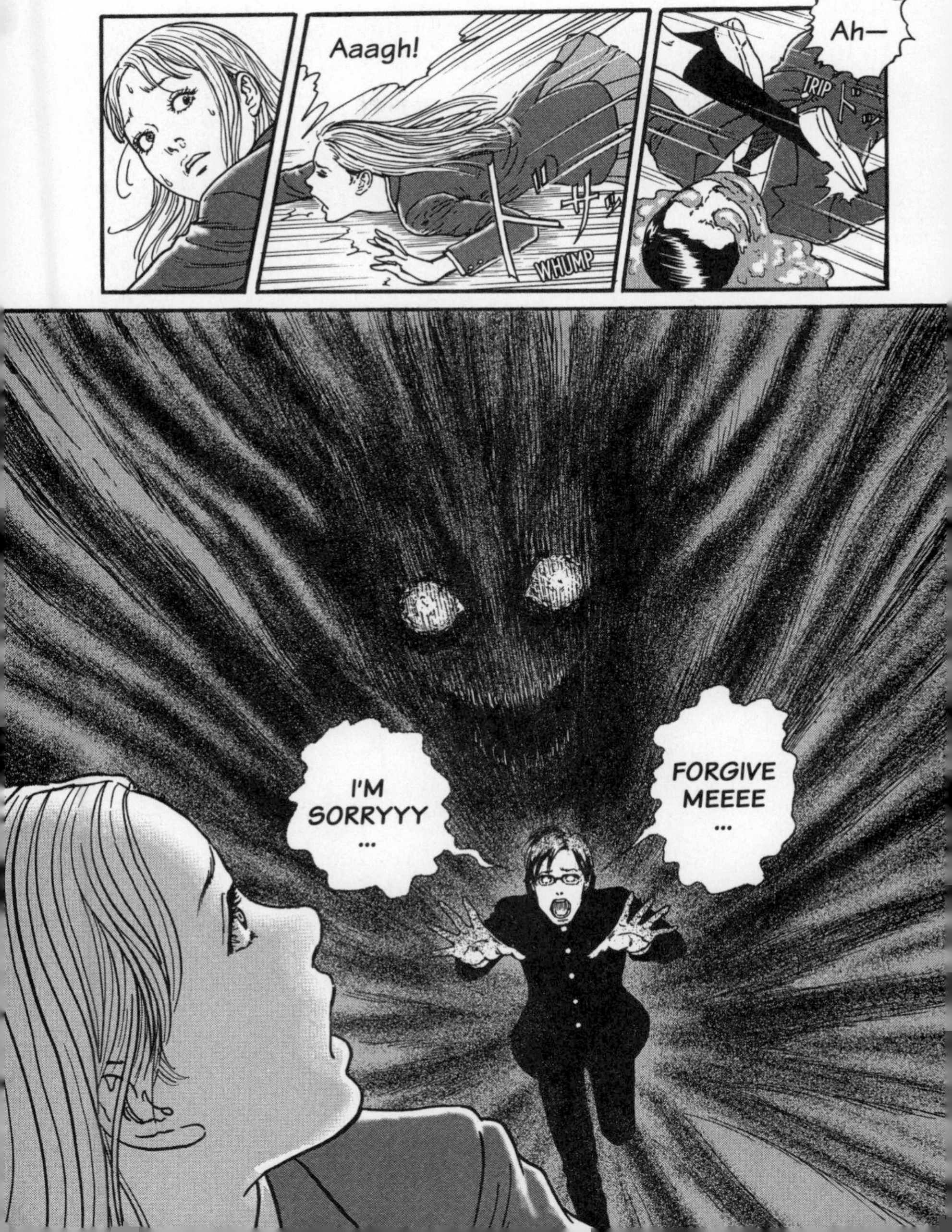
Ah—
TRIP
Aaagh!
WHUMP
FORGIVE MEEEE ...
I'M SORRYYY ...

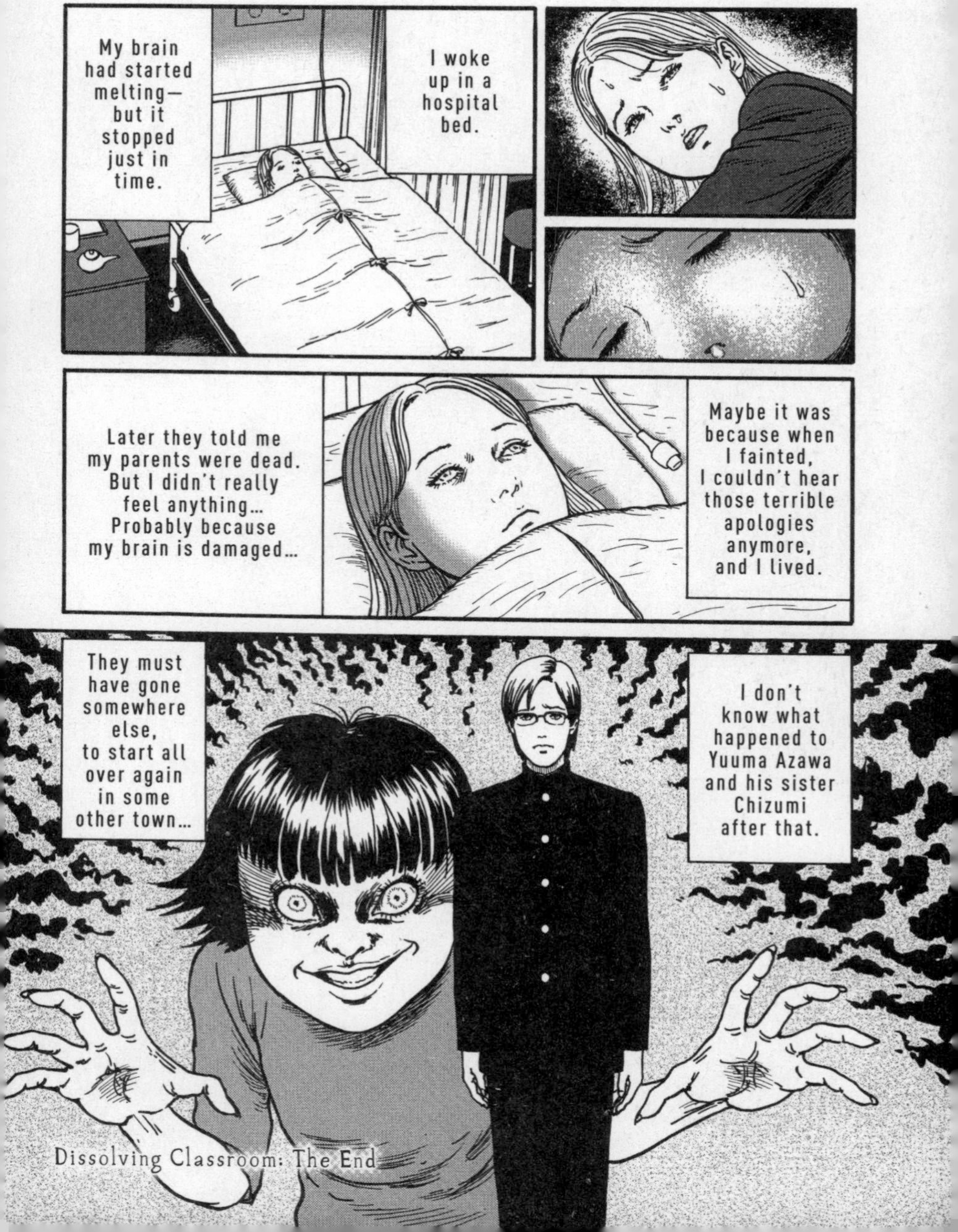
I woke up in a hospital bed.
My brain had started melting—but it stopped just in time.
Maybe it was because when I fainted, I couldn't hear those terrible apologies anymore, and I lived.
Later they told me my parents were dead. But I didn't really feel anything... Probably because my brain is damaged...
I don't know what happened to Yuuma Azawa and his sister Chizumi after that.
They must have gone somewhere else, to start all over again in some other town...
Dissolving Classroom: The End

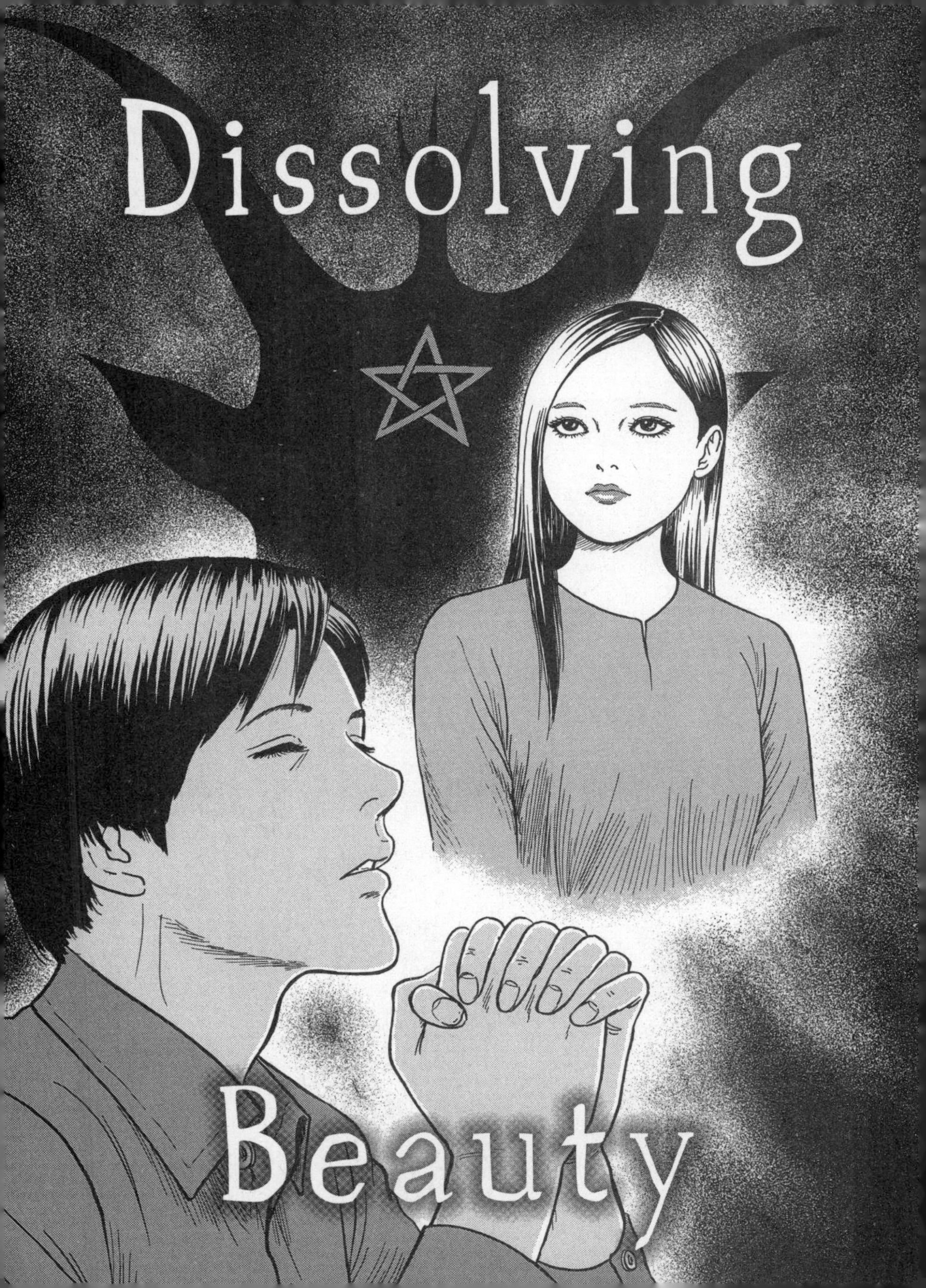
Dissolving
Beauty

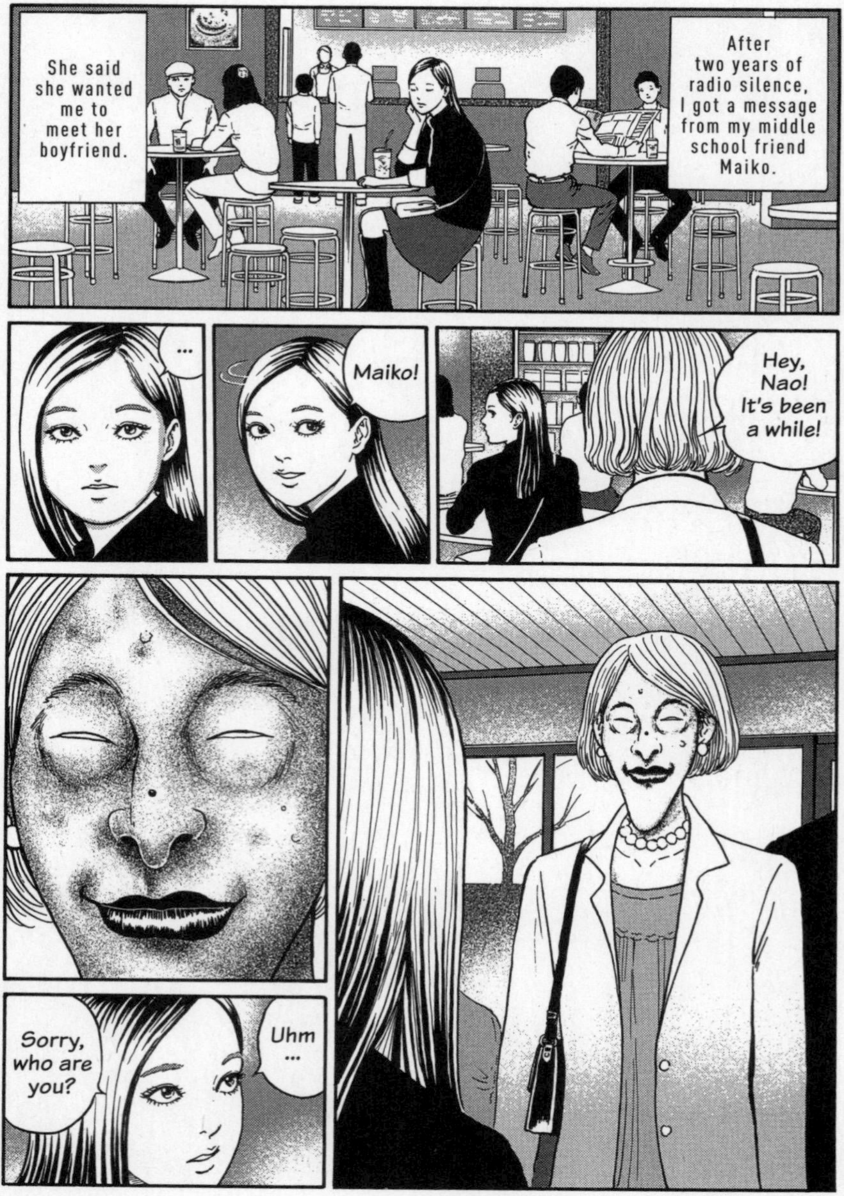
After two years of radio silence, I got a message from my middle school friend Maiko.
She said she wanted me to meet her boyfriend.
Hey, Nao! It's been a while!
Maiko!
...
Uhm ...
Sorry, who are you?

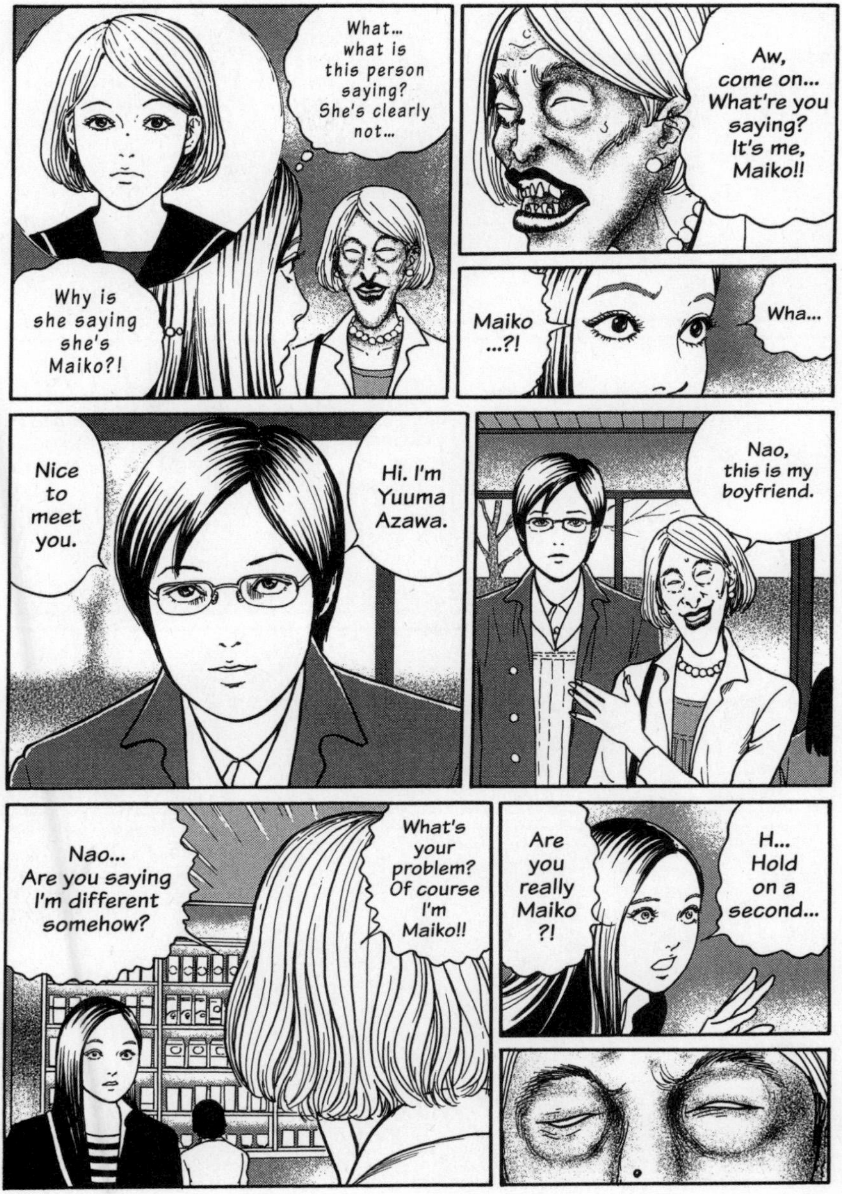
Aw, come on... What're you saying? It's me, Maiko!!
Wha...
Maiko ...?!
What... what is this person saying? She's clearly not...
Why is she saying she's Maiko?!
Nao, this is my boyfriend.
Hi. I'm Yuuma Azawa.
Nice to meet you.
H... Hold on a second...
Are you really Maiko ?!
What's your problem? Of course I'm Maiko!!
Nao... Are you saying I'm different somehow?

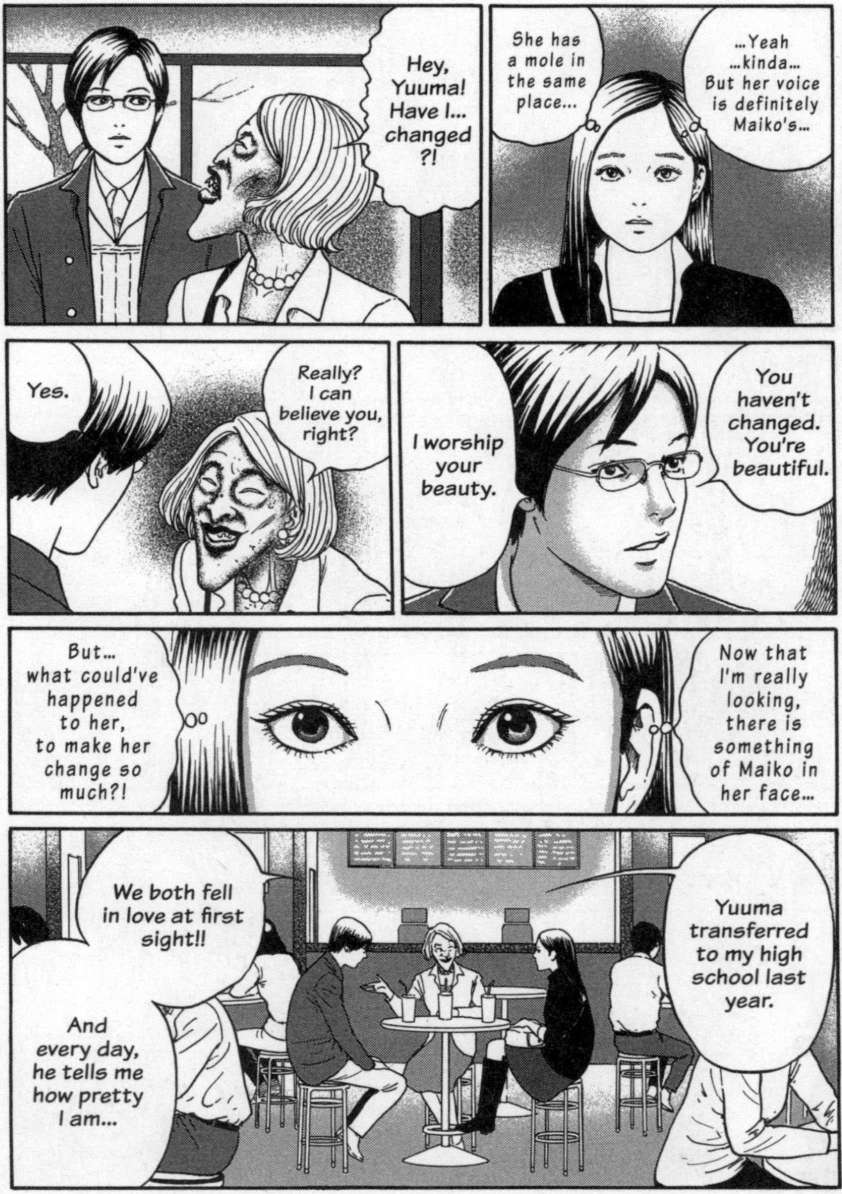
...Yeah ...kinda... But her voice is definitely Maiko's...
She has a mole in the same place...
Hey, Yuuma! Have I... changed ?!
You haven't changed. You're beautiful.
I worship your beauty.
Really? I can believe you, right?
Yes.
Now that I'm really looking, there is something of Maiko in her face...
But... what could've happened to her, to make her change so much?!
Yuuma transferred to my high school last year.
We both fell in love at first sight!!
And every day, he tells me how pretty I am...

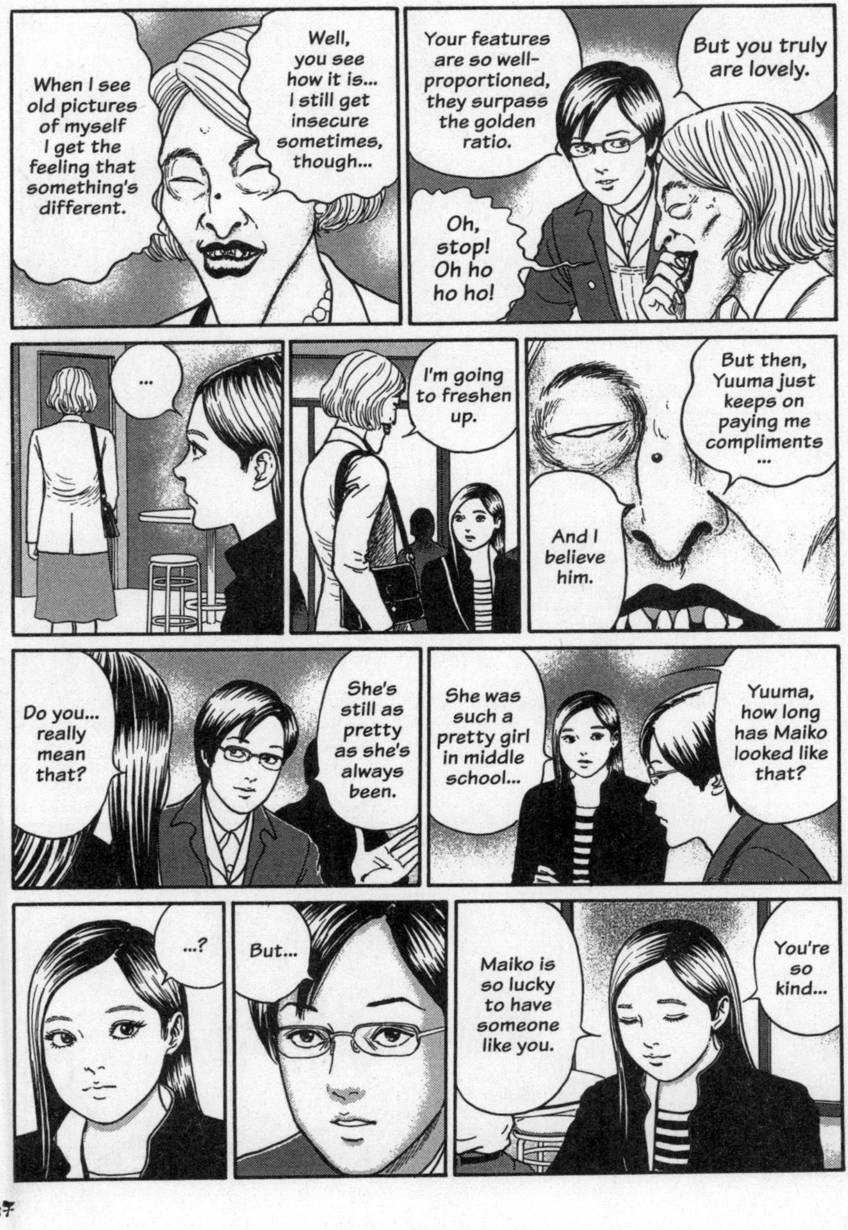
But you truly are lovely.
Your features are so well-proportioned, they surpass the golden ratio.
Oh, stop! Oh ho ho ho!
Well, you see how it is... I still get insecure sometimes, though...
When I see old pictures of myself I get the feeling that something's different.
But then, Yuuma just keeps on paying me compliments ...
And I believe him.
I'm going to freshen up.
...
Yuuma, how long has Maiko looked like that?
She was such a pretty girl in middle school...
She's still as pretty as she's always been.
Do you... really mean that?
You're so kind...
Maiko is so lucky to have someone like you.
But...
...?

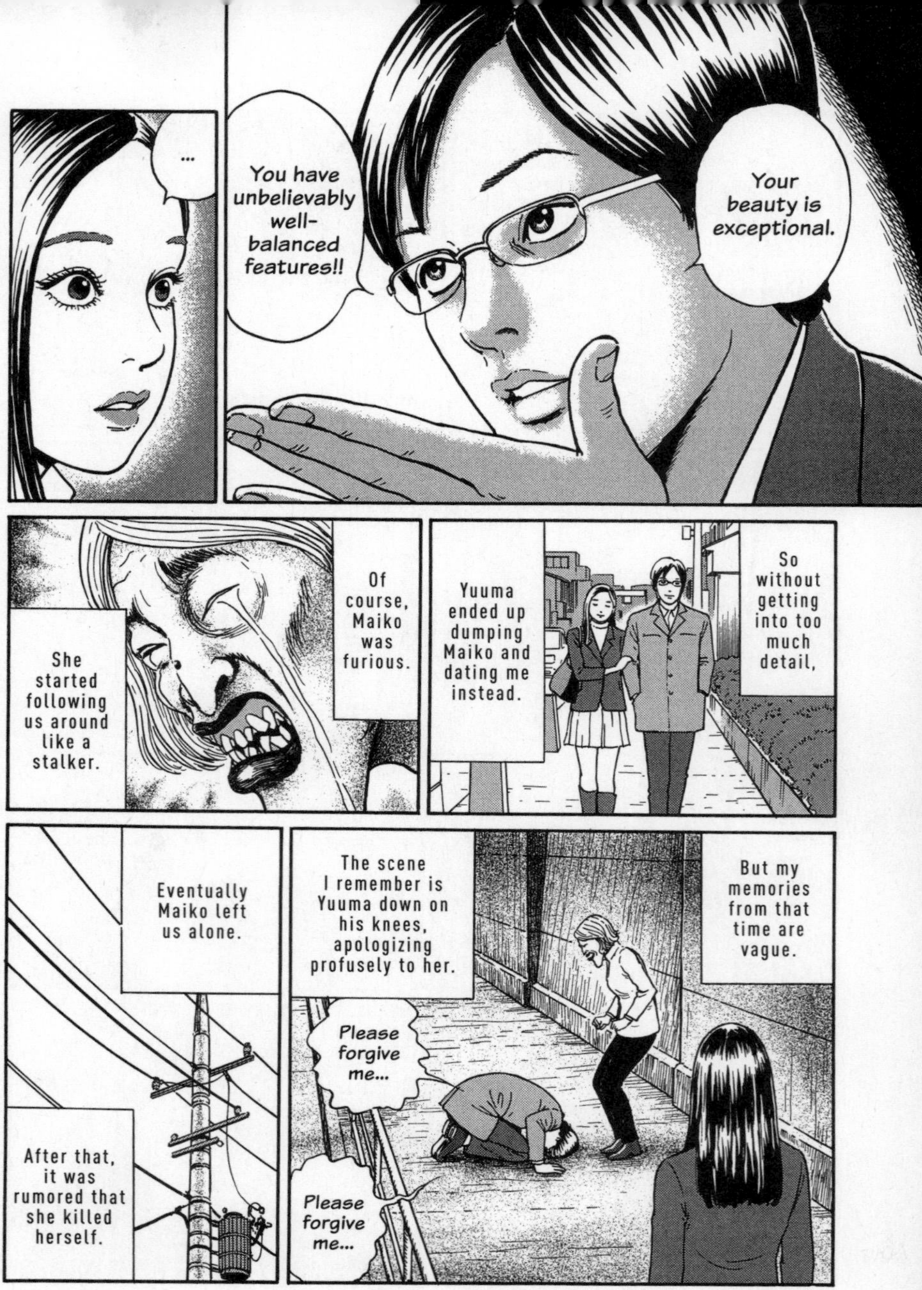
Your beauty is exceptional.
You have unbelievably well-balanced features!!
...
So without getting into too much detail,
Yuuma ended up dumping Maiko and dating me instead.
Of course, Maiko was furious.
She started following us around like a stalker.
But my memories from that time are vague.
The scene I remember is Yuuma down on his knees, apologizing profusely to her.
Please forgive me...
Please forgive me...
Eventually Maiko left us alone.
After that, it was rumored that she killed herself.

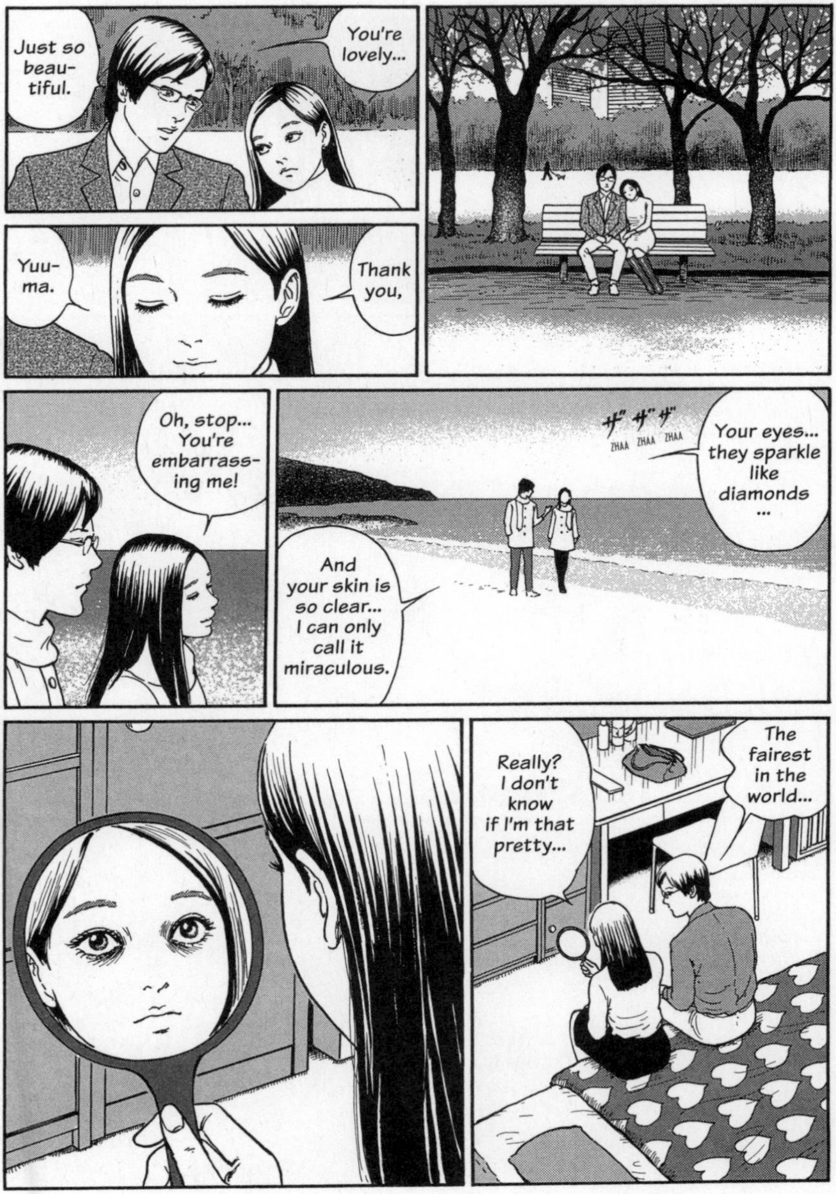
You're lovely...
Just so beau-tiful.
Thank you,
Yuu-ma.
Your eyes... they sparkle like diamonds...
ザザザ
ZHAA ZHAA ZHAA
And your skin is so clear... I can only call it miraculous.
Oh, stop... You're embarrass-ing me!
The fairest in the world...
Really? I don't know if I'm that pretty...

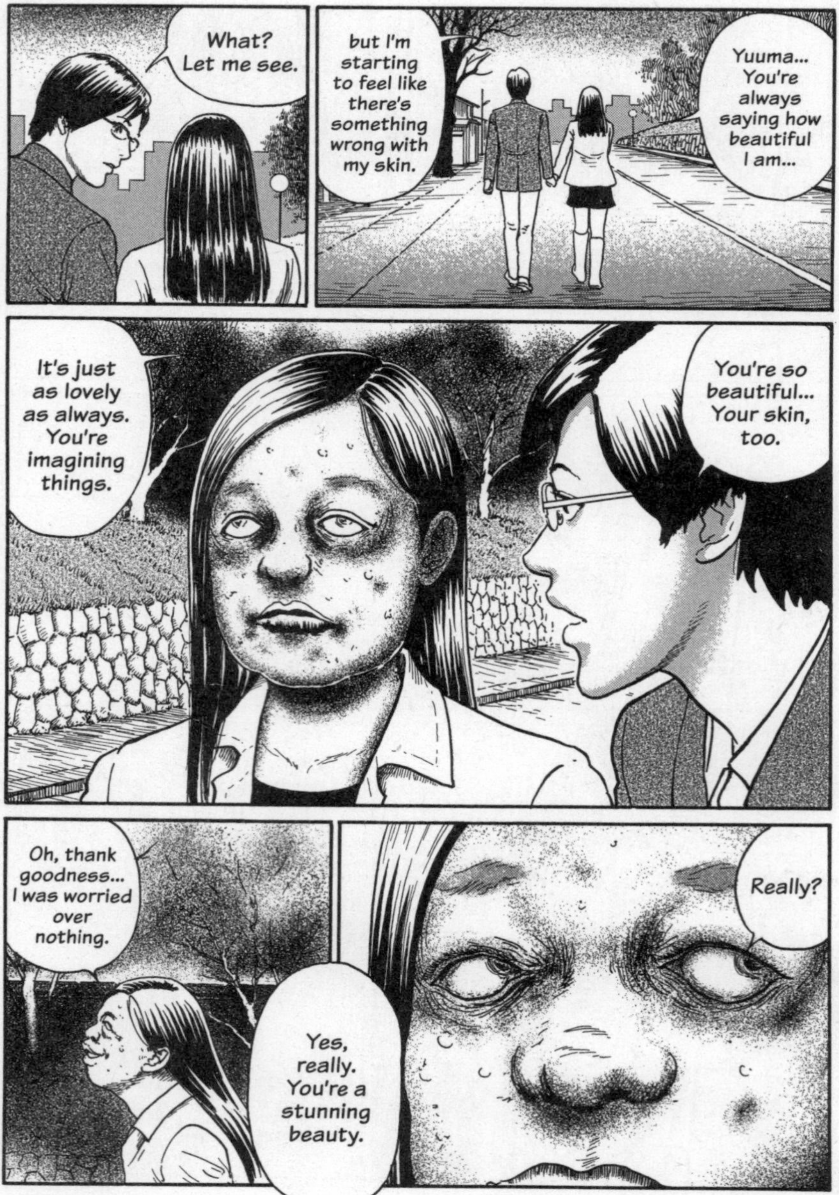
Yuuma... You're always saying how beautiful I am...
but I'm starting to feel like there's something wrong with my skin.
What? Let me see.
You're so beautiful... Your skin, too.
It's just as lovely as always. You're imagining things.
Really?
Yes, really. You're a stunning beauty.
Oh, thank goodness... I was worried over nothing.

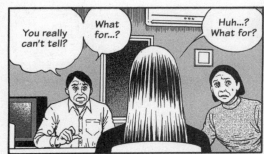

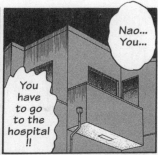

Nao... You...
You have to go to the hospital !!
Huh...? What for?
What for...?
You really can't tell?
We're worried. You might be seriously ill.
Your father's right, Nao. This can't be normal.
What're you talking about? Aren't I just as pretty as ever?
He tells me so every day.
...

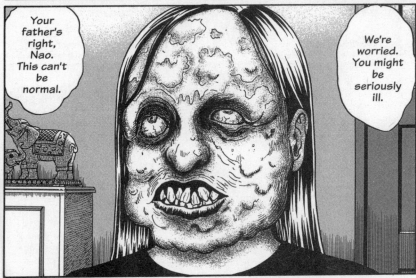

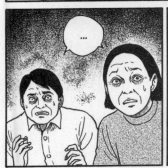

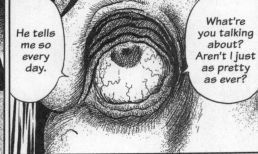

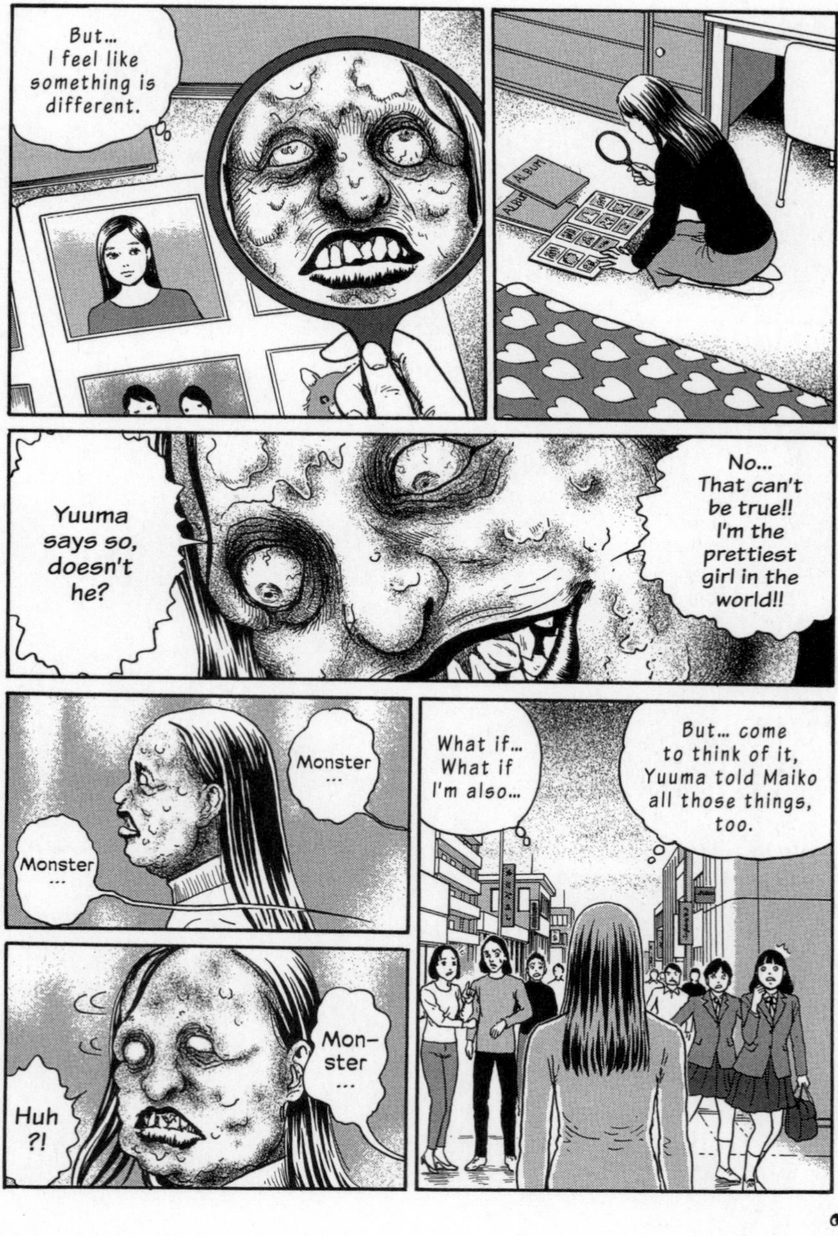
But... I feel like something is different.
No... That can't be true!! I'm the prettiest girl in the world!!
Yuuma says so, doesn't he?
But... come to think of it, Yuuma told Maiko all those things, too.
What if... What if I'm also...
Monster ...
Monster ...
Mon-ster ...
Huh ?!

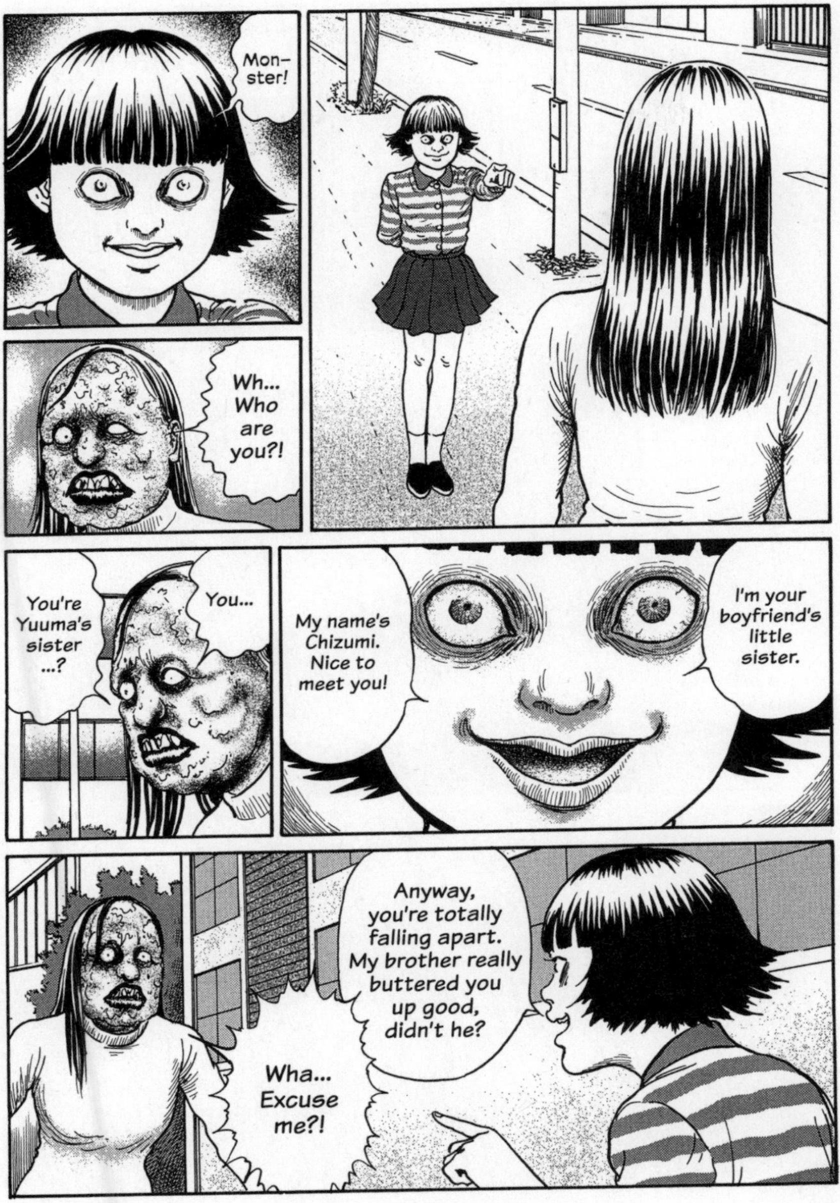
Mon–ster!
Wh... Who are you?!
I'm your boyfriend's little sister.
My name's Chizumi. Nice to meet you!
You...
You're Yuuma's sister ...?
Anyway, you're totally falling apart. My brother really buttered you up good, didn't he?
Wha... Excuse me?!

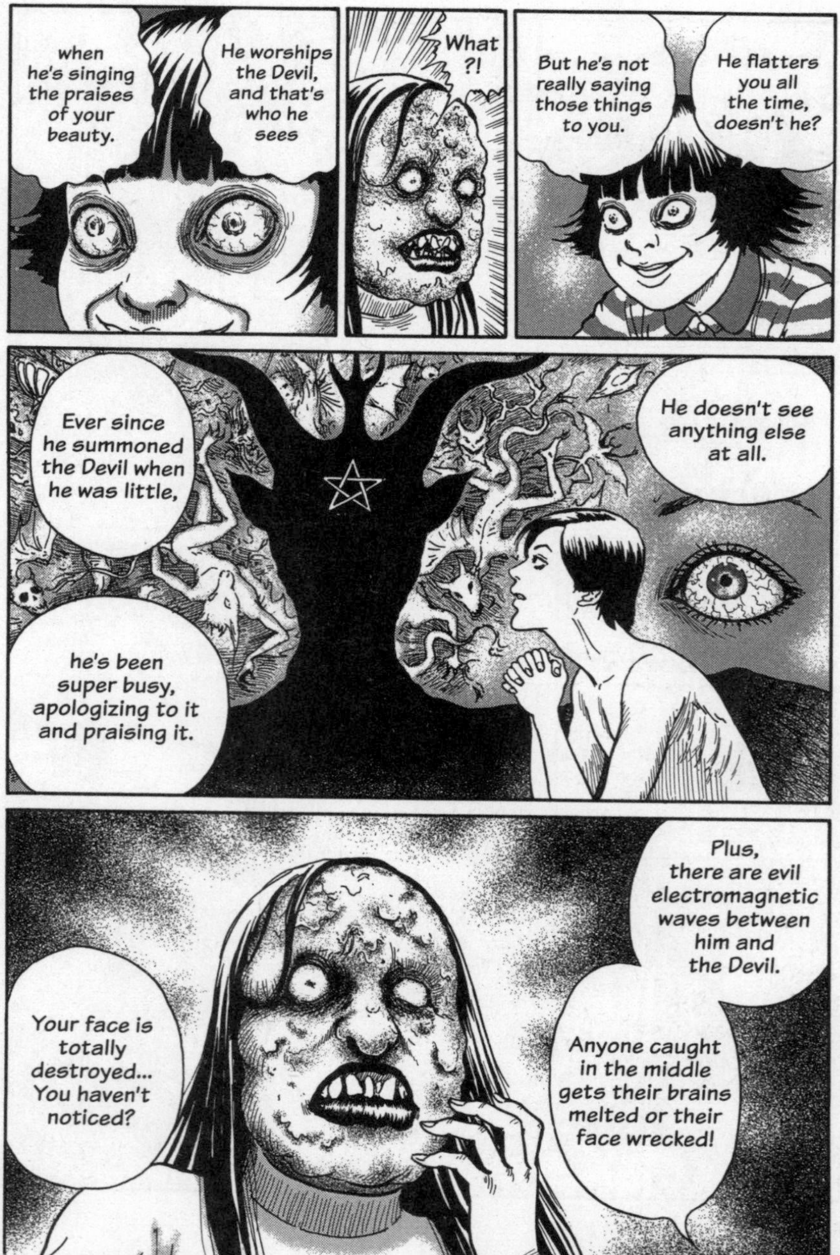

He flatters you all the time, doesn't he?
But he's not really saying those things to you.
What ?!
He worships the Devil, and that's who he sees
when he's singing the praises of your beauty.
He doesn't see anything else at all.
Ever since he summoned the Devil when he was little,
he's been super busy, apologizing to it and praising it.
Plus, there are evil electromagnetic waves between him and the Devil.
Anyone caught in the middle gets their brains melted or their face wrecked!
Your face is totally destroyed... You haven't noticed?

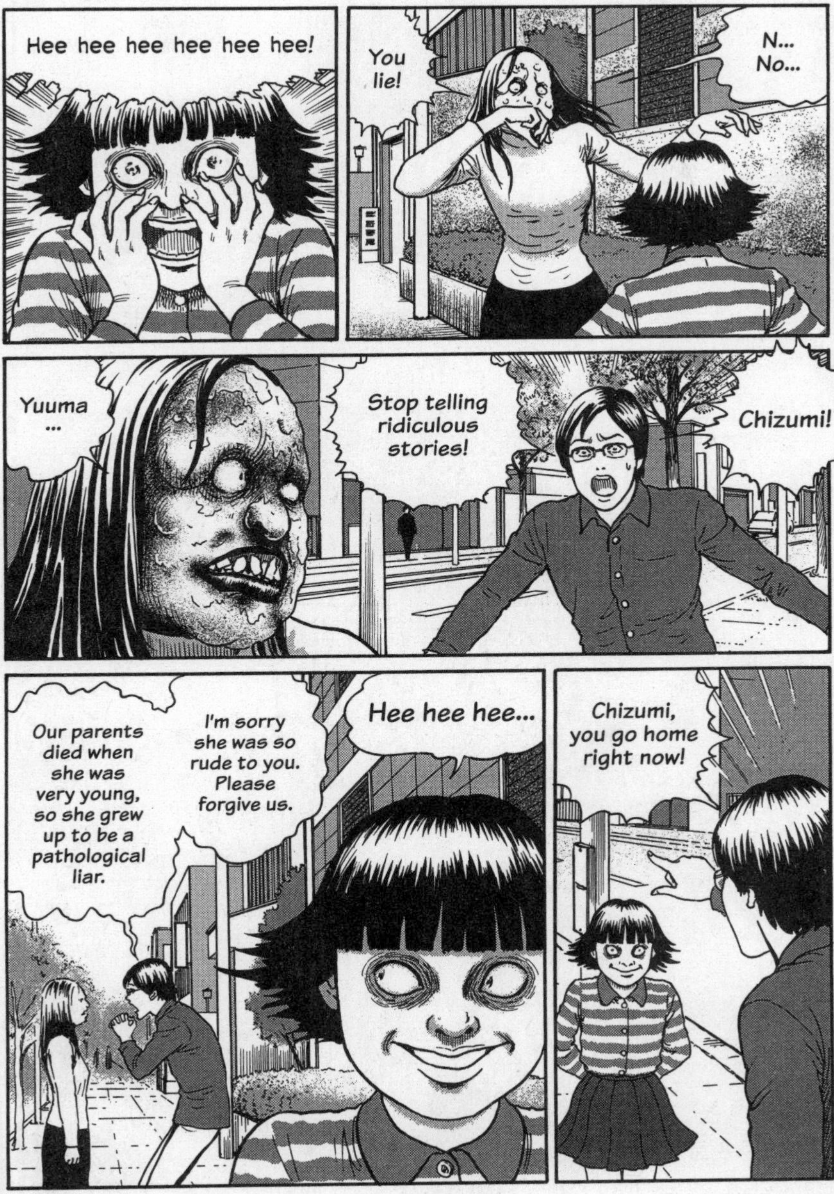
N... No...
You lie!
Hee hee hee hee hee hee!
Chizumi!
Stop telling ridiculous stories!
Yuuma ...
Chizumi, you go home right now!
Hee hee hee...
I'm sorry she was so rude to you. Please forgive us.
Our parents died when she was very young, so she grew up to be a pathological liar.

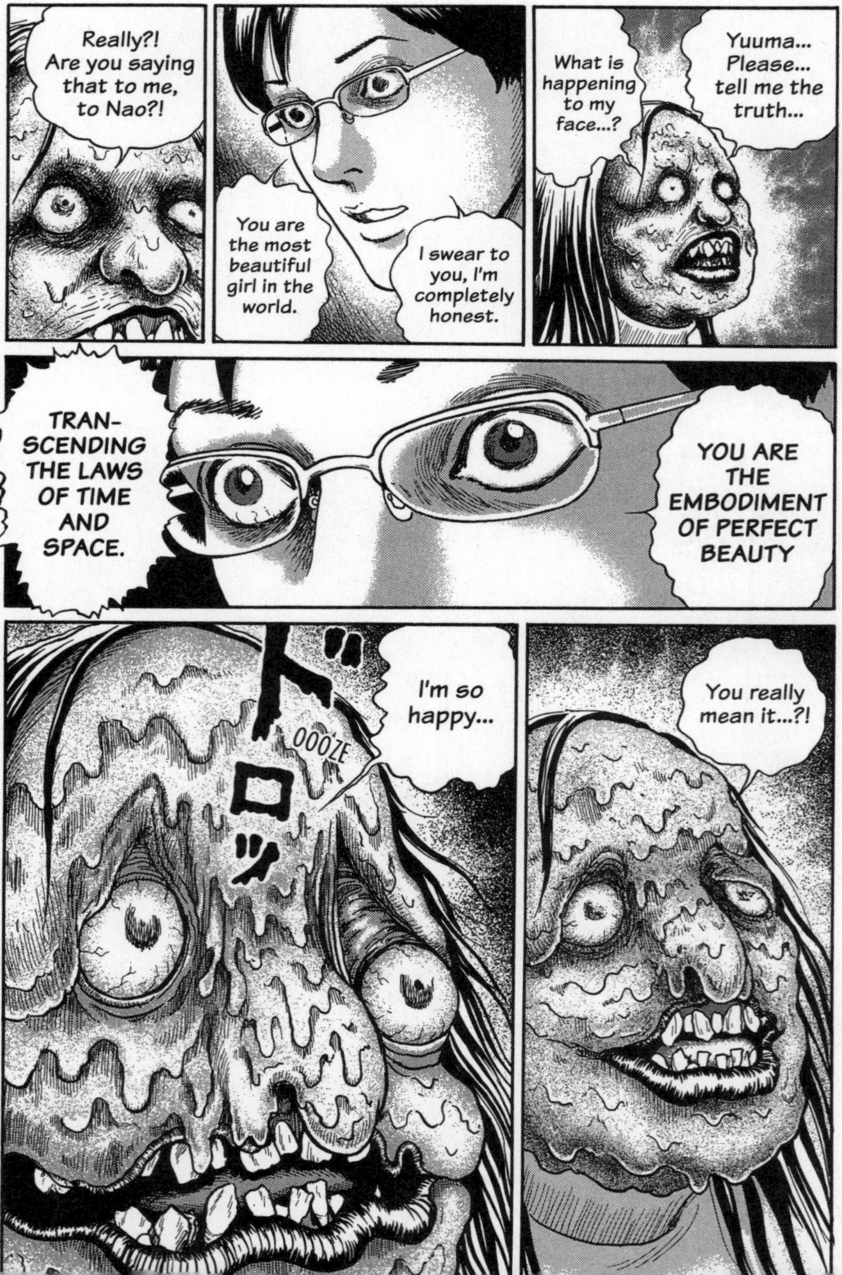
Yuuma... Please... tell me the truth...
What is happening to my face...?
You are the most beautiful girl in the world.
I swear to you, I'm completely honest.
Really?! Are you saying that to me, to Nao?!
YOU ARE THE EMBODIMENT OF PERFECT BEAUTY
TRAN-SCENDING THE LAWS OF TIME AND SPACE.
You really mean it...?!
I'm so happy...
OOOZE

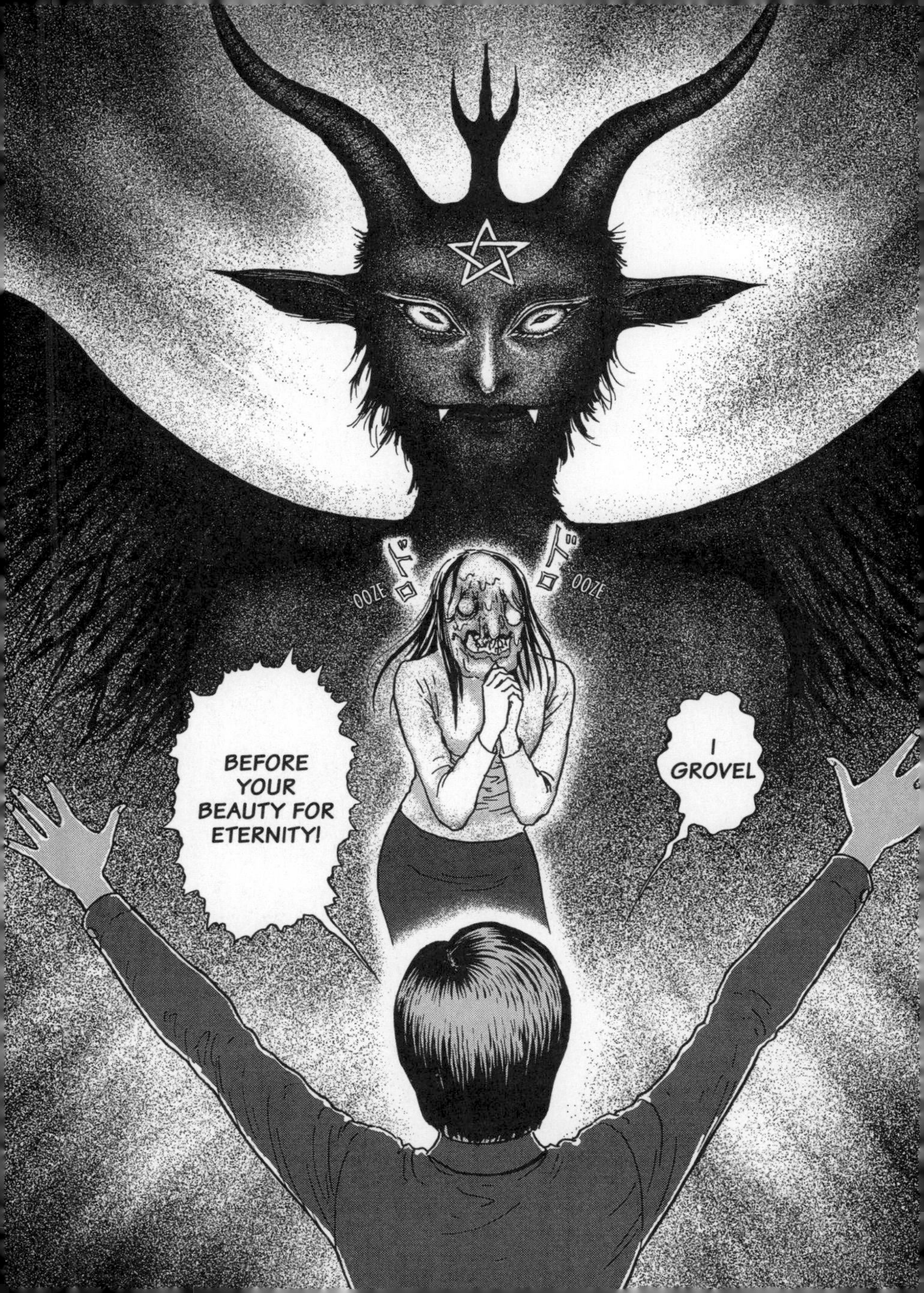
ドロ
OOZE
ドロ
OOZE
I GROVEL
BEFORE YOUR BEAUTY FOR ETERNITY!

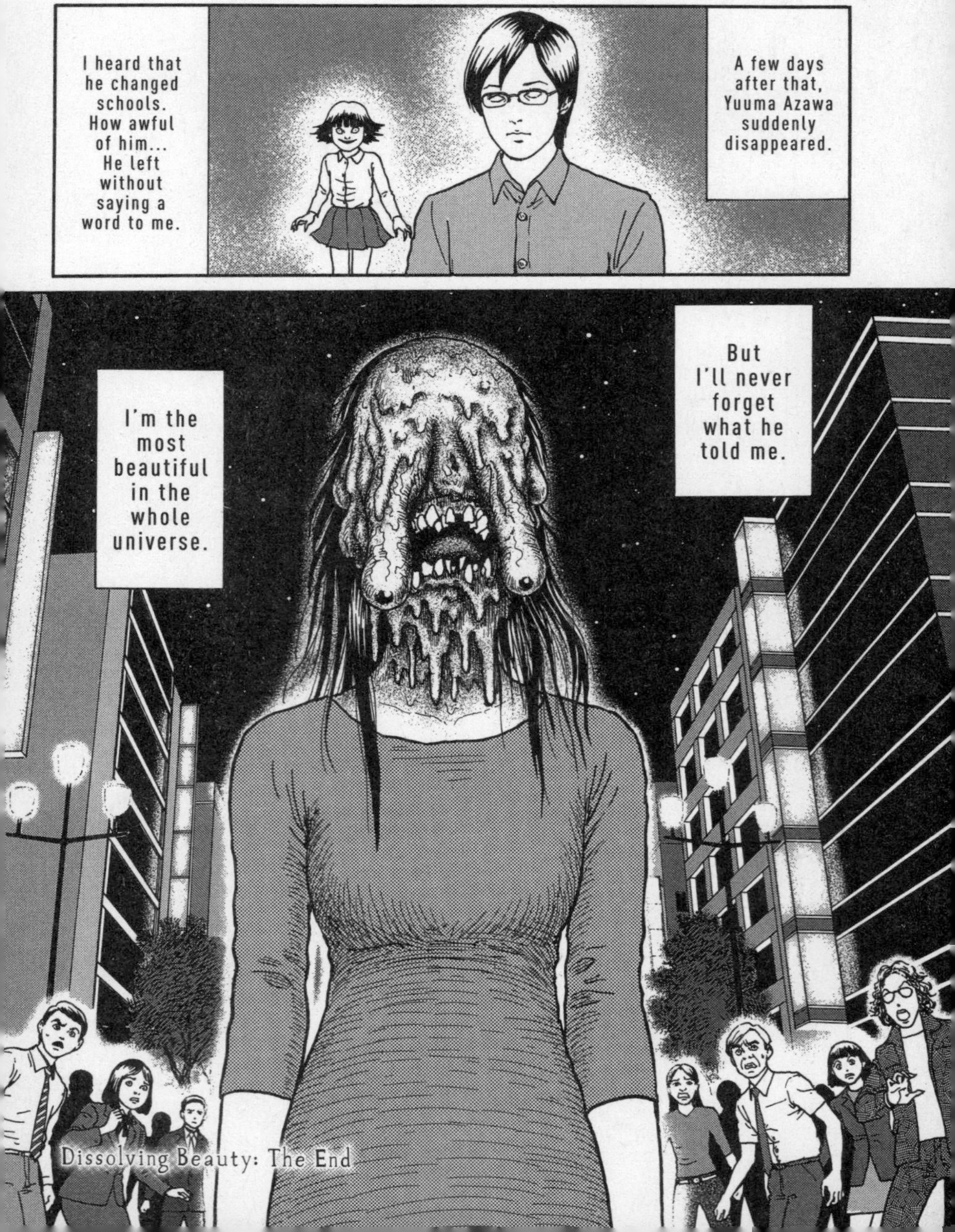
A few days after that, Yuuma Azawa suddenly disappeared.
I heard that he changed schools. How awful of him... He left without saying a word to me.
But I'll never forget what he told me.
I'm the most beautiful in the whole universe.
Dissolving Beauty: The End

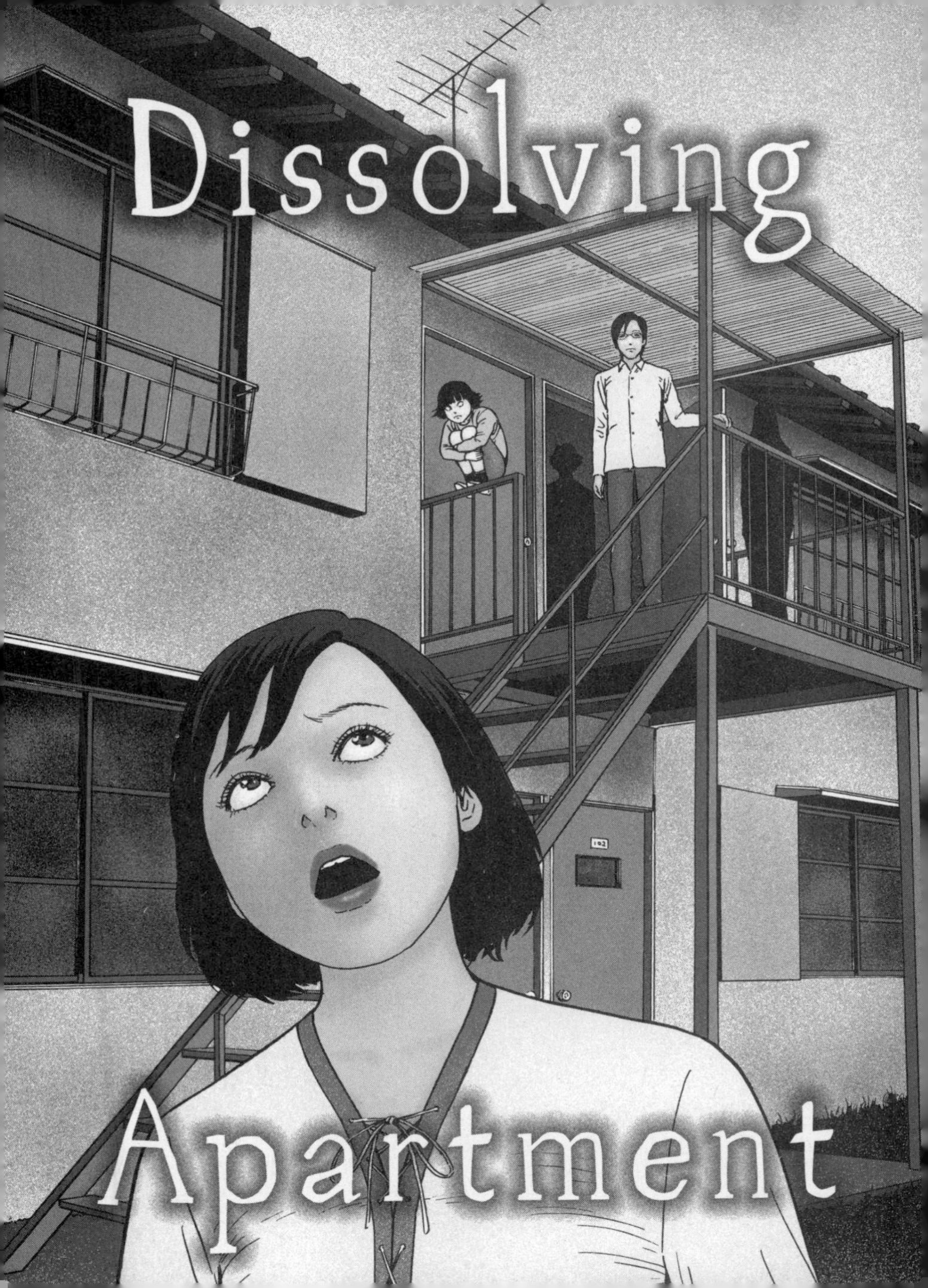
Dissolving
Apartment

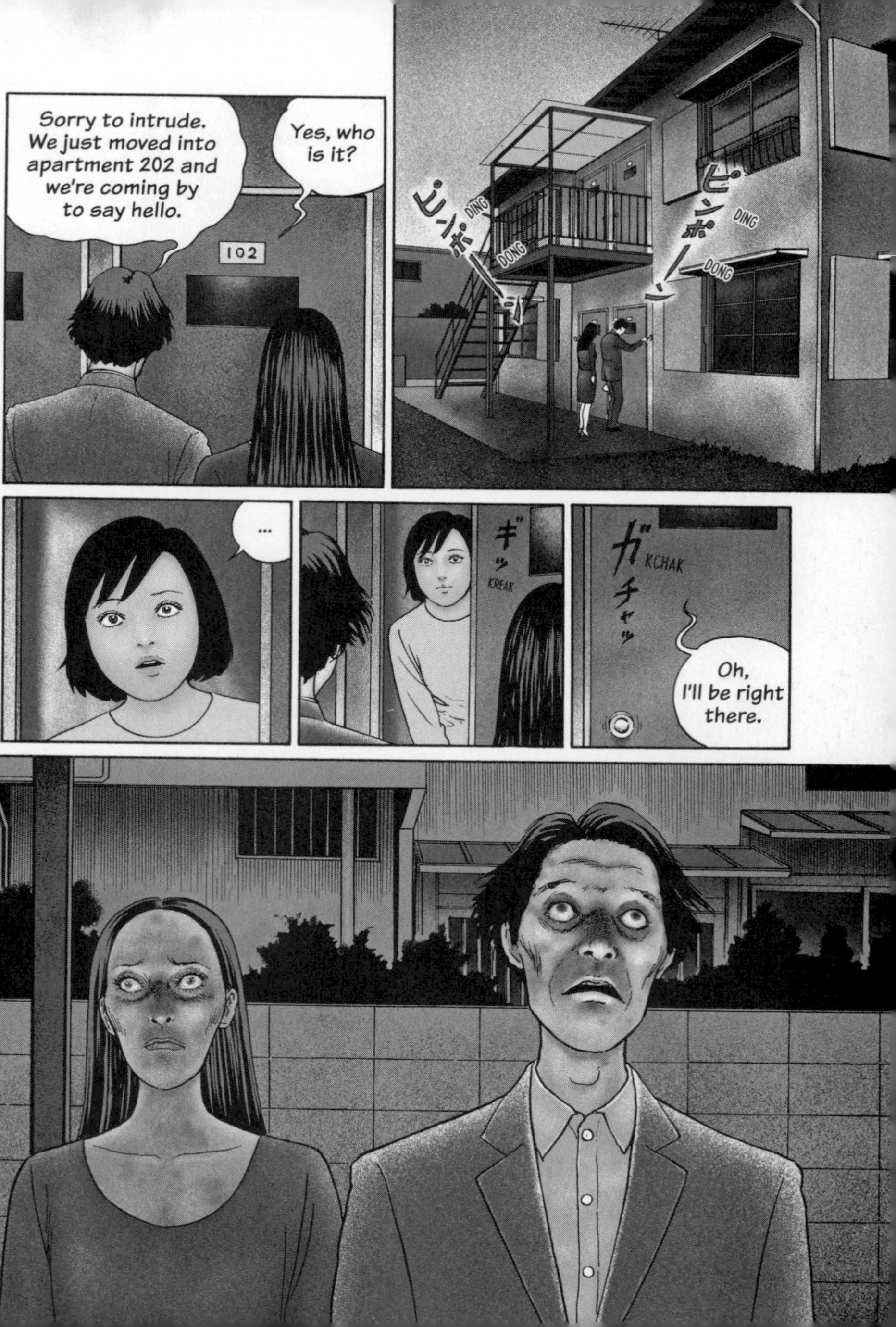
ピンポーン
DING
DONG
ピンポーン
DING
DONG
Yes, who is it?
Sorry to intrude. We just moved into apartment 202 and we're coming by to say hello.
102
ガチャッ
KCHAK
Oh, I'll be right there.
ギッ
KREAK
...

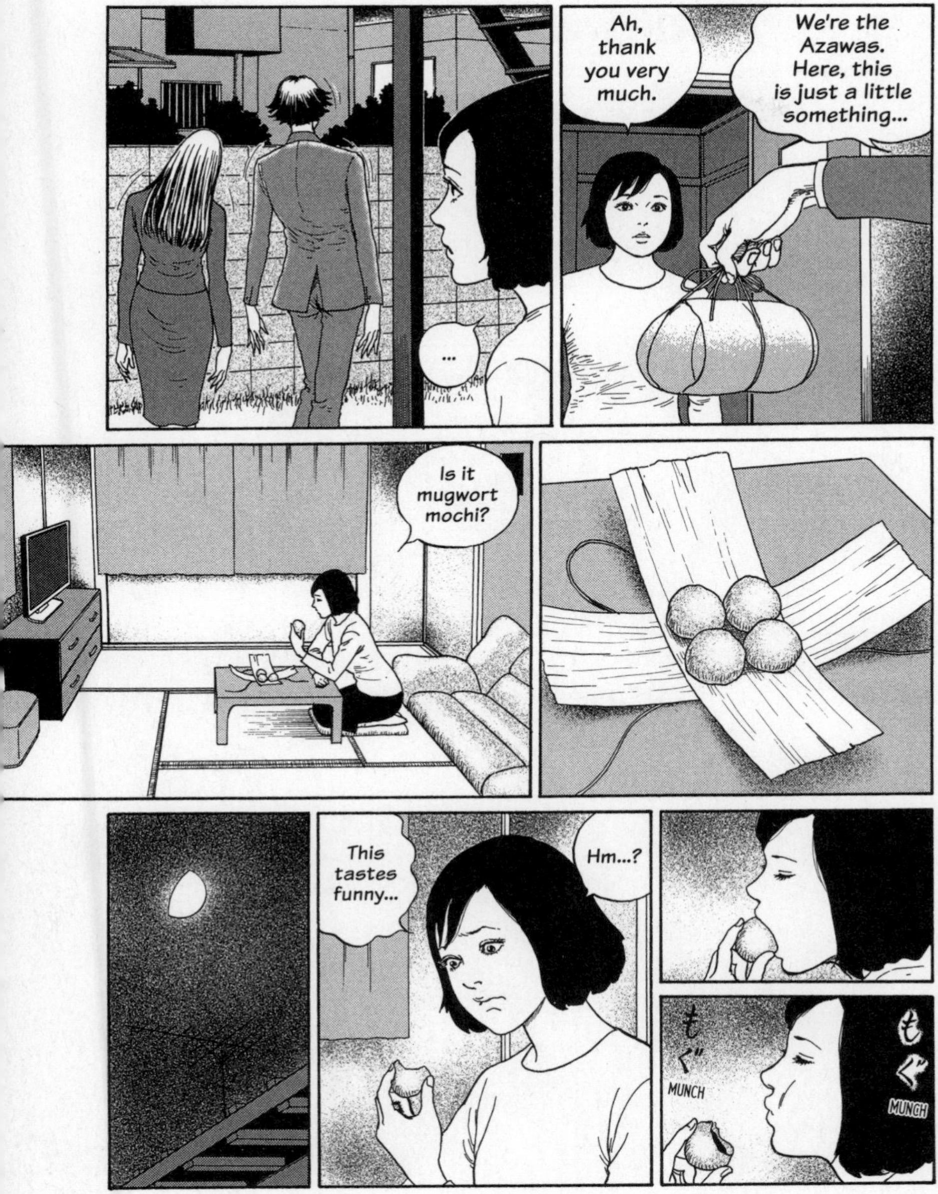
We're the Azawas. Here, this is just a little something...
Ah, thank you very much.
...
Is it mugwort mochi?
もぐ
MUNCH
もぐ
MUNCH
Hm...?
This tastes funny...

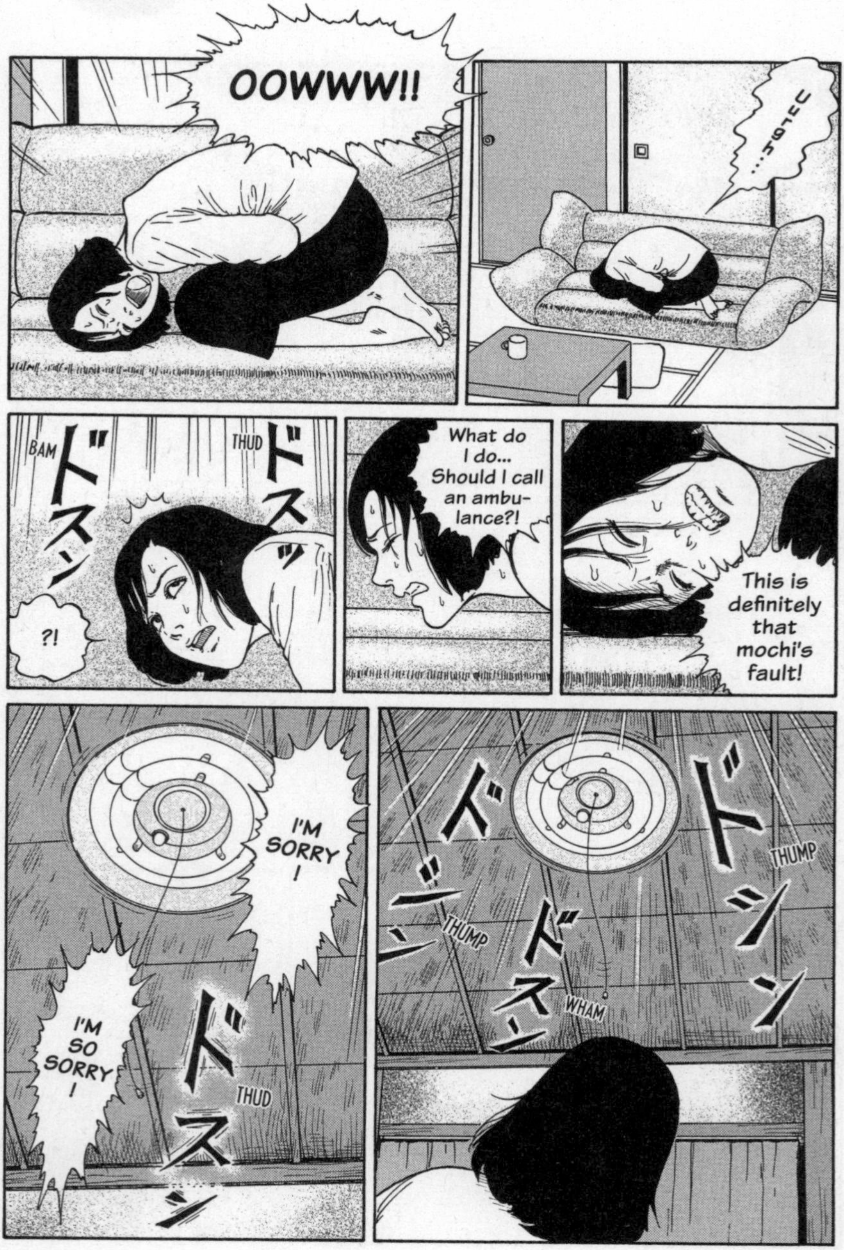
Uuugh...
OOWWW!!
This is definitely that mochi's fault!
What do I do... Should I call an ambulance?!
ドスッ
THUD
ドスン
BAM
?!
THUMP
THUMP
WHAM
I'M SORRY!
I'M SO SORRY!
ドスン
THUD

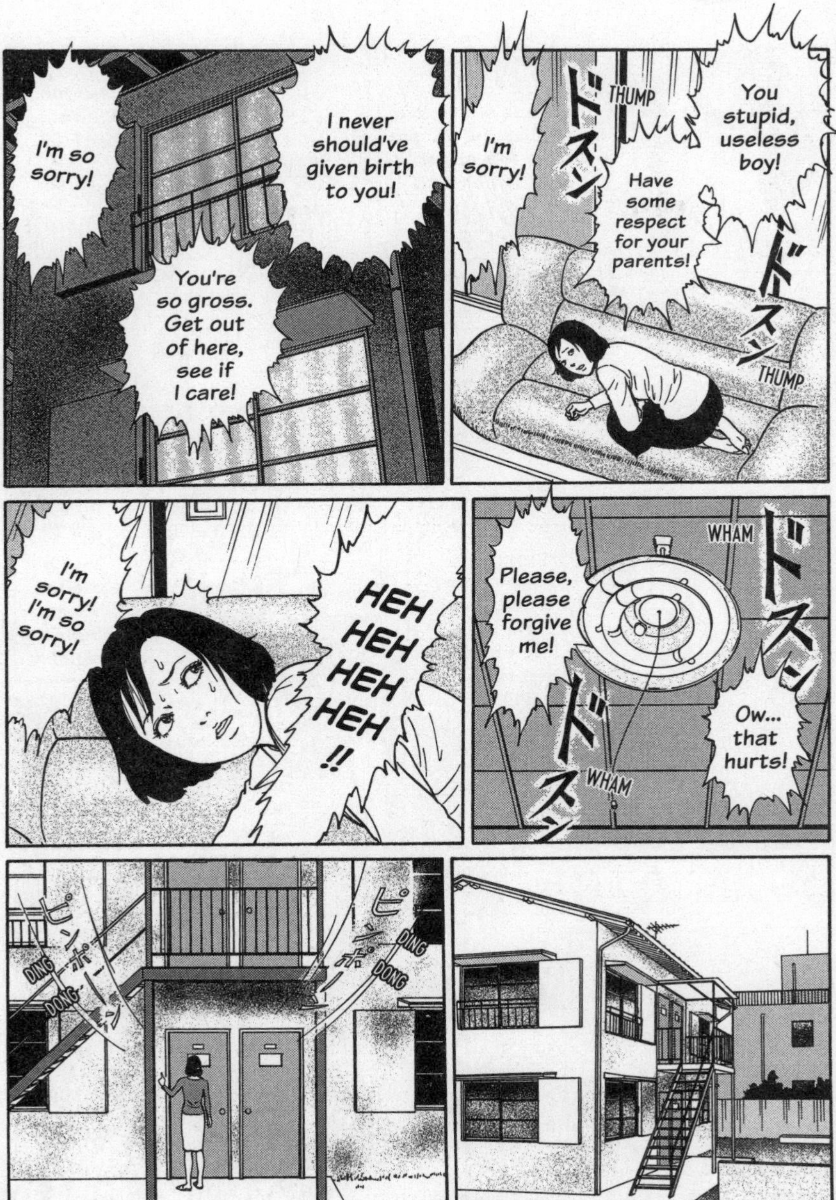
You stupid, useless boy!
THUMP
ドスン
I'm sorry!
Have some respect for your parents!
ドスン
THUMP
I never should've given birth to you!
I'm so sorry!
You're so gross. Get out of here, see if I care!
WHAM
ドスン
Please, please forgive me!
ドスン
WHAM
Ow... that hurts!
HEH HEH HEH HEH !!
I'm sorry! I'm so sorry!
ピンポーン
DING DONG
ピンポーン
DING DONG

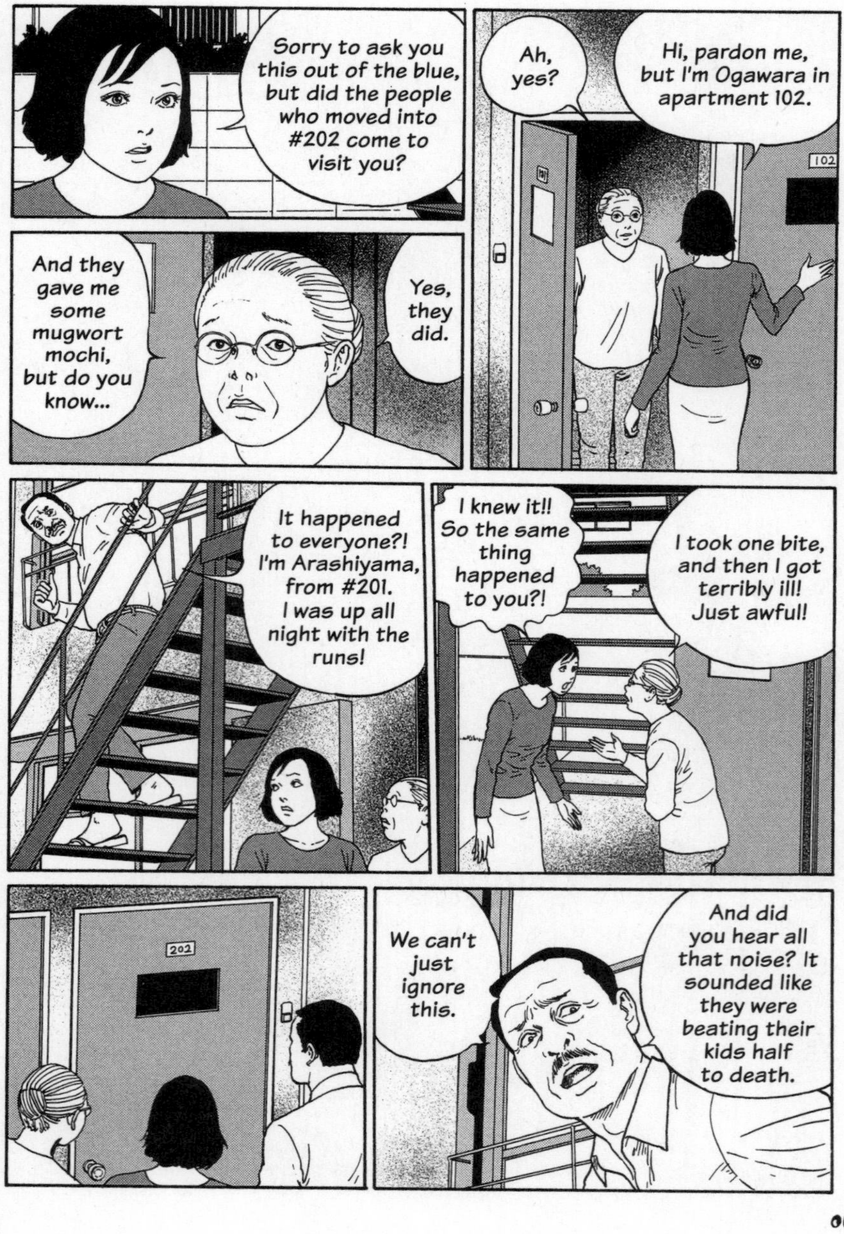
Hi, pardon me, but I'm Ogawara in apartment 102.
Ah, yes?
102
Sorry to ask you this out of the blue, but did the people who moved into #202 come to visit you?
Yes, they did.
And they gave me some mugwort mochi, but do you know...
I took one bite, and then I got terribly ill! Just awful!
I knew it!! So the same thing happened to you?!
It happened to everyone?! I'm Arashiyama, from #201. I was up all night with the runs!
And did you hear all that noise? It sounded like they were beating their kids half to death.
We can't just ignore this.
202

ピンポーン
DING
DONG
ピンポーン
DING
DONG
ガチャッ
KCHAK
202
ギイイ
KREEEAK
Oh, dear... Your face......
Hey, is your mom or dad around...?

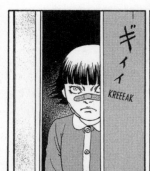

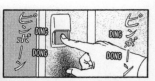

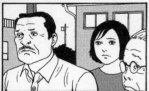

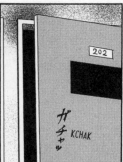

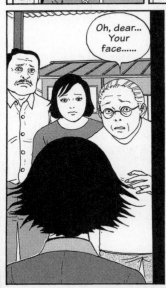

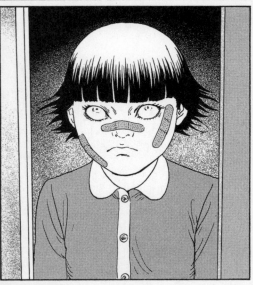

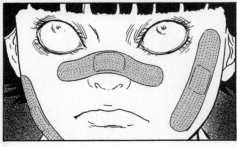

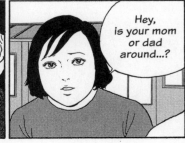

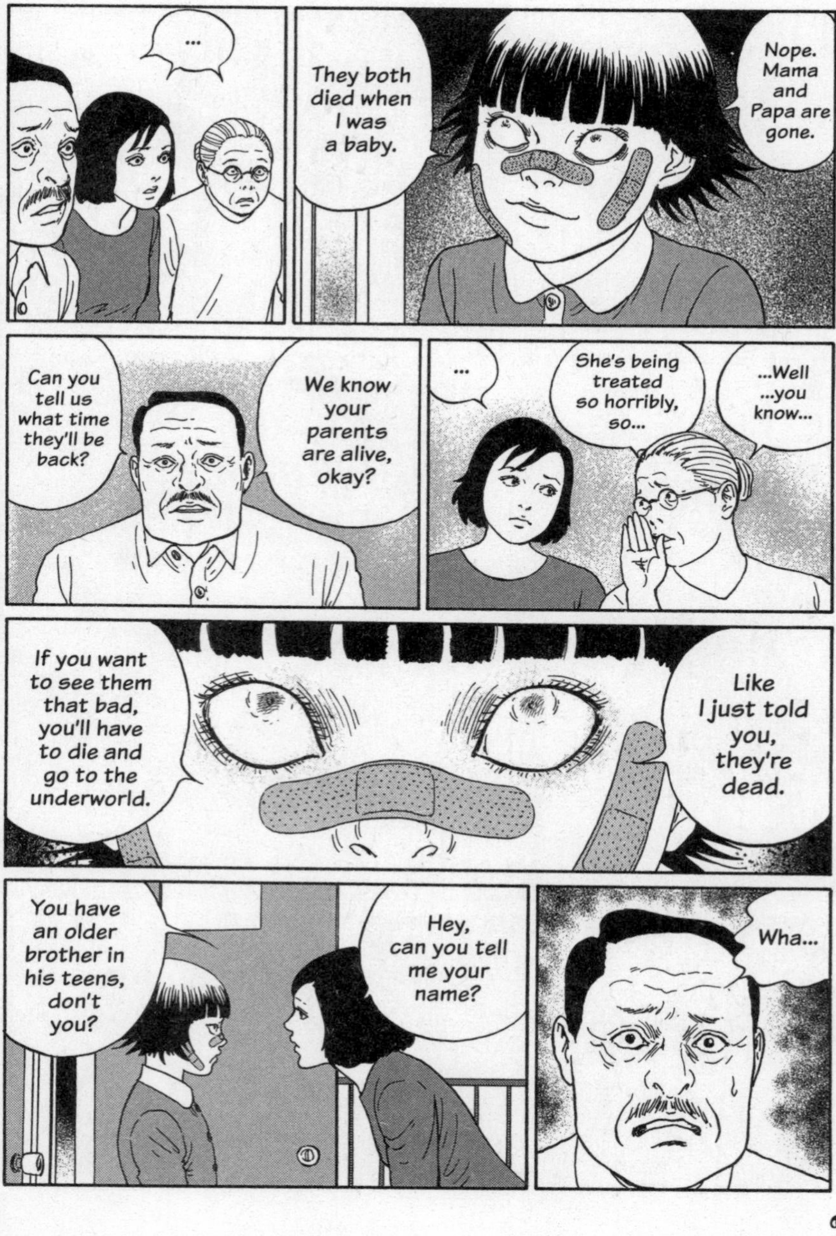
Nope. Mama and Papa are gone.
They both died when I was a baby.
...
...Well ...you know...
She's being treated so horribly, so...
...
We know your parents are alive, okay?
Can you tell us what time they'll be back?
Like I just told you, they're dead.
If you want to see them that bad, you'll have to die and go to the underworld.
Wha...
Hey, can you tell me your name?
You have an older brother in his teens, don't you?

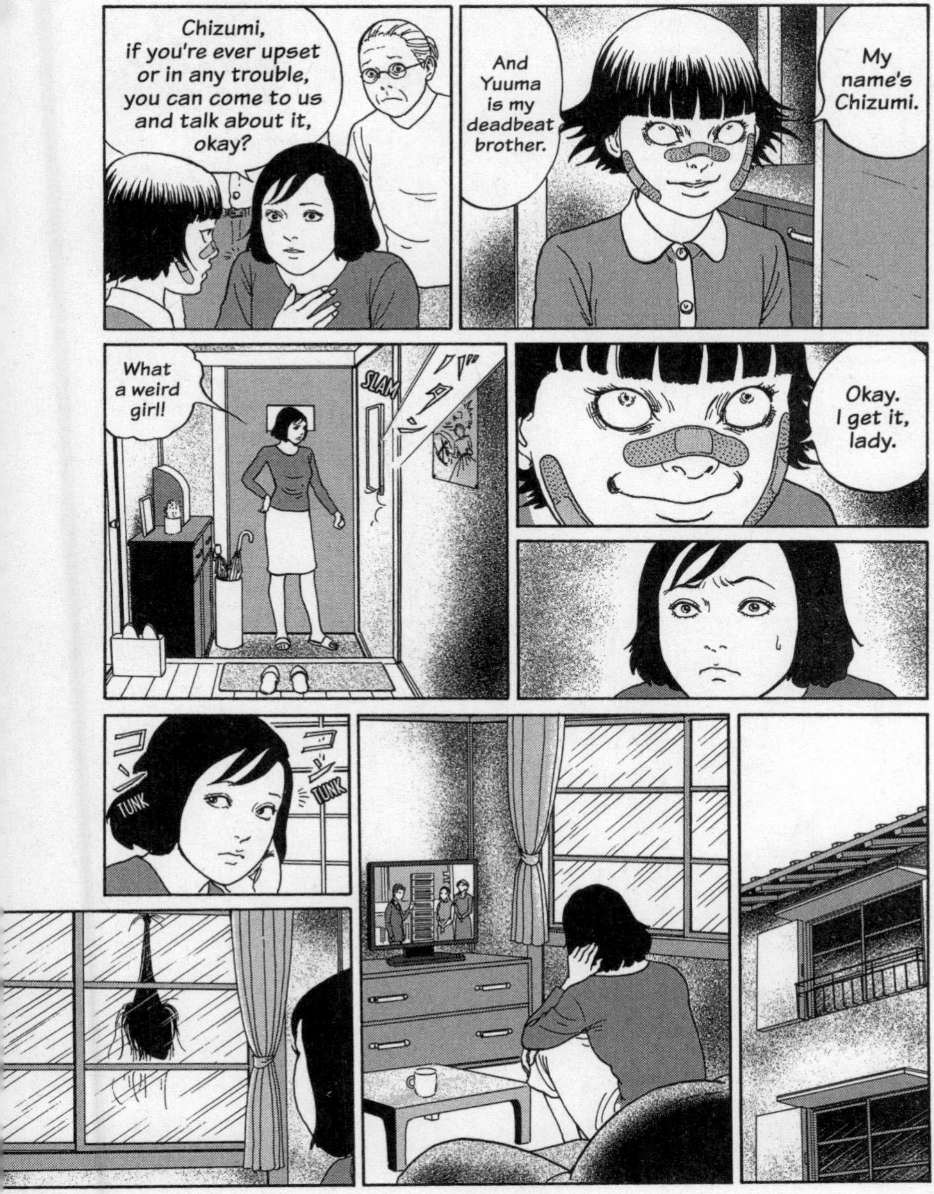
My name's Chizumi.
And Yuuma is my deadbeat brother.
Chizumi, if you're ever upset or in any trouble, you can come to us and talk about it, okay?
Okay. I get it, lady.
SLAM
What a weird girl!
TUNK
TUNK

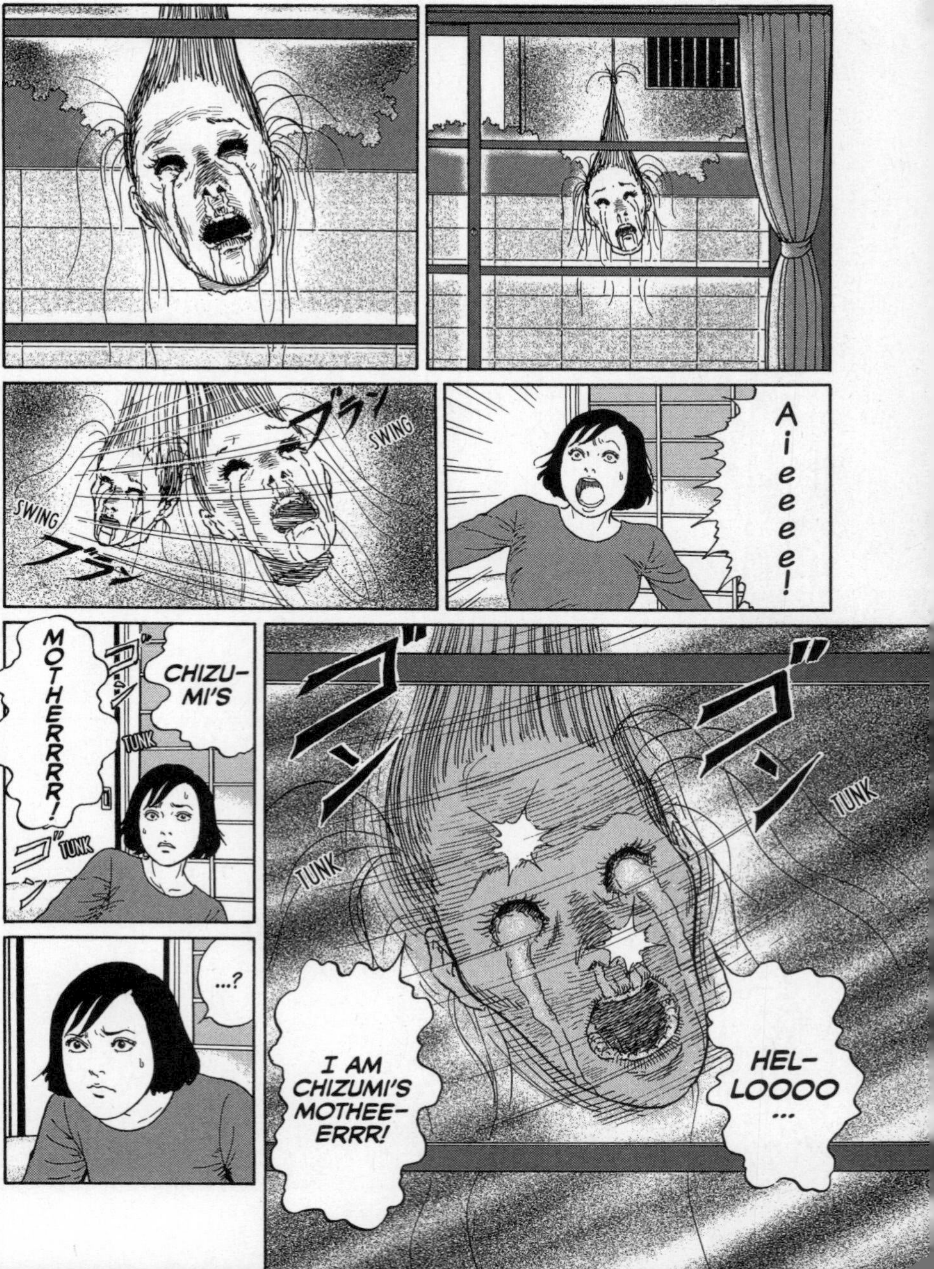
Aieeeee!
SWING
SWING
TUNK
TUNK
HEL-LOOOO ...
I AM CHIZUMI'S MOTHEE-ERRR!
CHIZU-MI'S
MOTHERRRR!
TUNK
TUNK
...?

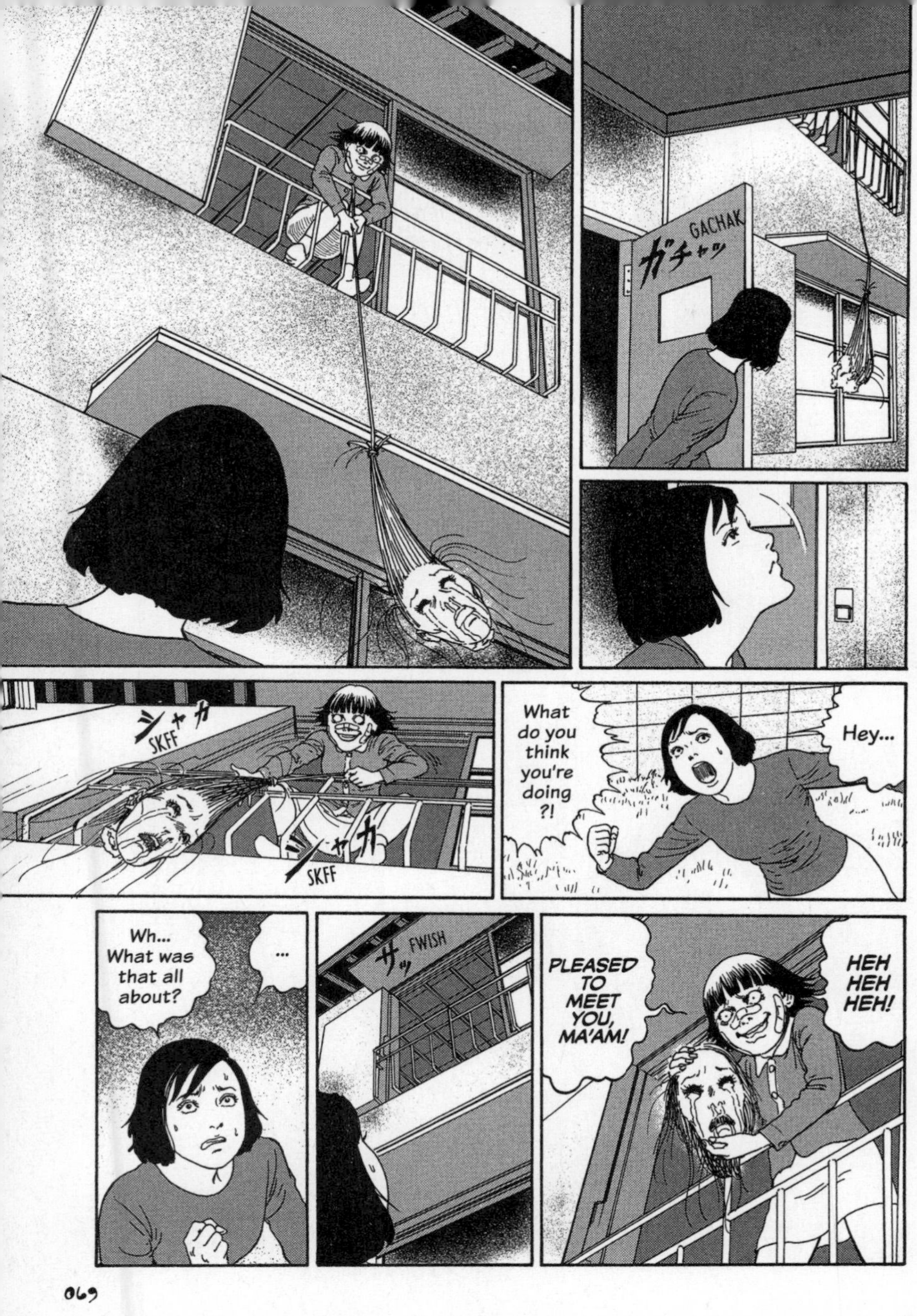
GACHAK
ガチャッ
Hey...
What do you think you're doing?!
シャカ
SKFF
シャカ
SKFF
HEH HEH HEH!
PLEASED TO MEET YOU, MA'AM!
サッ
FWISH
...
Wh... What was that all about?

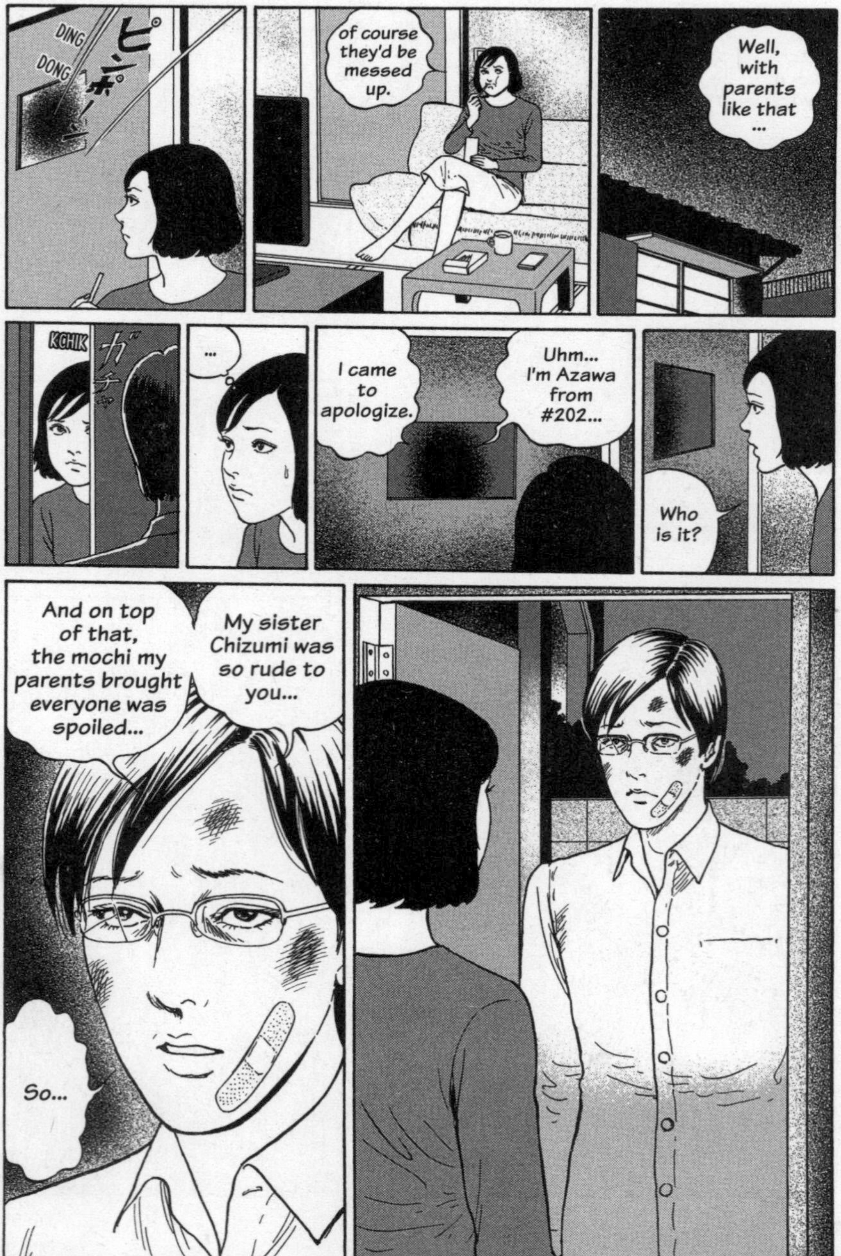
Well, with parents like that ...
of course they'd be messed up.
DING DONG
ピンポーン
Who is it?
Uhm... I'm Azawa from #202...
I came to apologize.
...
KCHIK
ガチャ
My sister Chizumi was so rude to you...
And on top of that, the mochi my parents brought everyone was spoiled...
So...

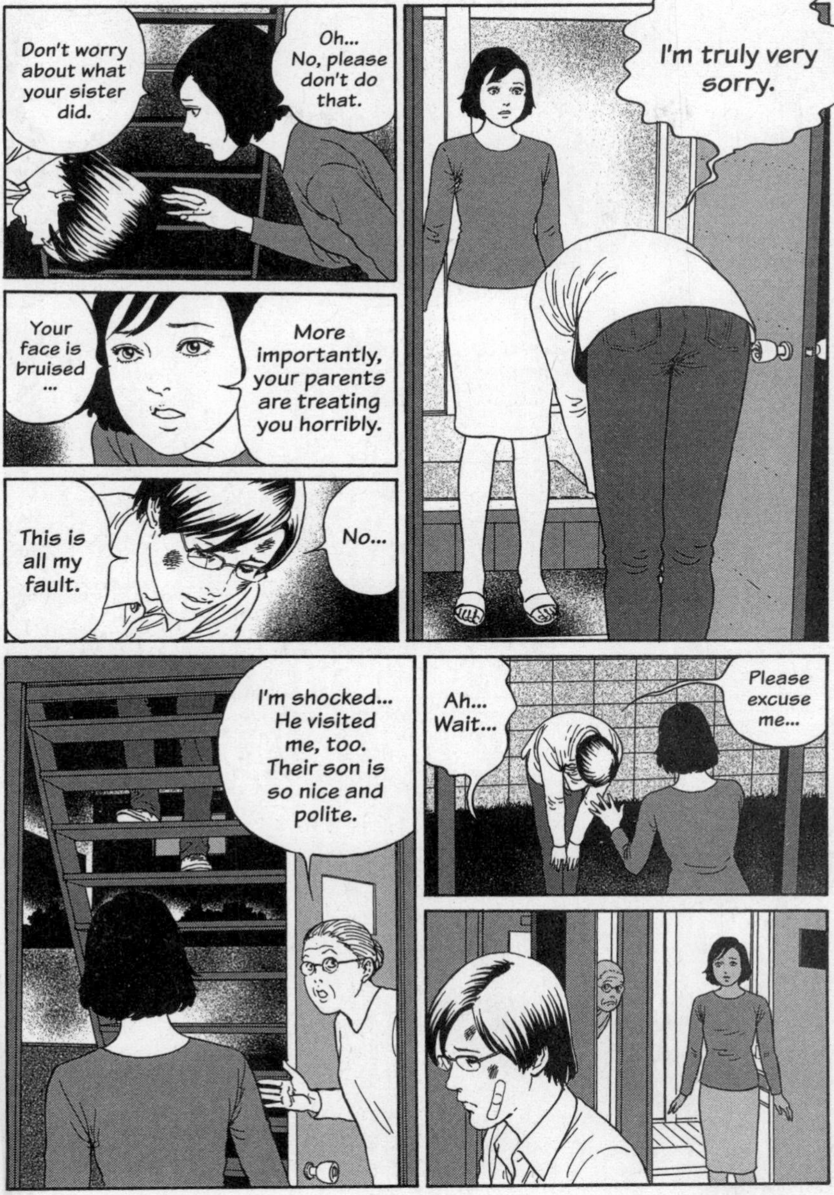
I'm truly very sorry.
Oh... No, please don't do that.
Don't worry about what your sister did.
More importantly, your parents are treating you horribly.
Your face is bruised ...
No...
This is all my fault.
Please excuse me...
Ah... Wait...
I'm shocked... He visited me, too. Their son is so nice and polite.

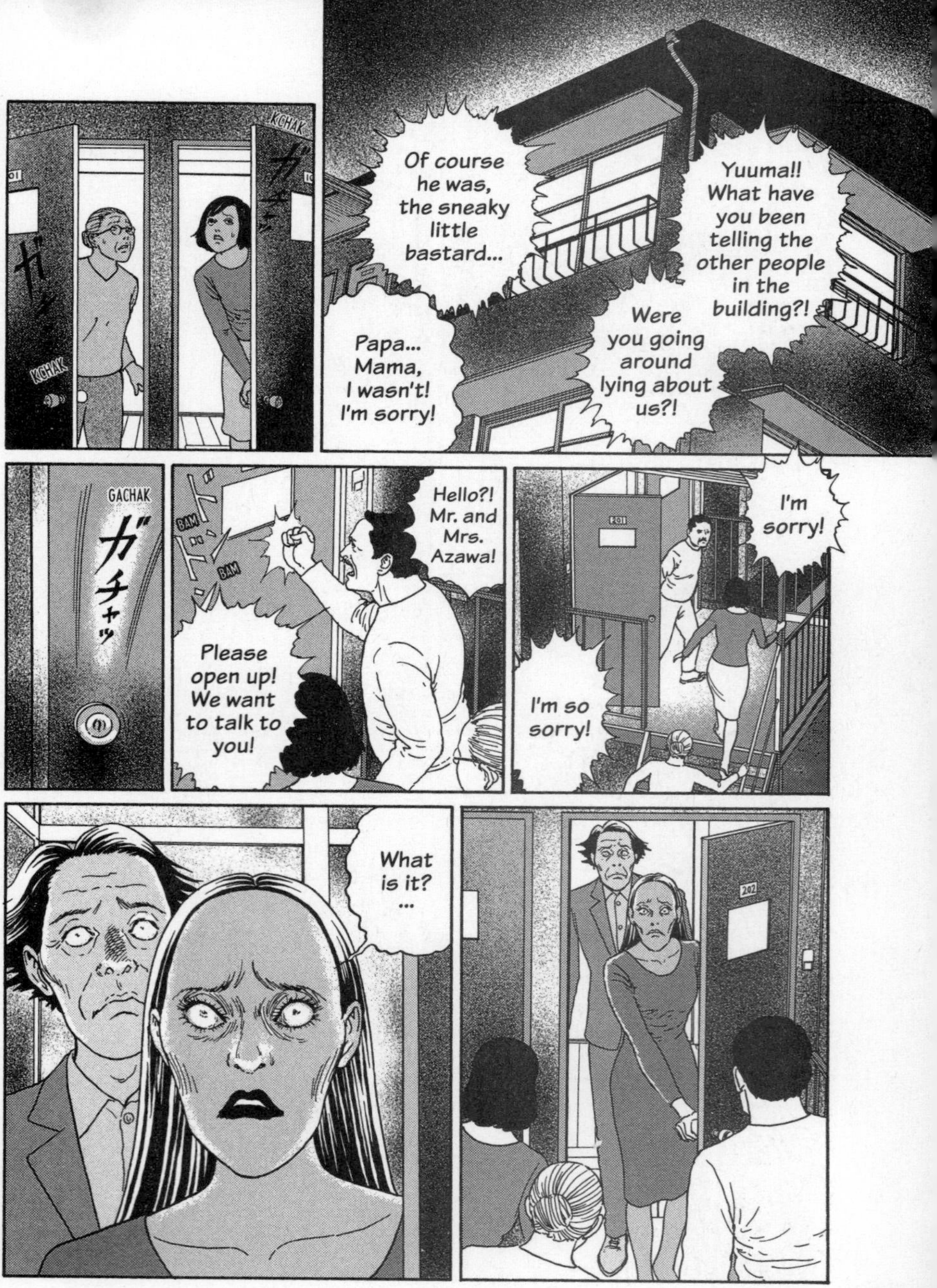
Yuuma!! What have you been telling the other people in the building?!
Of course he was, the sneaky little bastard...
Were you going around lying about us?!
Papa... Mama, I wasn't! I'm sorry!
KCHAK
KCHAK
I'm sorry!
I'm so sorry!
Hello?! Mr. and Mrs. Azawa!
BAM
BAM
Please open up! We want to talk to you!
GACHAK
ガチャッ
What is it? ...

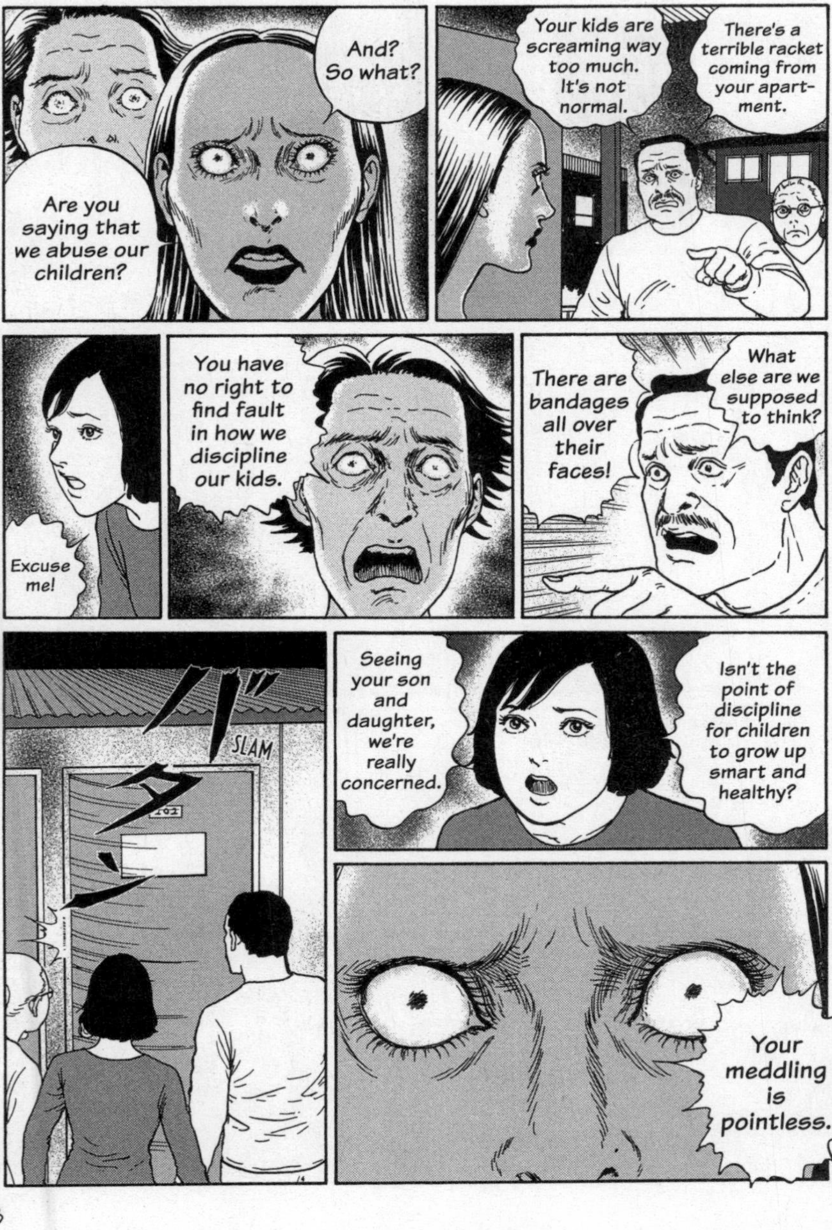
There's a terrible racket coming from your apartment.
Your kids are screaming way too much. It's not normal.
And? So what?
Are you saying that we abuse our children?
What else are we supposed to think?
There are bandages all over their faces!
You have no right to find fault in how we discipline our kids.
Excuse me!
Isn't the point of discipline for children to grow up smart and healthy?
Seeing your son and daughter, we're really concerned.
Your meddling is pointless.
バタン
SLAM

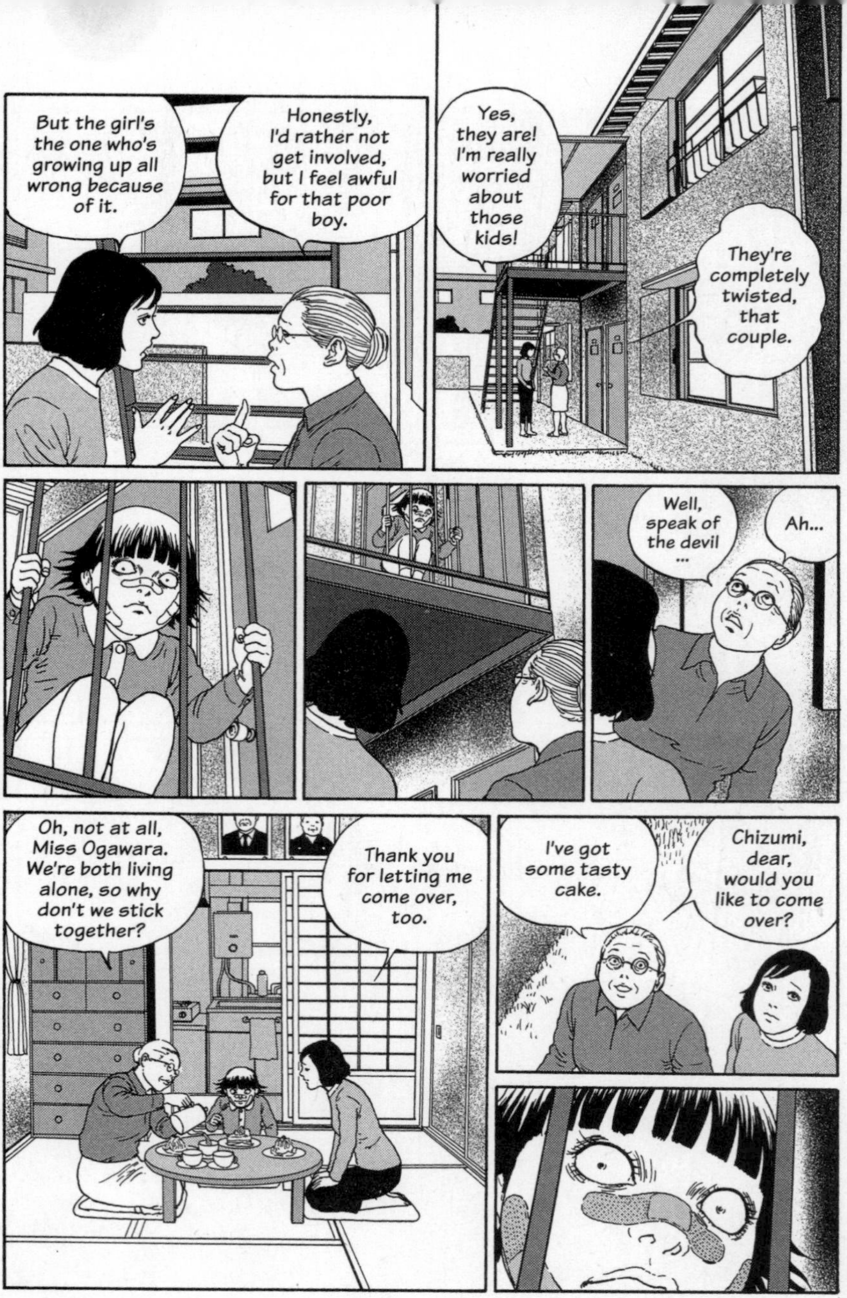
Yes, they are! I'm really worried about those kids!
They're completely twisted, that couple.
Honestly, I'd rather not get involved, but I feel awful for that poor boy.
But the girl's the one who's growing up all wrong because of it.
Ah...
Well, speak of the devil ...
Chizumi, dear, would you like to come over?
I've got some tasty cake.
Thank you for letting me come over, too.
Oh, not at all, Miss Ogawara. We're both living alone, so why don't we stick together?

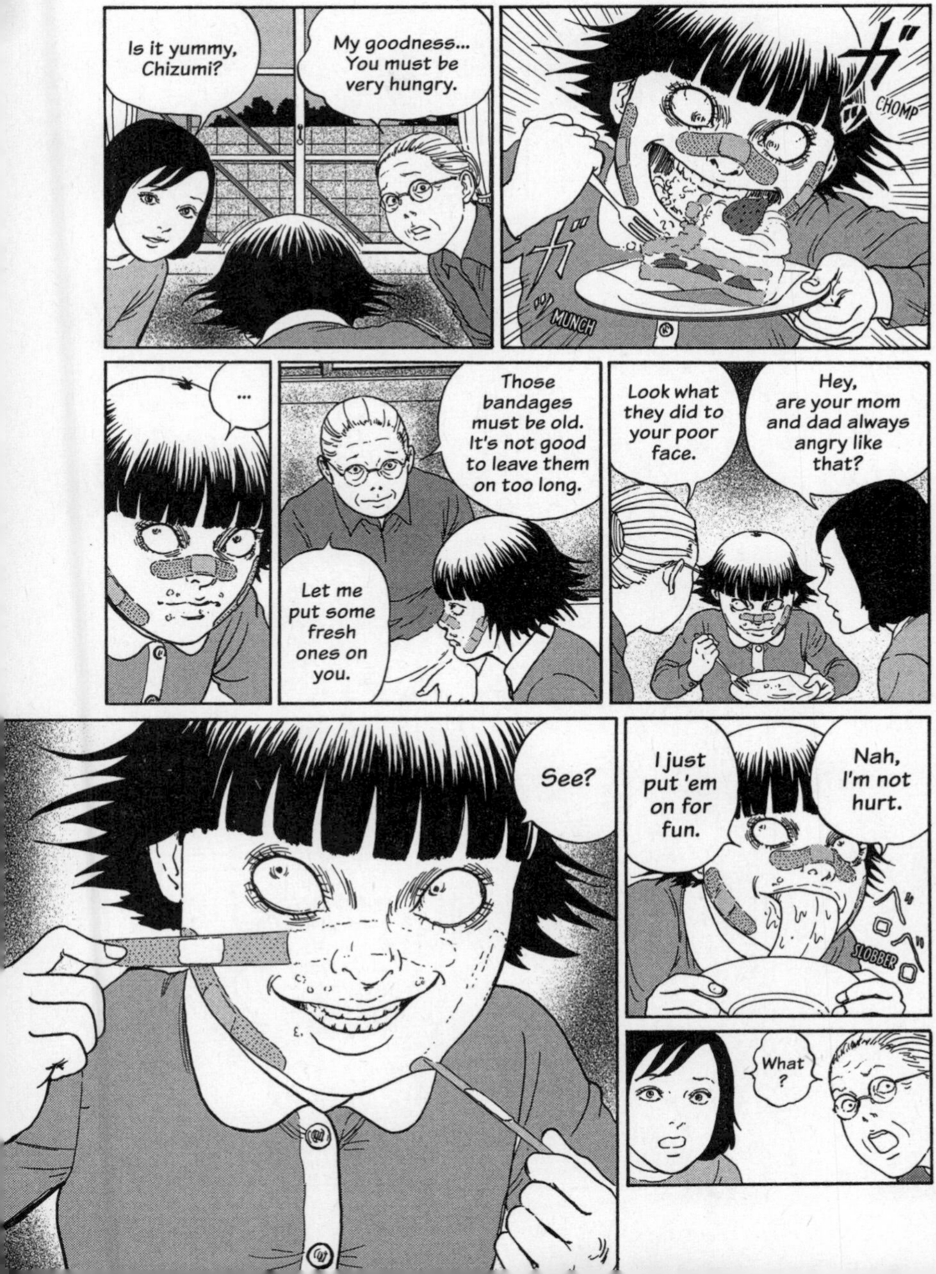
ガ
CHOMP
ガ
MUNCH
My goodness... You must be very hungry.
Is it yummy, Chizumi?
Hey, are your mom and dad always angry like that?
Look what they did to your poor face.
Those bandages must be old. It's not good to leave them on too long.
Let me put some fresh ones on you.
...
Nah, I'm not hurt.
I just put 'em on for fun.
SLOBBER
What?
See?

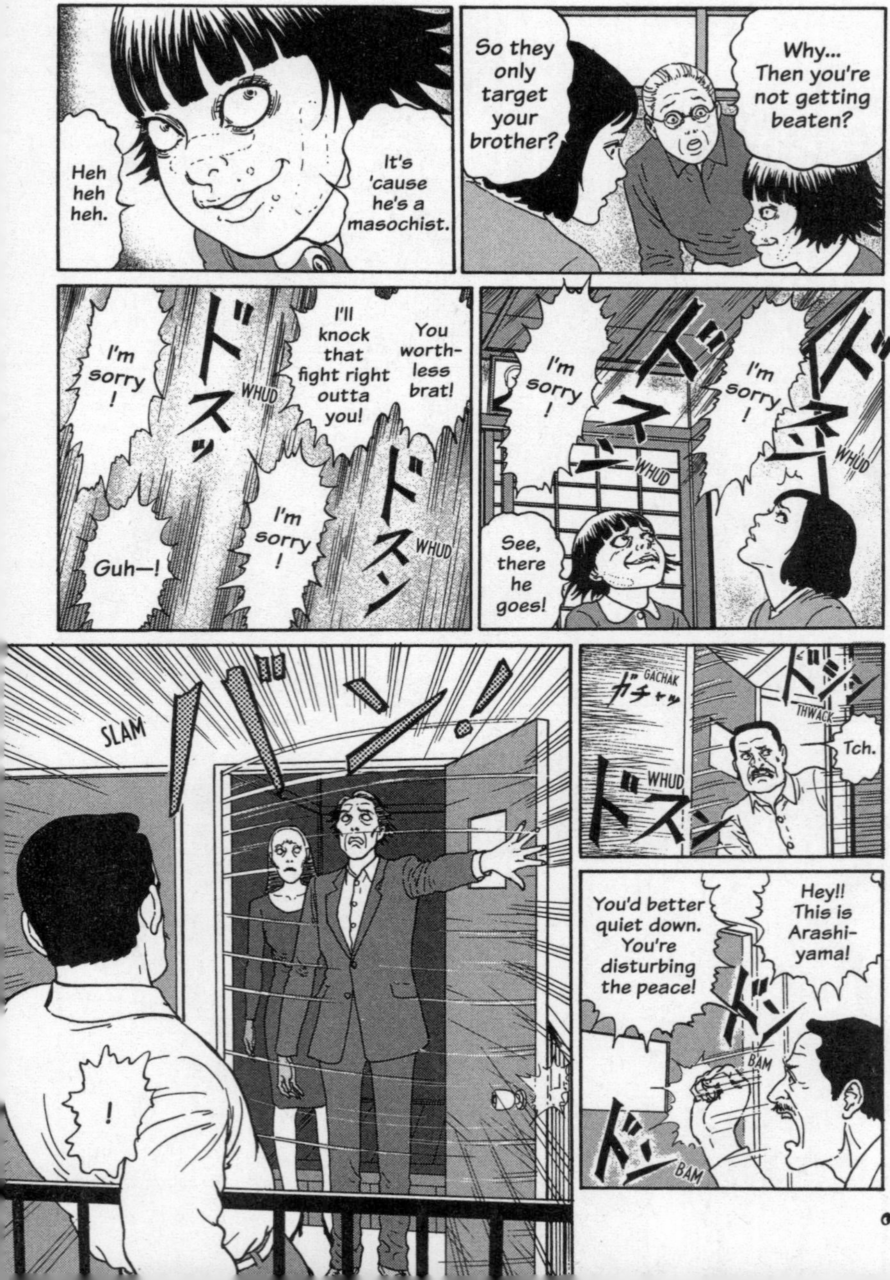
Why... Then you're not getting beaten?
So they only target your brother?
It's 'cause he's a masochist.
Heh heh heh.
ドスン
WHUD
I'm sorry!
ドスン
WHUD
I'm sorry!
See, there he goes!
You worthless brat!
I'll knock that fight right outta you!
ドスッ
WHUD
I'm sorry!
ドスン
WHUD
I'm sorry!
Guh—!
ドッ
THWACK
ガチャッ
GACHAK
Tch.
ドスン
WHUD
Hey!! This is Arashi-yama!
You'd better quiet down. You're disturbing the peace!
ドン
BAM
ドン
BAM
バンッ!!
SLAM
!

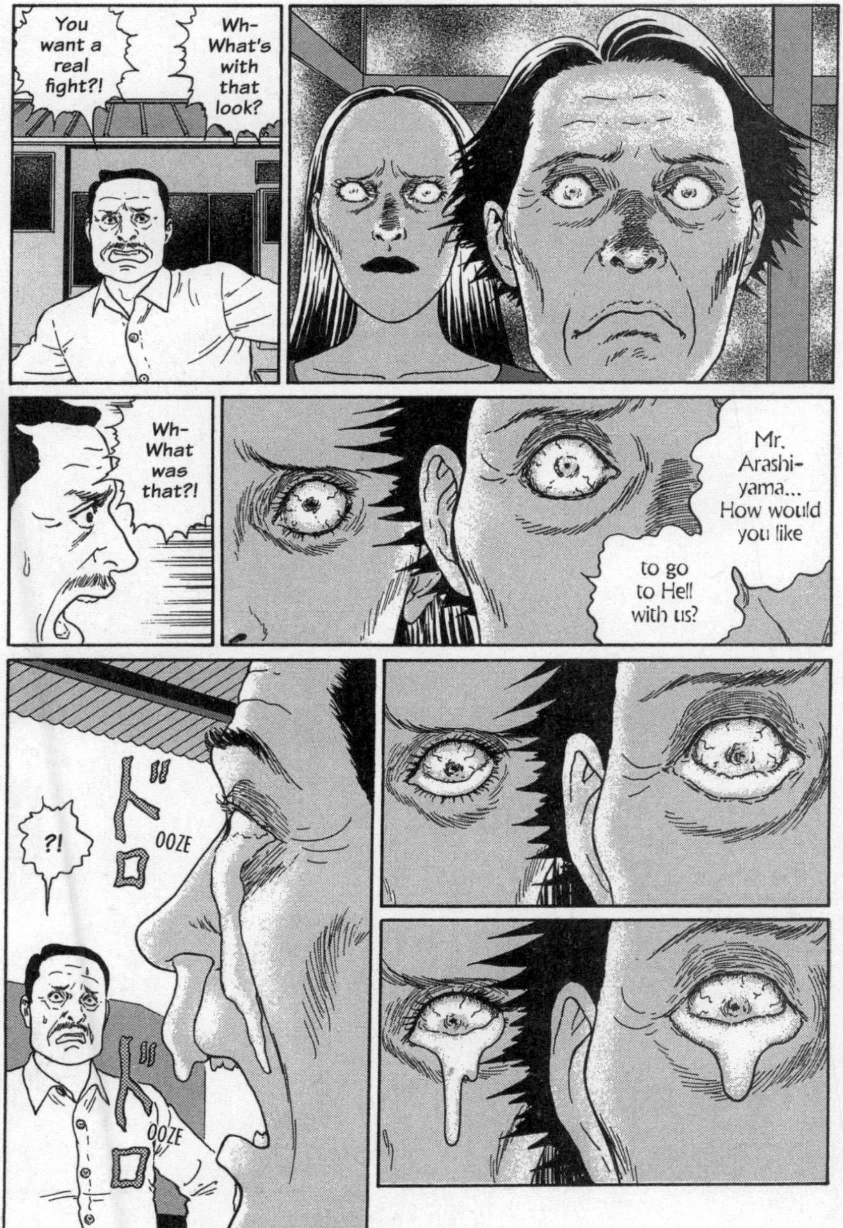
Wh- What's with that look?
You want a real fight?!
Mr. Arashi-yama... How would you like
to go to Hell with us?
Wh- What was that?!
ドロ
OOZE
?!
ドロ
OOZE

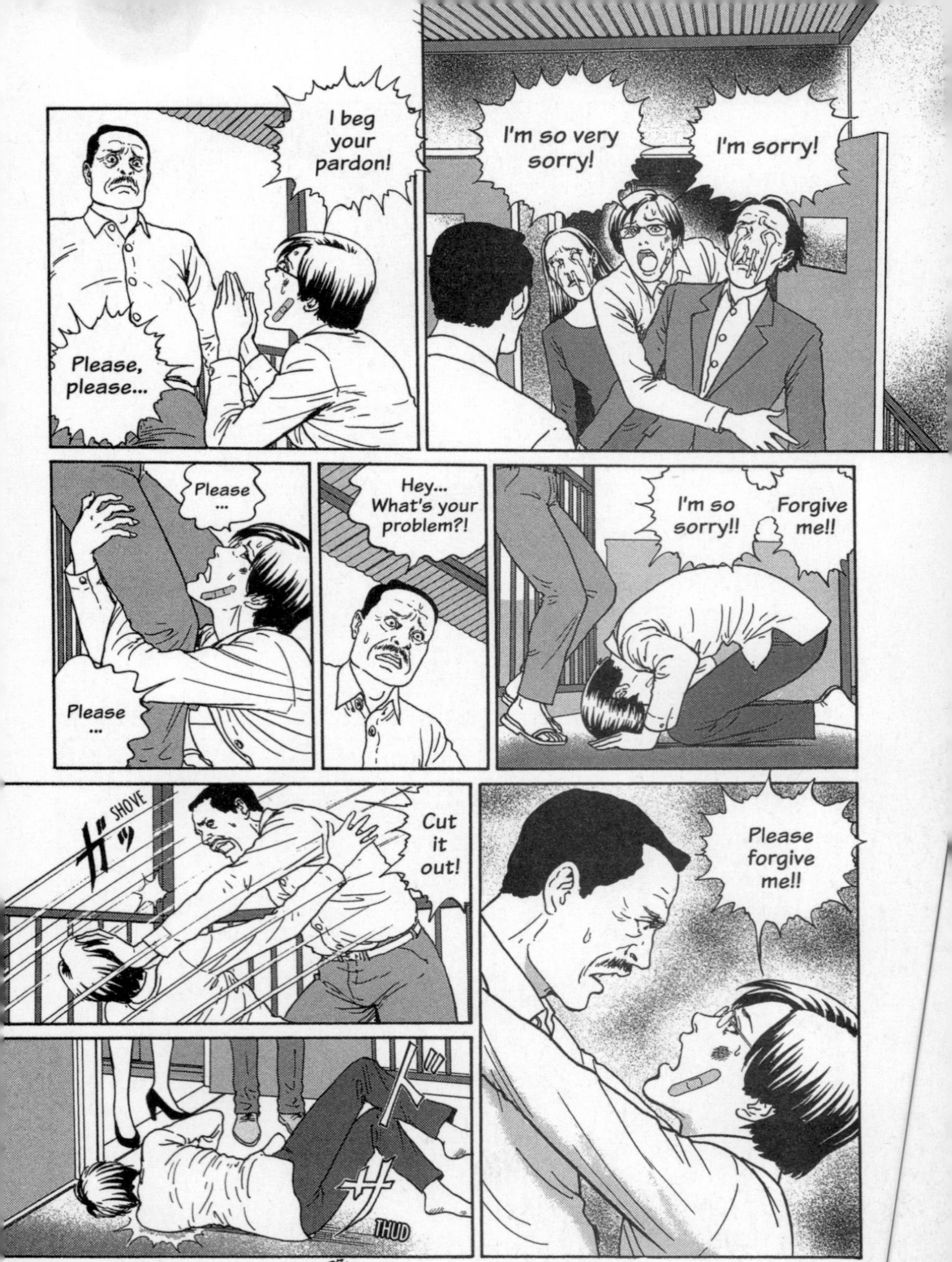
I'm sorry!
I'm so very sorry!
I beg your pardon!
Please, please...
Forgive me!!
I'm so sorry!!
Hey... What's your problem?!
Please ...
Please ...
Please forgive me!!
Cut it out!
ガッ
SHOVE
THUD

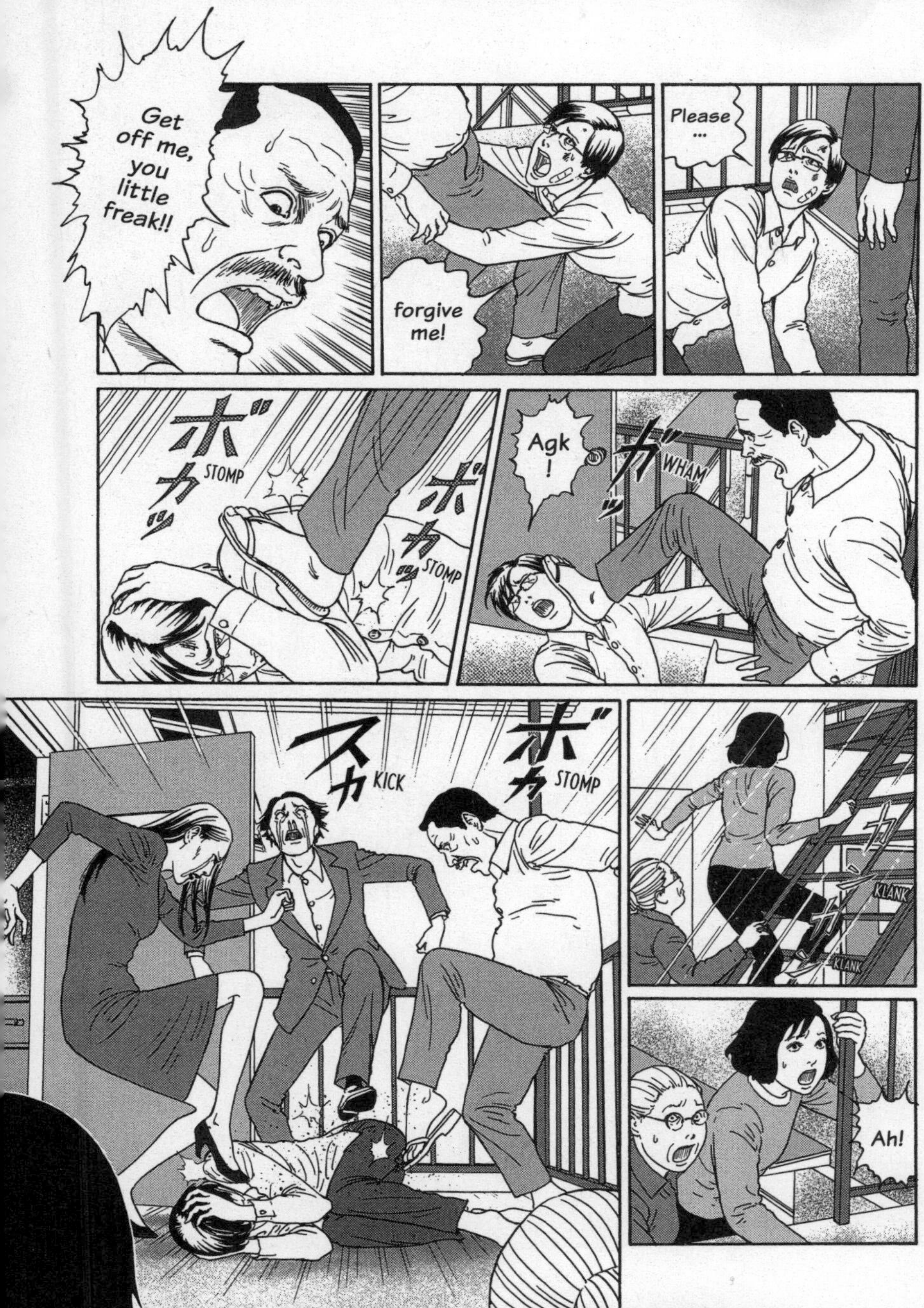

Please ...
forgive me!
Get off me, you little freak!!
Agk !
ガッ
WHAM
ボカッ
STOMP
ボカ
STOMP
KLANK
KLANK
Ah!
スカ
KICK
ボカ
STOMP

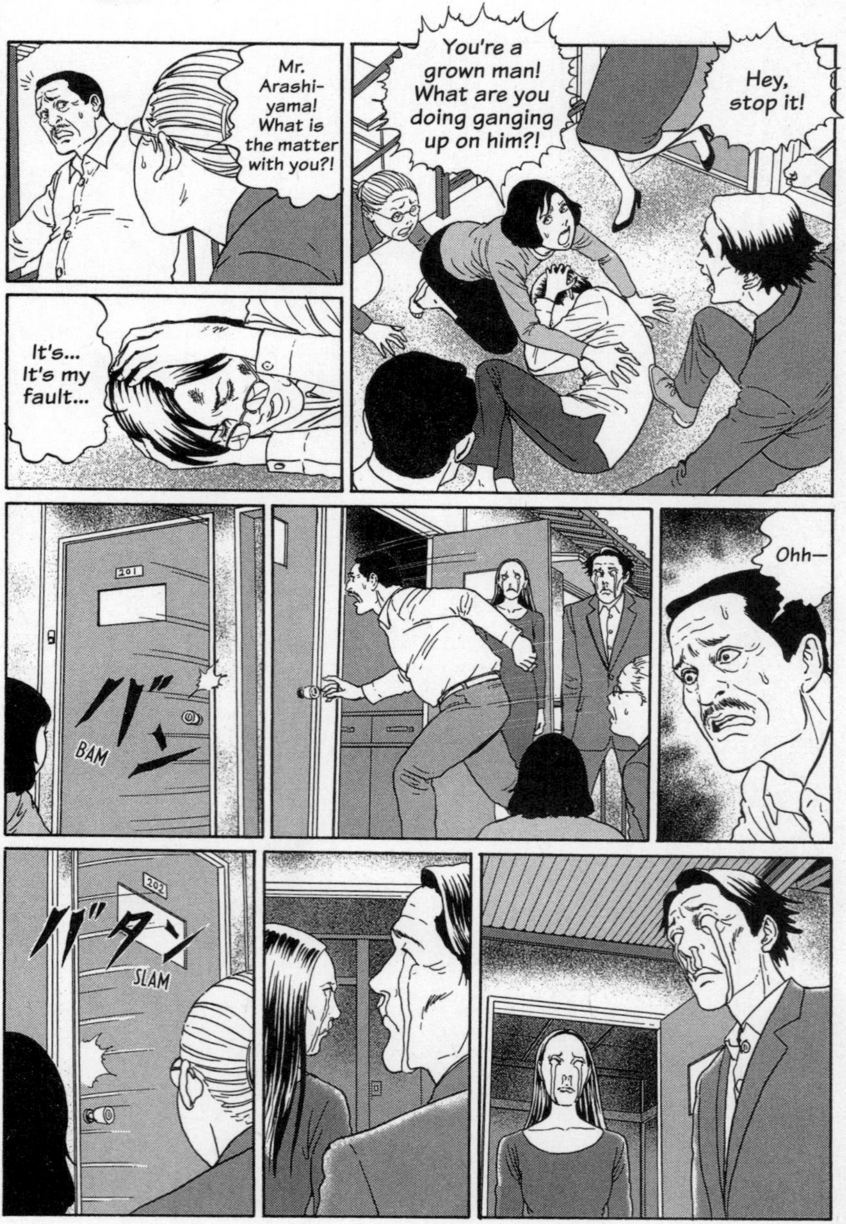
Hey, stop it!
You're a grown man! What are you doing ganging up on him?!
Mr. Arashi-yama! What is the matter with you?!
It's... It's my fault...
Ohh—
バン
BAM
バタン
SLAM

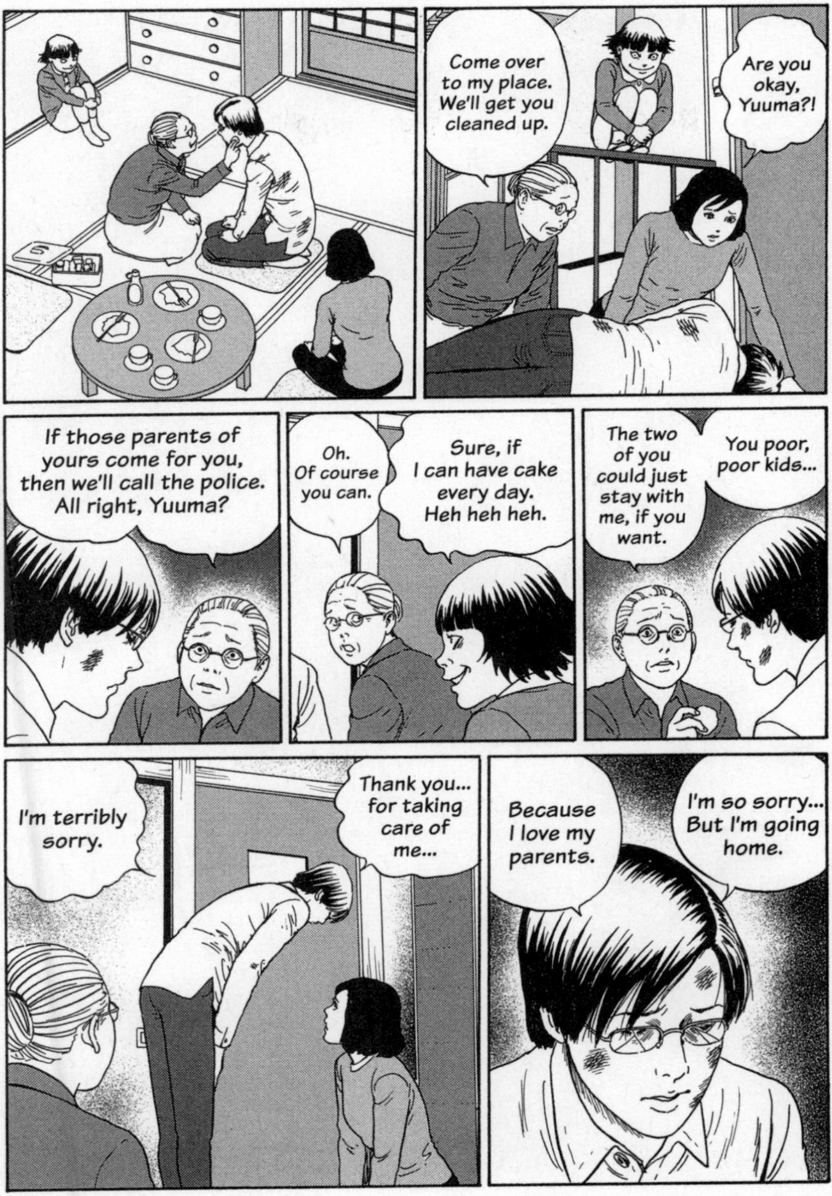
Are you okay, Yuuma?!
Come over to my place. We'll get you cleaned up.
You poor, poor kids...
The two of you could just stay with me, if you want.
Sure, if I can have cake every day. Heh heh heh.
Oh. Of course you can.
If those parents of yours come for you, then we'll call the police. All right, Yuuma?
I'm so sorry... But I'm going home.
Because I love my parents.
Thank you... for taking care of me...
I'm terribly sorry.

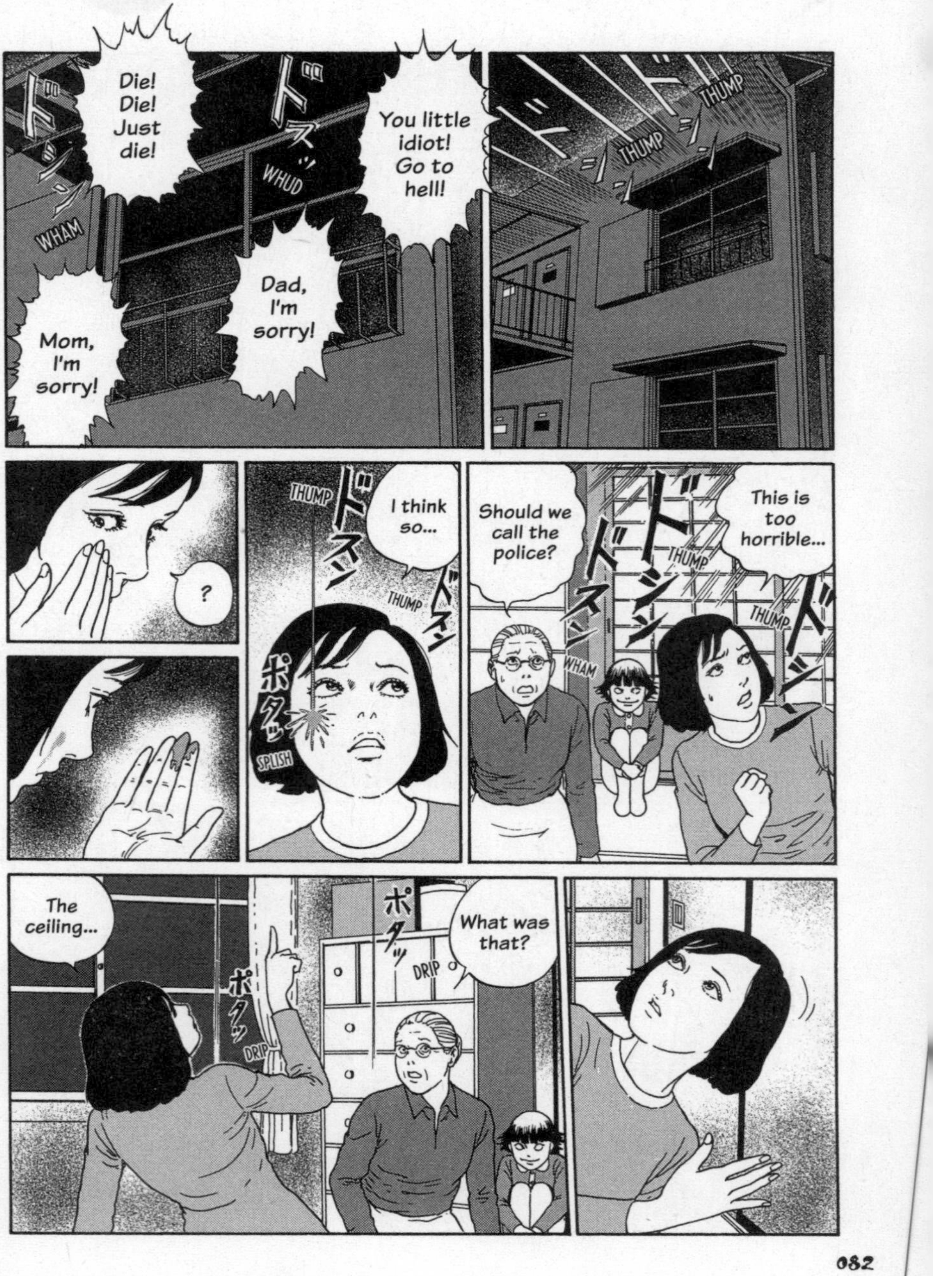
THUMP
THUMP
You little idiot! Go to hell!
WHUD
Die! Die! Just die!
WHAM
Dad, I'm sorry!
Mom, I'm sorry!
This is too horrible...
THUMP
THUMP
Should we call the police?
WHAM
I think so...
THUMP
THUMP
ポタッ
SPLISH
?
What was that?
ポタッ
DRIP
The ceiling...
ポタッ
DRIP

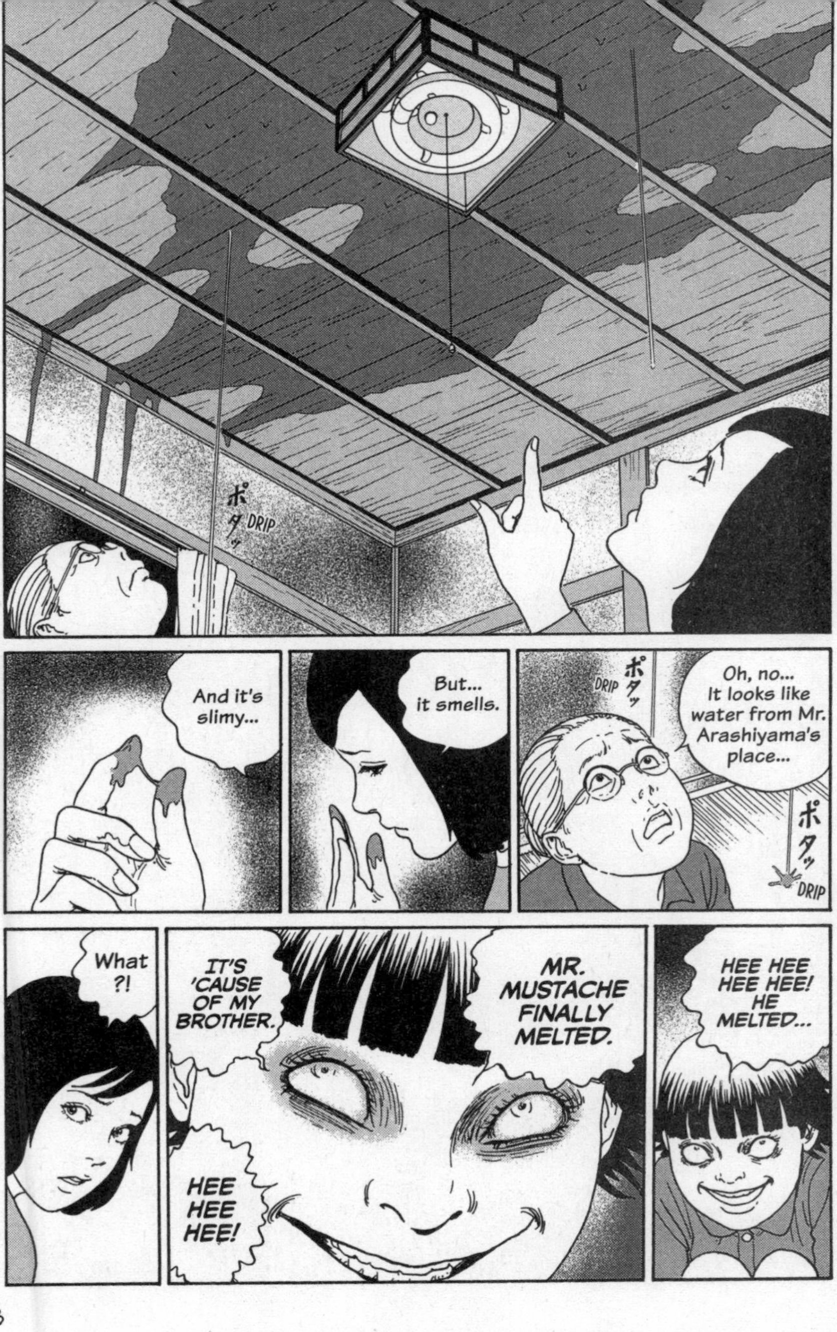
ポタッ
DRIP
ポタッ
DRIP
Oh, no... It looks like water from Mr. Arashiyama's place...
ポタッ
DRIP
But... it smells.
And it's slimy...
HEE HEE HEE HEE! HE MELTED...
MR. MUSTACHE FINALLY MELTED.
IT'S 'CAUSE OF MY BROTHER.
HEE HEE HEE!
What ?!

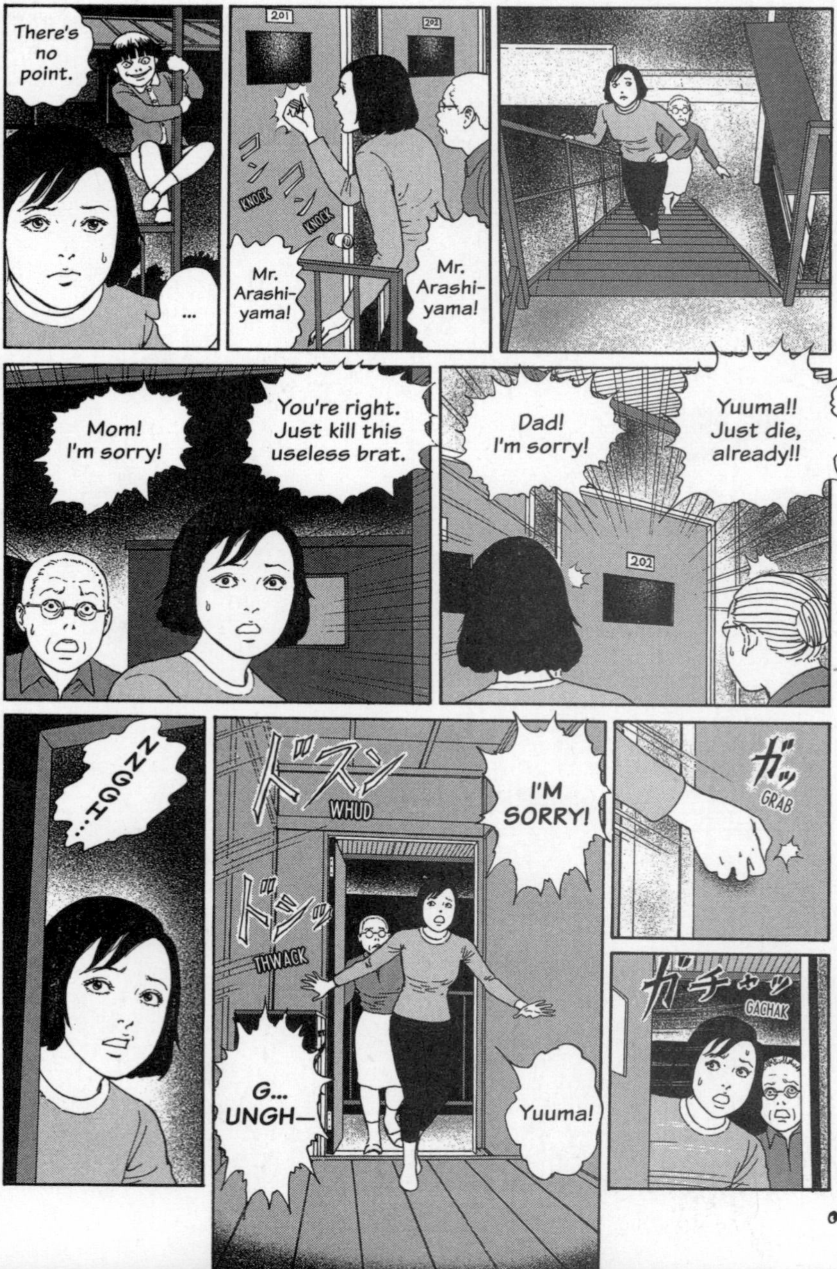

Mr. Arashi-yama!
コン
コン
KNOCK
KNOCK
Mr. Arashi-yama!
There's no point.
...
Yuuma!! Just die, already!!
Dad! I'm sorry!
You're right. Just kill this useless brat.
Mom! I'm sorry!
ガッ
GRAB
ガチャッ
GACHAK
I'M SORRY!
ドスン
WHUD
ドシッ
THWACK
Yuuma!
G... UNGH—
...IGGZZ

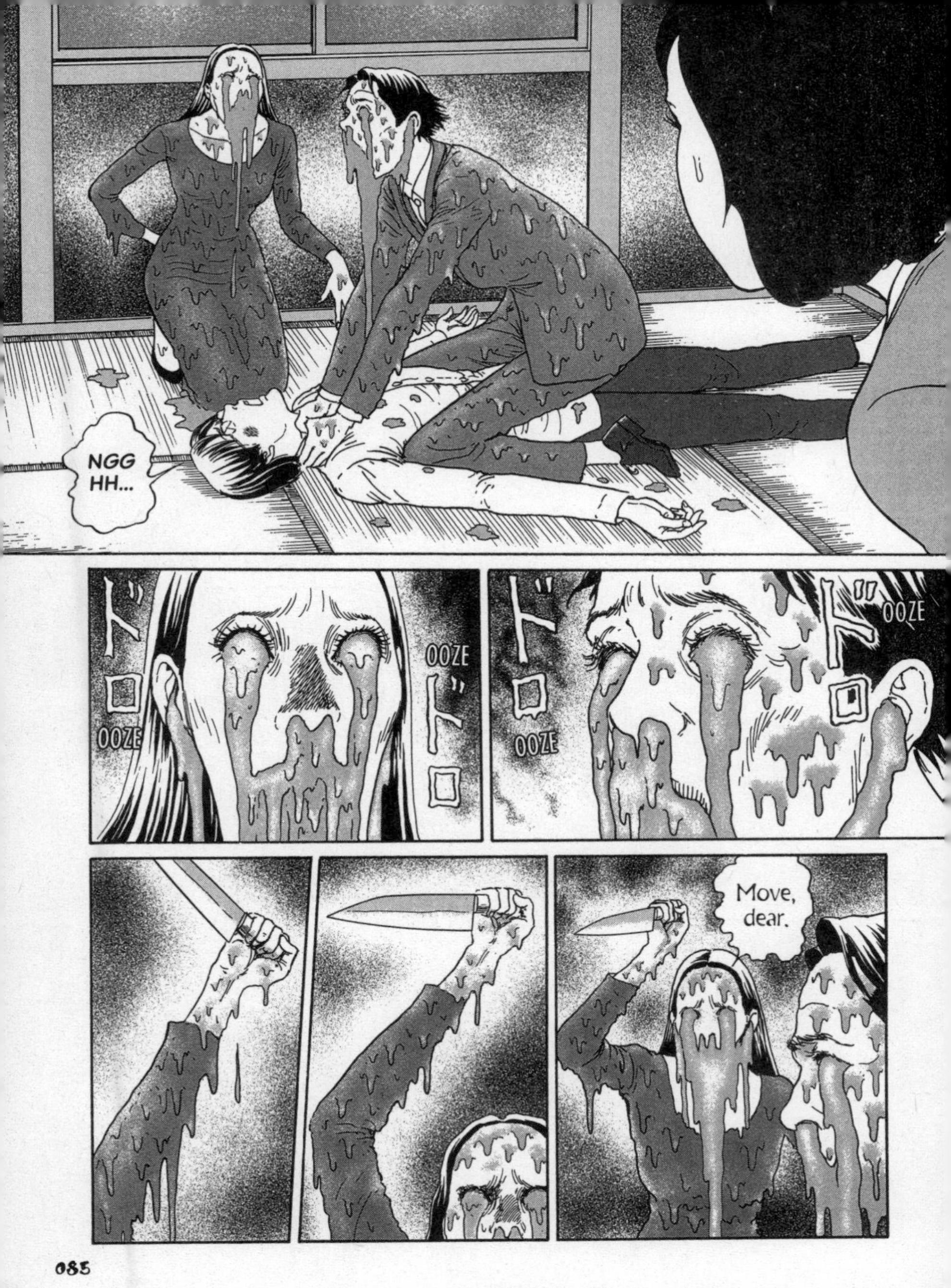
NGG HH...
ドロ
OOZE
ドロ
OOZE
ドロ
OOZE
ドロ
OOZE
Move, dear.

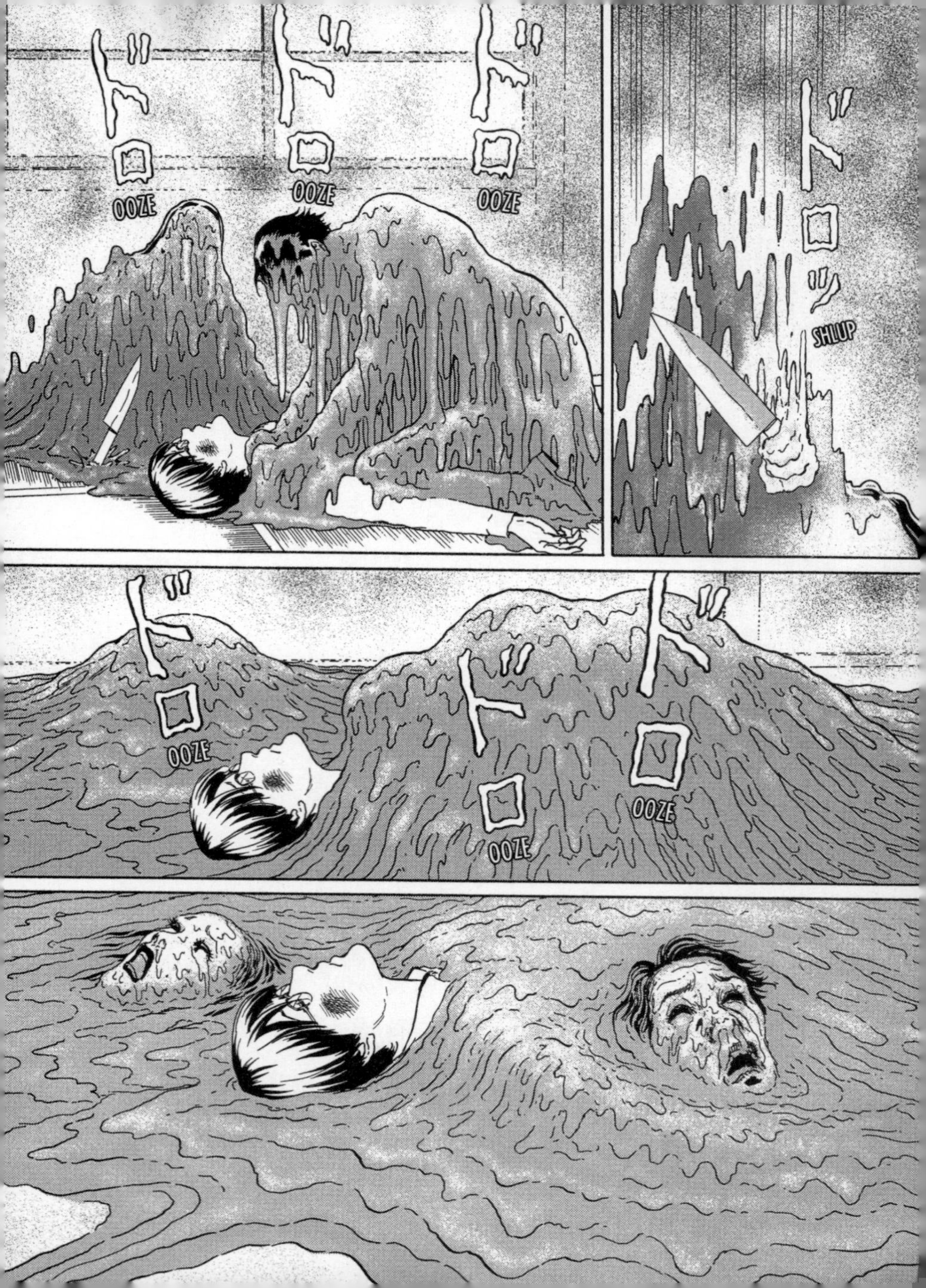
ドロッ
SHLUP
ドロ
OOZE
ドロ
OOZE
ドロ
OOZE
ドロ
OOZE
ドロ
OOZE
ドロ
OOZE

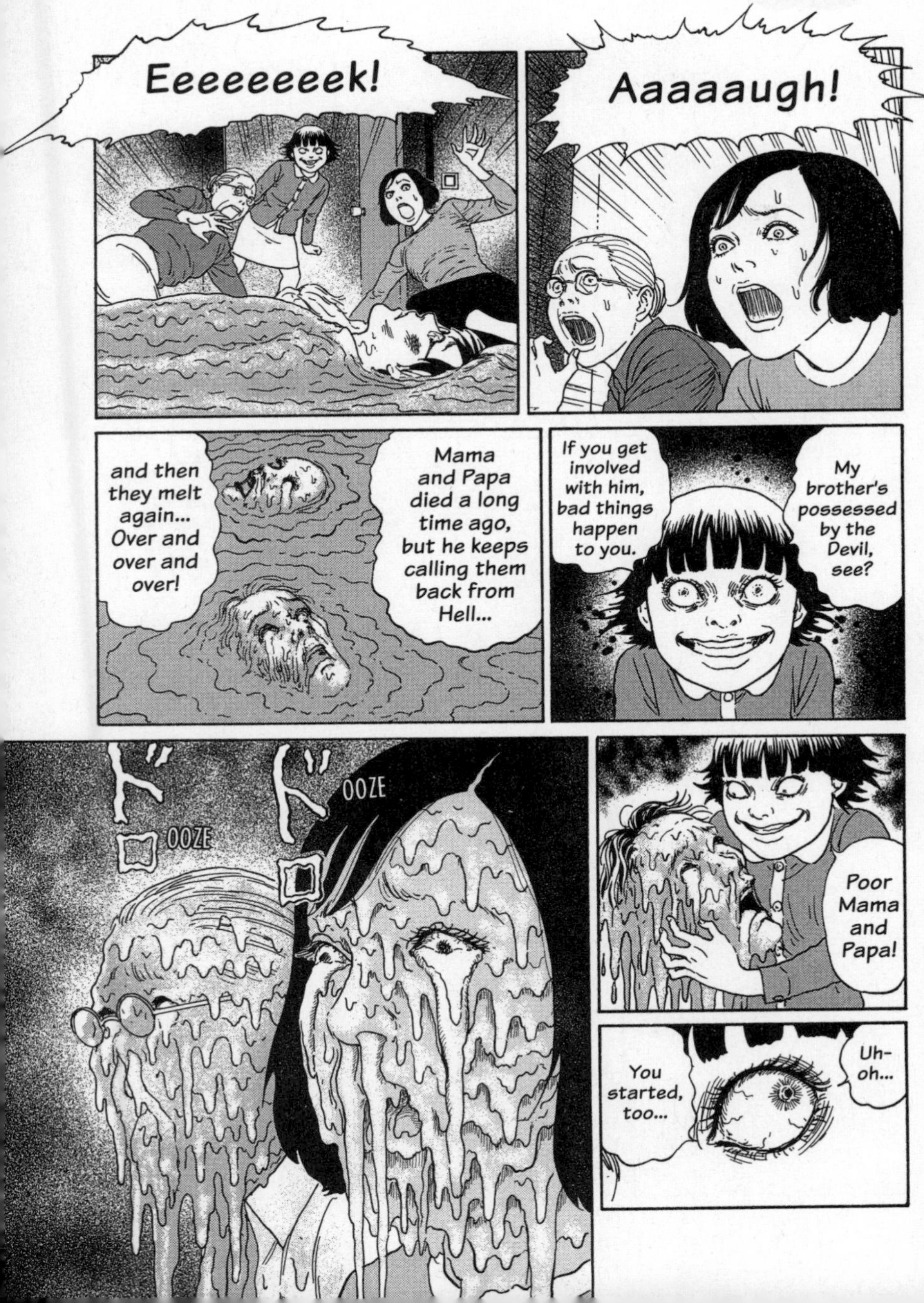
Aaaaaugh!
Eeeeeeeek!
My brother's possessed by the Devil, see?
If you get involved with him, bad things happen to you.
Mama and Papa died a long time ago, but he keeps calling them back from Hell...
and then they melt again... Over and over and over!
Poor Mama and Papa!
Uh-oh...
You started, too...
ドロ
OOZE
ドロ
OOZE

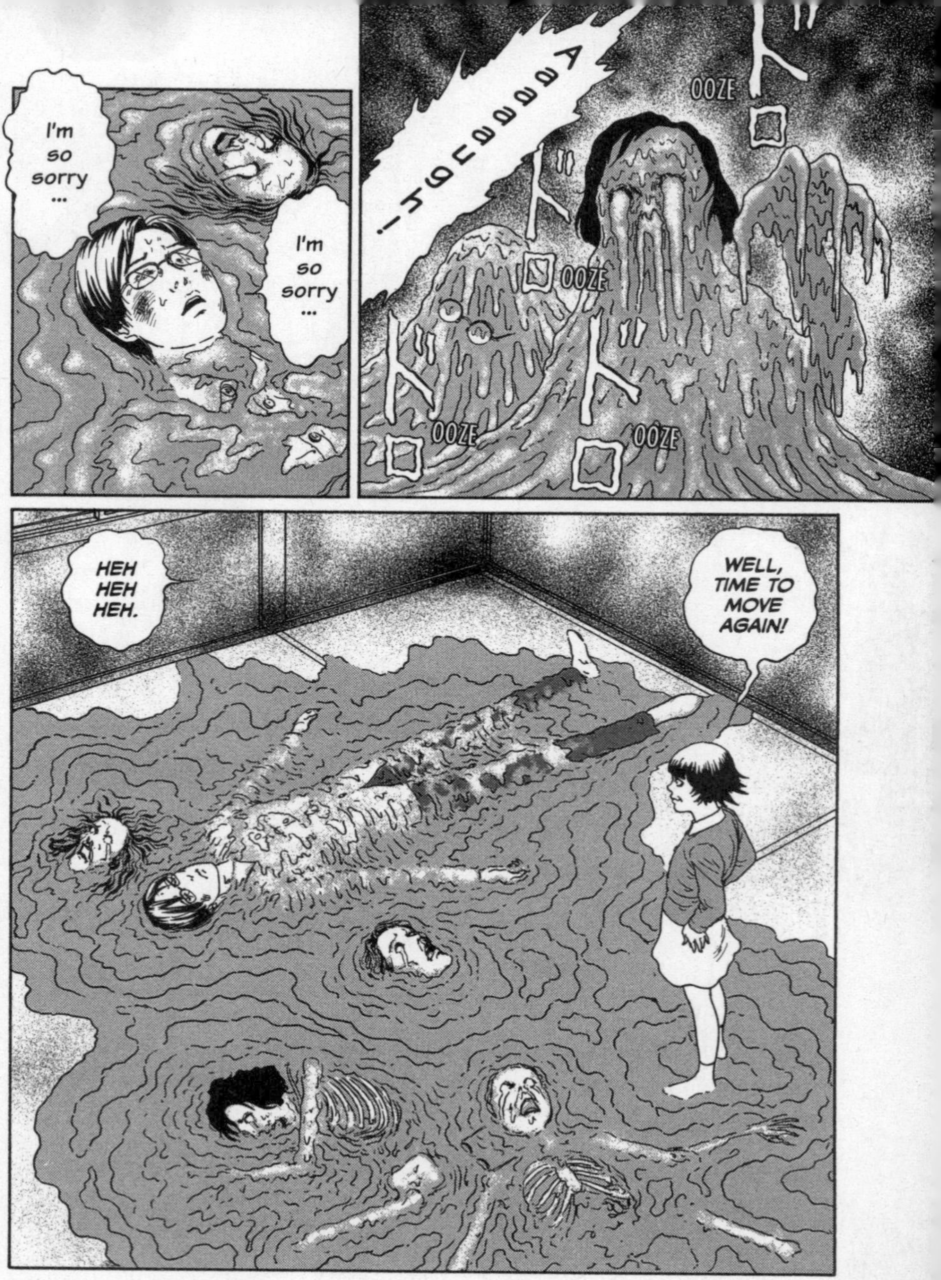
Aaaaaugh!
OOZE
OOZE
OOZE
OOZE
I'm so sorry ...
I'm so sorry ...
WELL, TIME TO MOVE AGAIN!
HEH HEH HEH.

Dissolving Apartment: The End

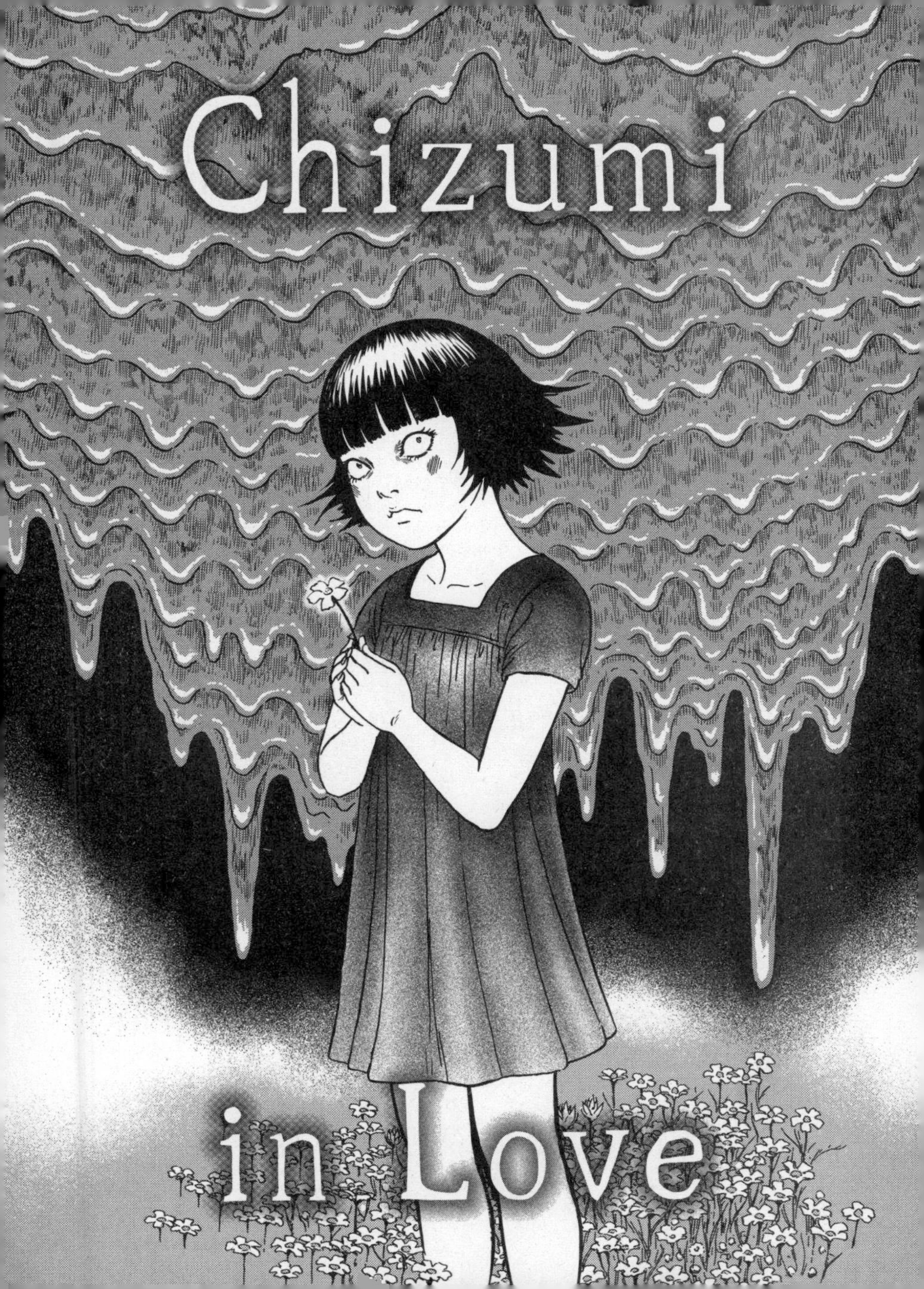
Chizumi
in Love

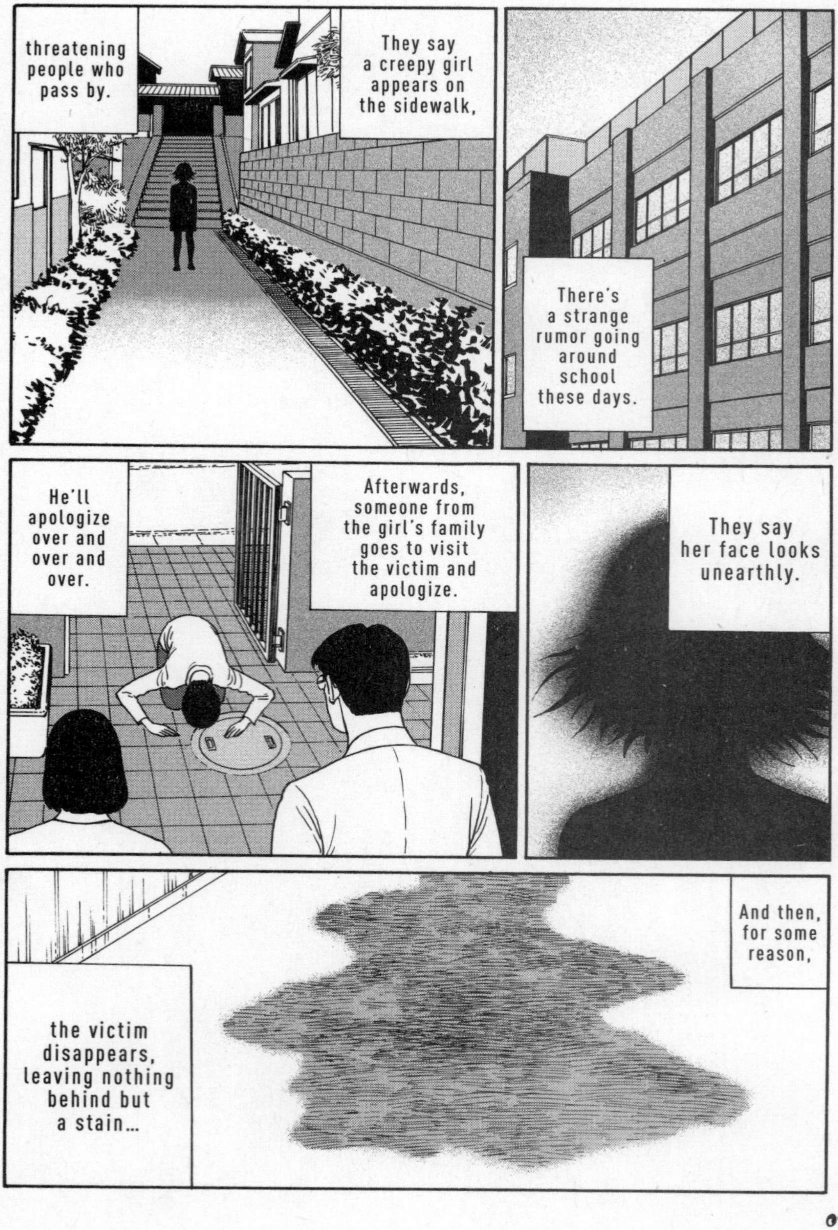
There's a strange rumor going around school these days.
They say a creepy girl appears on the sidewalk,
threatening people who pass by.
They say her face looks unearthly.
Afterwards, someone from the girl's family goes to visit the victim and apologize.
He'll apologize over and over and over.
And then, for some reason,
the victim disappears, leaving nothing behind but a stain...

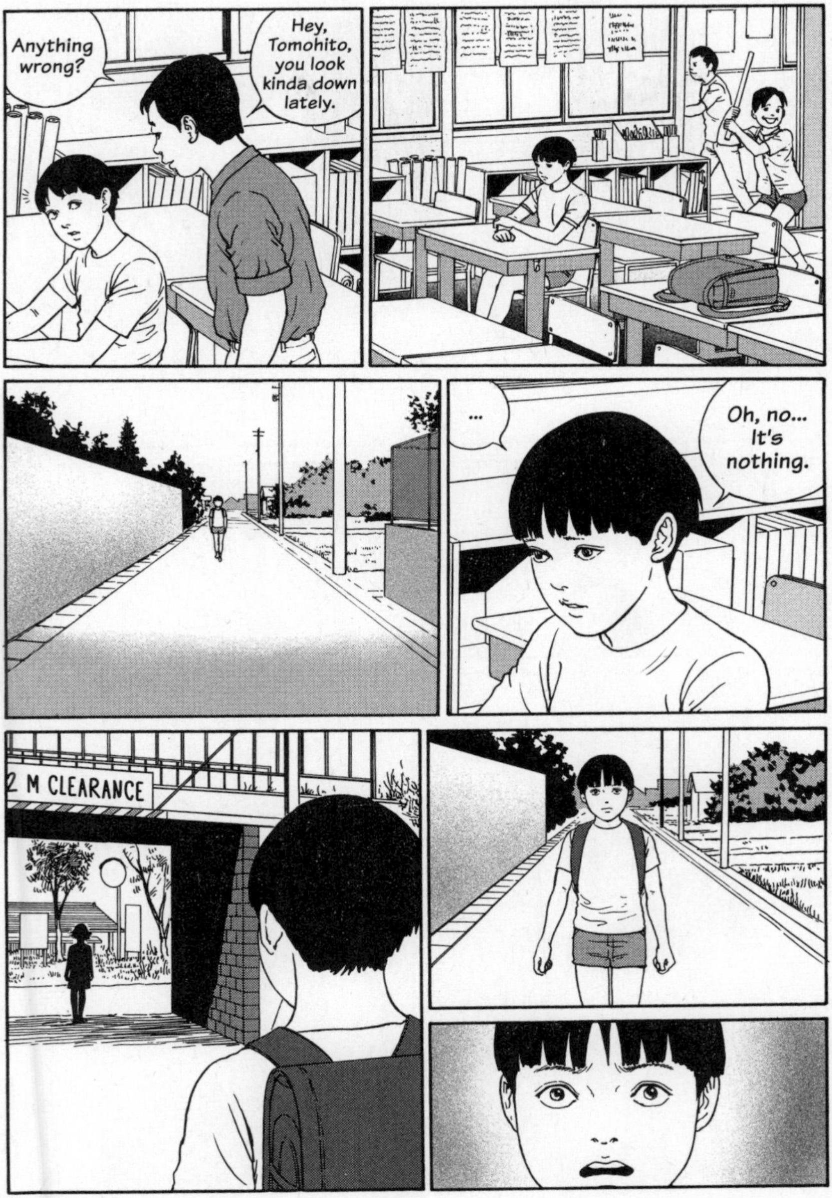
Hey, Tomohito, you look kinda down lately.
Anything wrong?
Oh, no... It's nothing.
...
2 M CLEARANCE

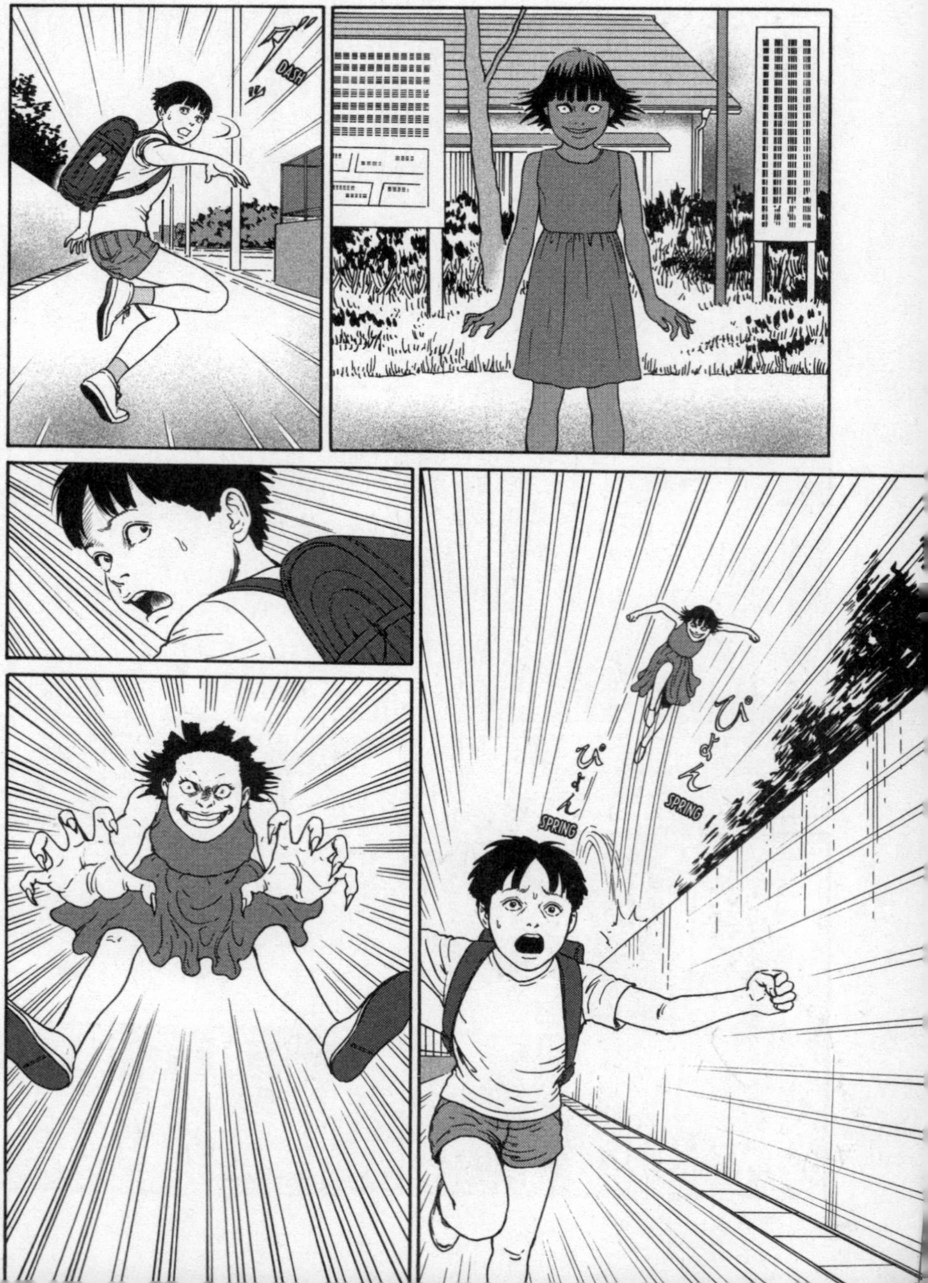
ダッ
DASH
ぴょん
SPRING
ぴょん
SPRING

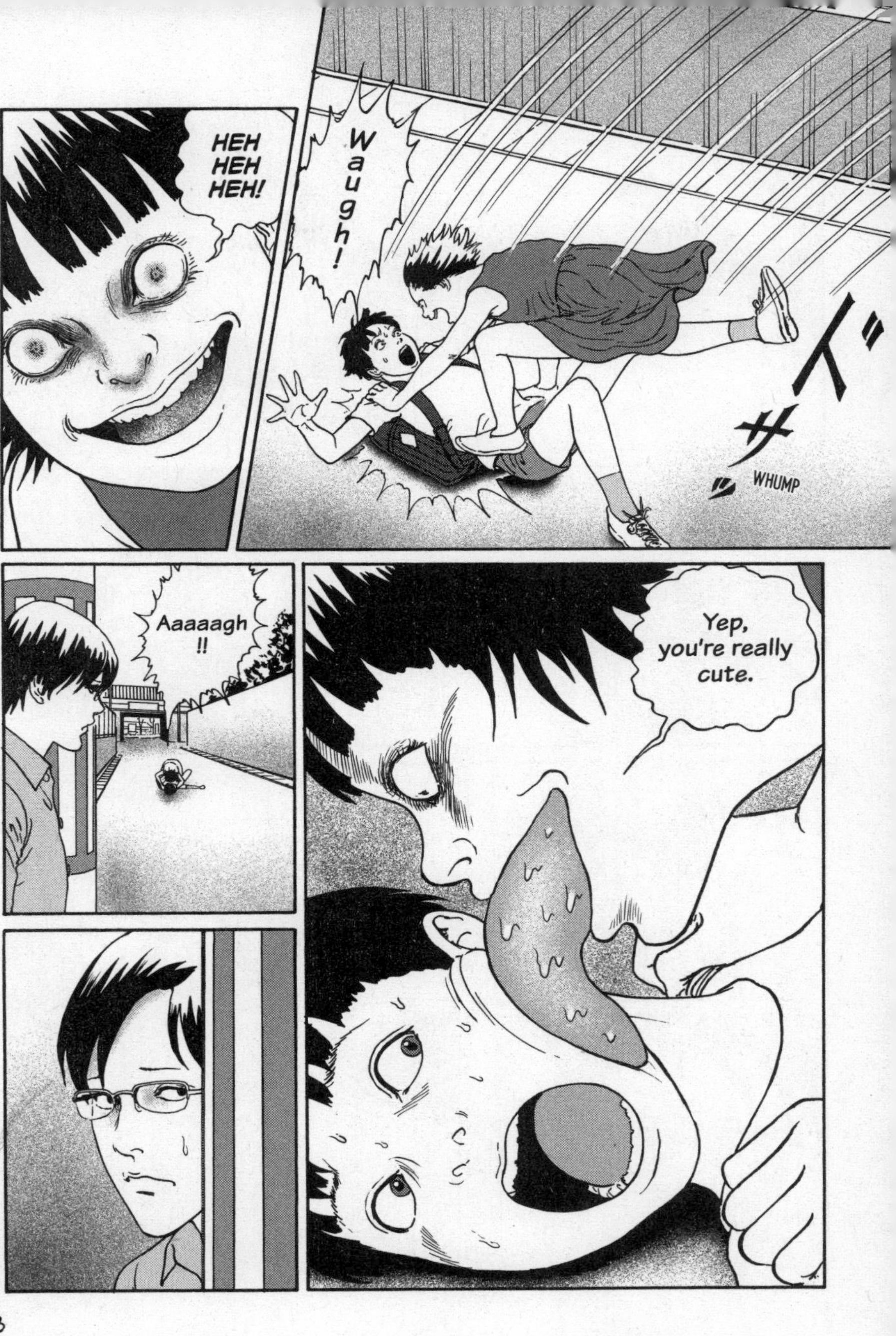
Waugh!
ドサ
WHUMP
HEH HEH HEH!
Yep, you're really cute.
Aaaaagh !!

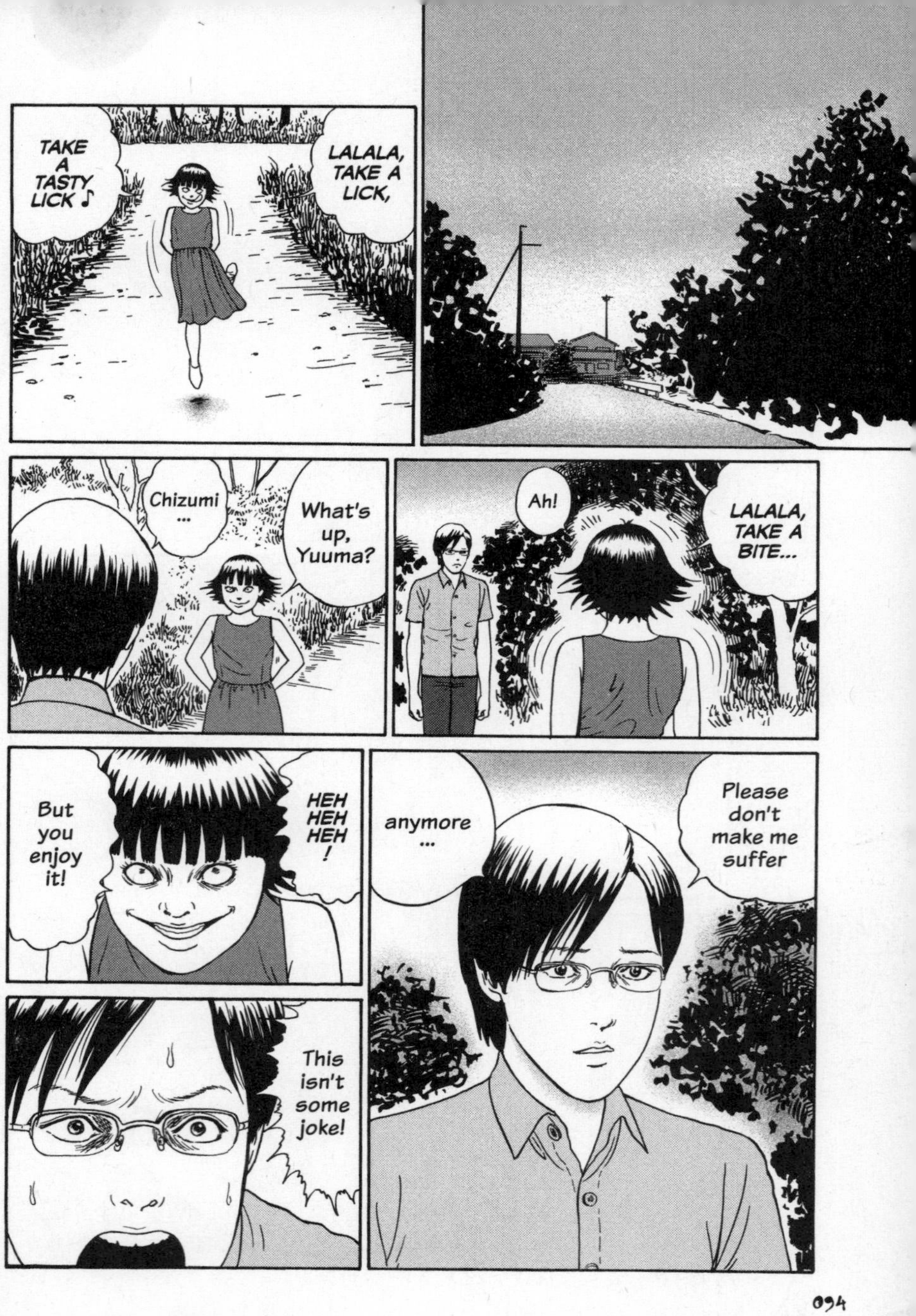
LALALA, TAKE A LICK,
TAKE A TASTY LICK ♪
LALALA, TAKE A BITE...
Ah!
What's up, Yuuma?
Chizumi ...
Please don't make me suffer
anymore ...
HEH HEH HEH !
But you enjoy it!
This isn't some joke!

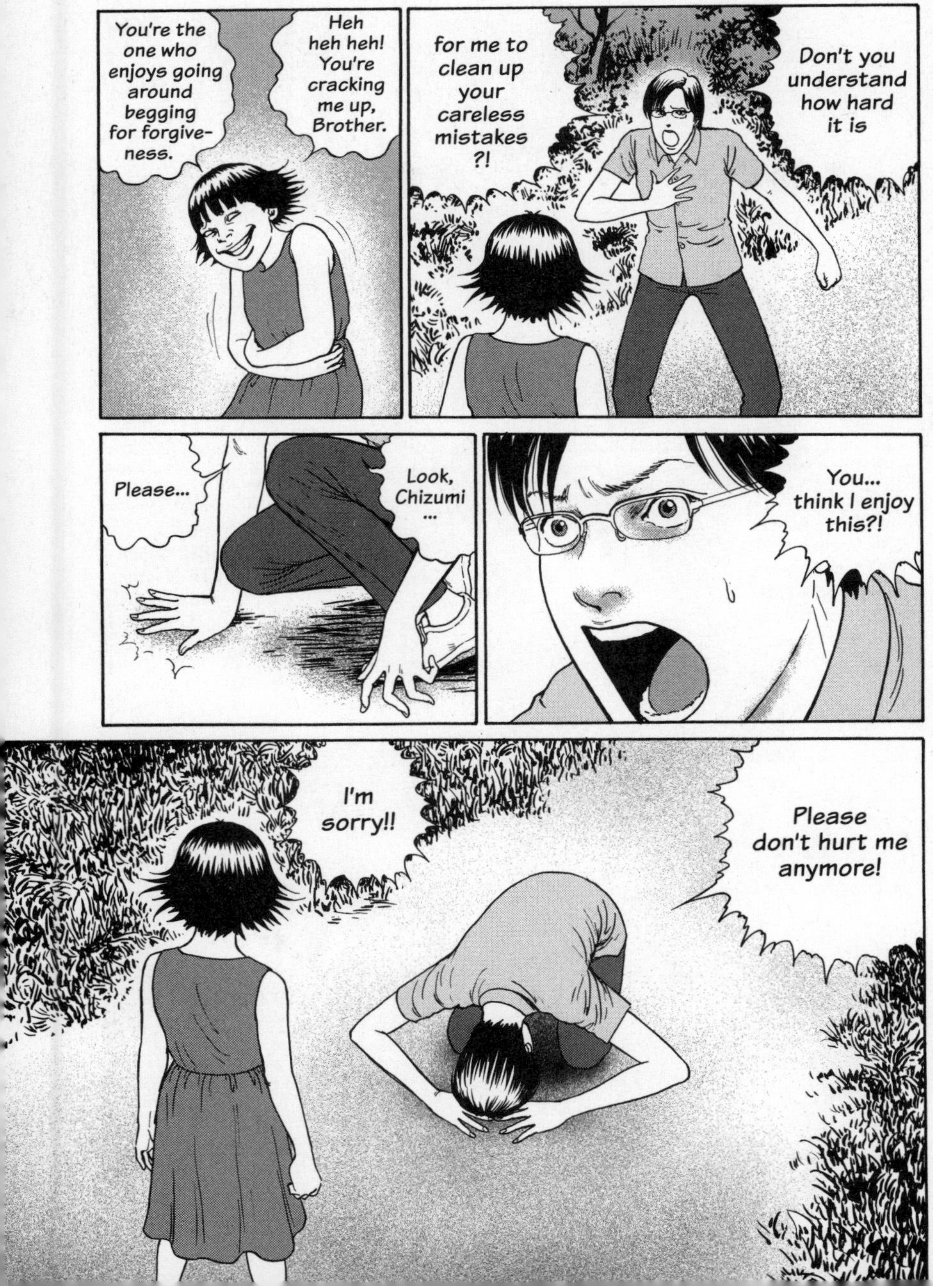
Don't you understand how hard it is
for me to clean up your careless mistakes ?!
Heh heh heh! You're cracking me up, Brother.
You're the one who enjoys going around begging for forgive-ness.
You... think I enjoy this?!
Look, Chizumi ...
Please...
I'm sorry!!
Please don't hurt me anymore!

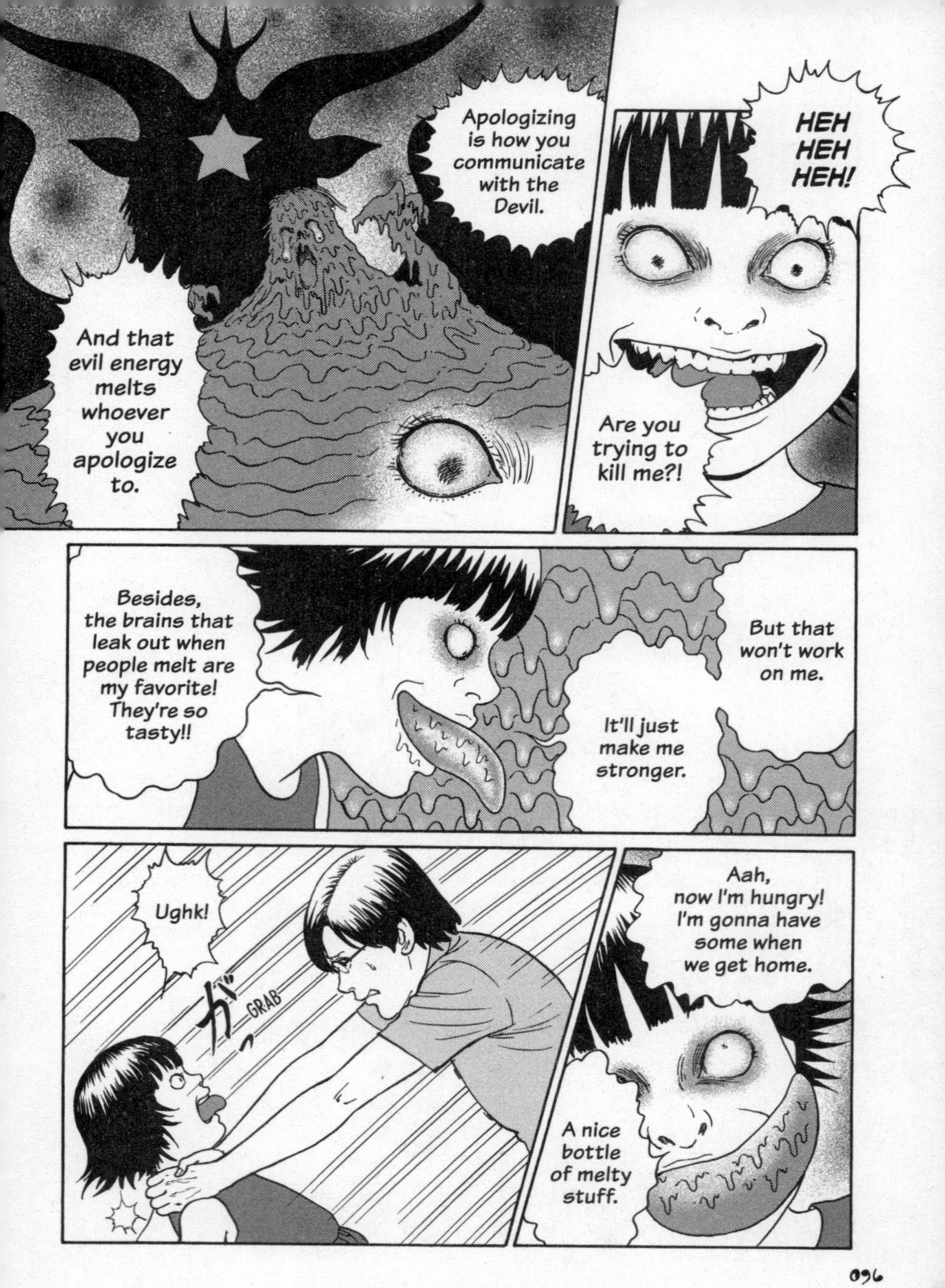
HEH HEH HEH!
Are you trying to kill me?!
Apologizing is how you communicate with the Devil.
And that evil energy melts whoever you apologize to.
But that won't work on me.
It'll just make me stronger.
Besides, the brains that leak out when people melt are my favorite! They're so tasty!!
Aah, now I'm hungry! I'm gonna have some when we get home.
A nice bottle of melty stuff.
Ughk!
ガッ
GRAB

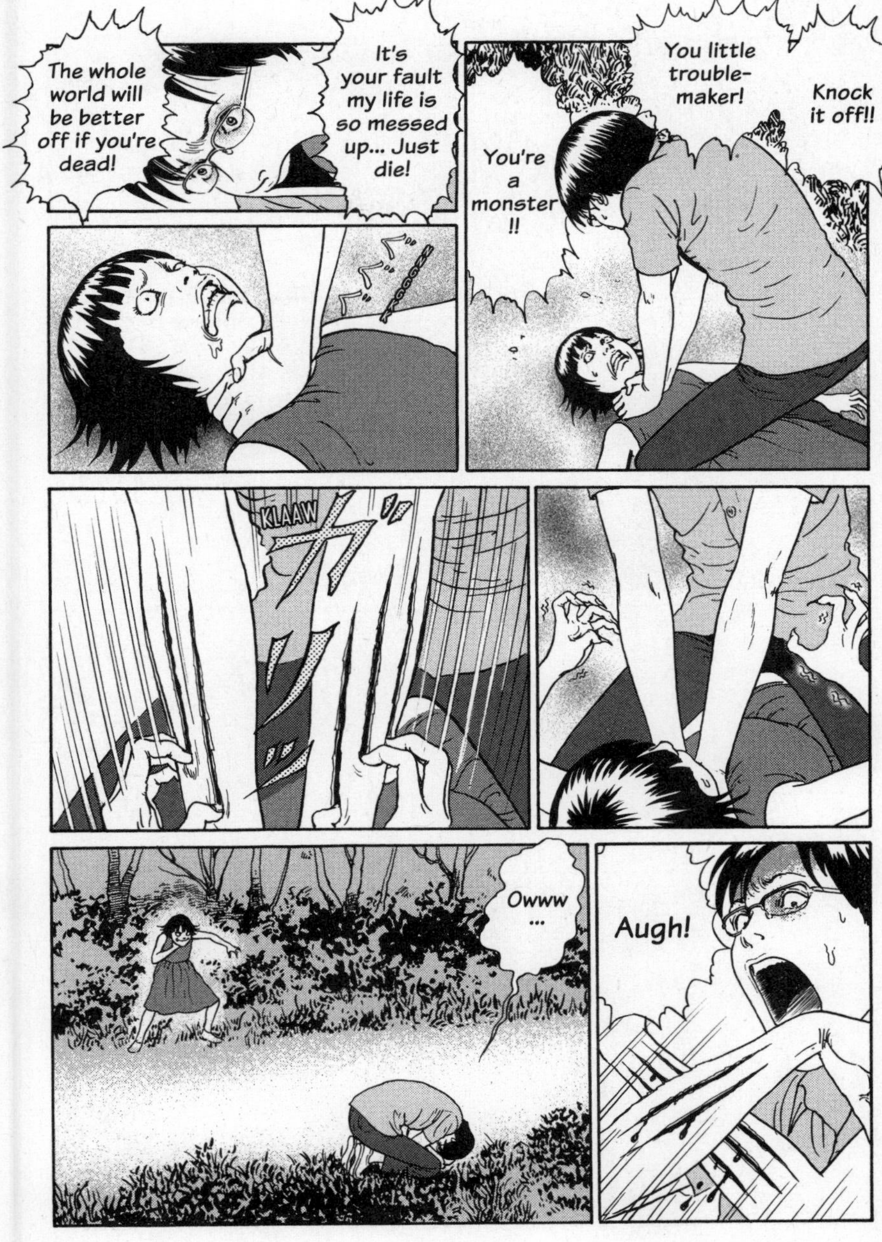
Knock it off!!
You little trouble-maker!
You're a monster!!
It's your fault my life is so messed up... Just die!
The whole world will be better off if you're dead!
NNGGGKK
KLAAW
Augh!
Owww ...

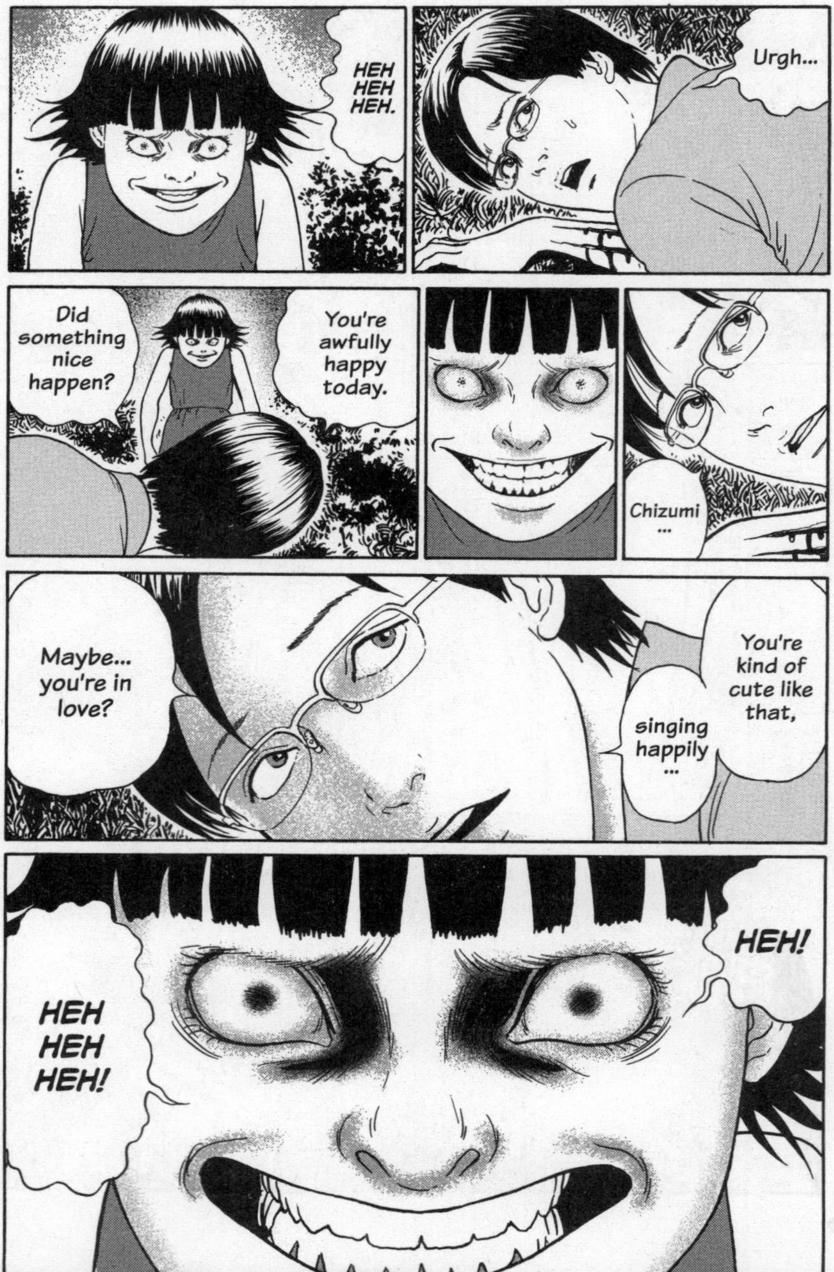
Urgh...
HEH HEH HEH.
Chizumi ...
You're awfully happy today.
Did something nice happen?
You're kind of cute like that,
singing happily ...
Maybe... you're in love?
HEH!
HEH HEH HEH!

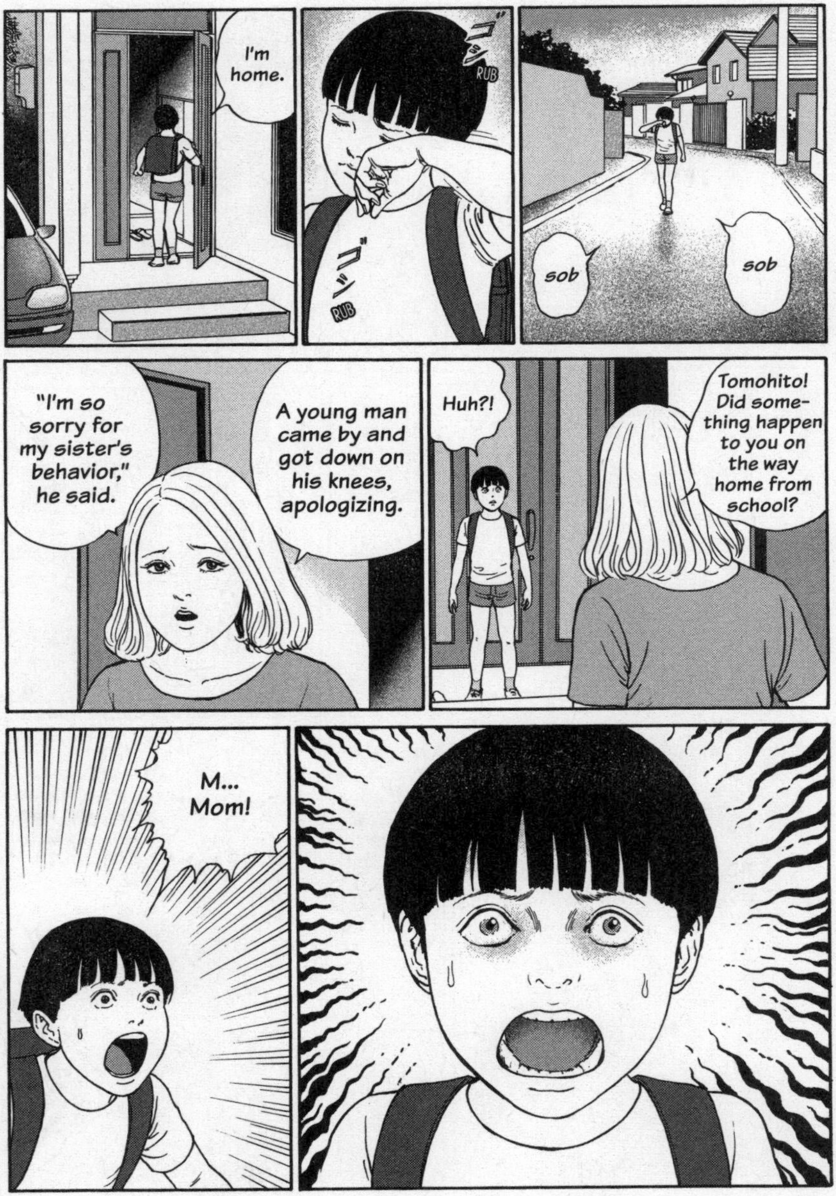
sob
sob
RUB
RUB
I'm home.
Tomohito! Did some-thing happen to you on the way home from school?
Huh?!
A young man came by and got down on his knees, apologizing.
"I'm so sorry for my sister's behavior," he said.
M... Mom!

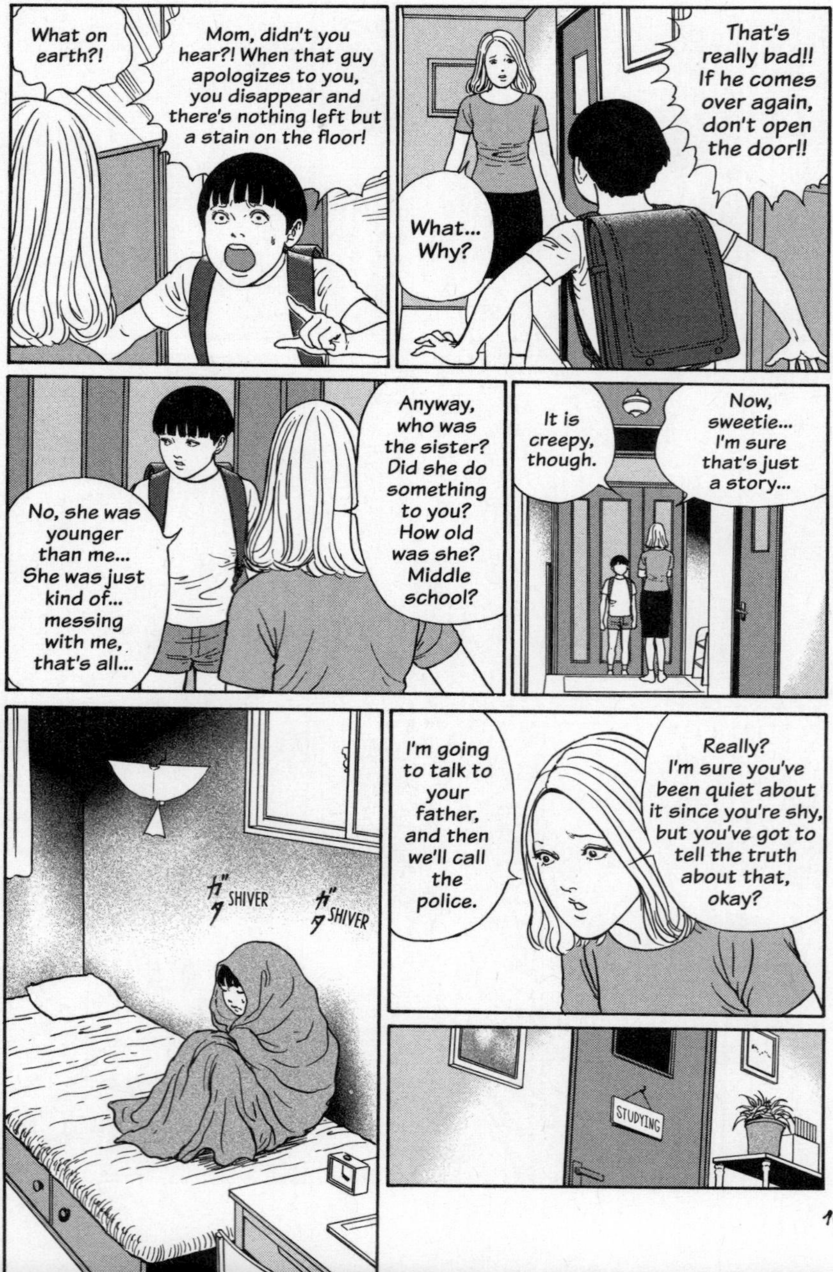
That's really bad!! If he comes over again, don't open the door!!
What... Why?
Mom, didn't you hear?! When that guy apologizes to you, you disappear and there's nothing left but a stain on the floor!
What on earth?!
Now, sweetie... I'm sure that's just a story...
It is creepy, though.
Anyway, who was the sister? Did she do something to you? How old was she? Middle school?
No, she was younger than me... She was just kind of... messing with me, that's all...
Really? I'm sure you've been quiet about it since you're shy, but you've got to tell the truth about that, okay?
I'm going to talk to your father, and then we'll call the police.
STUDYING
ガタ SHIVER
ガタ SHIVER

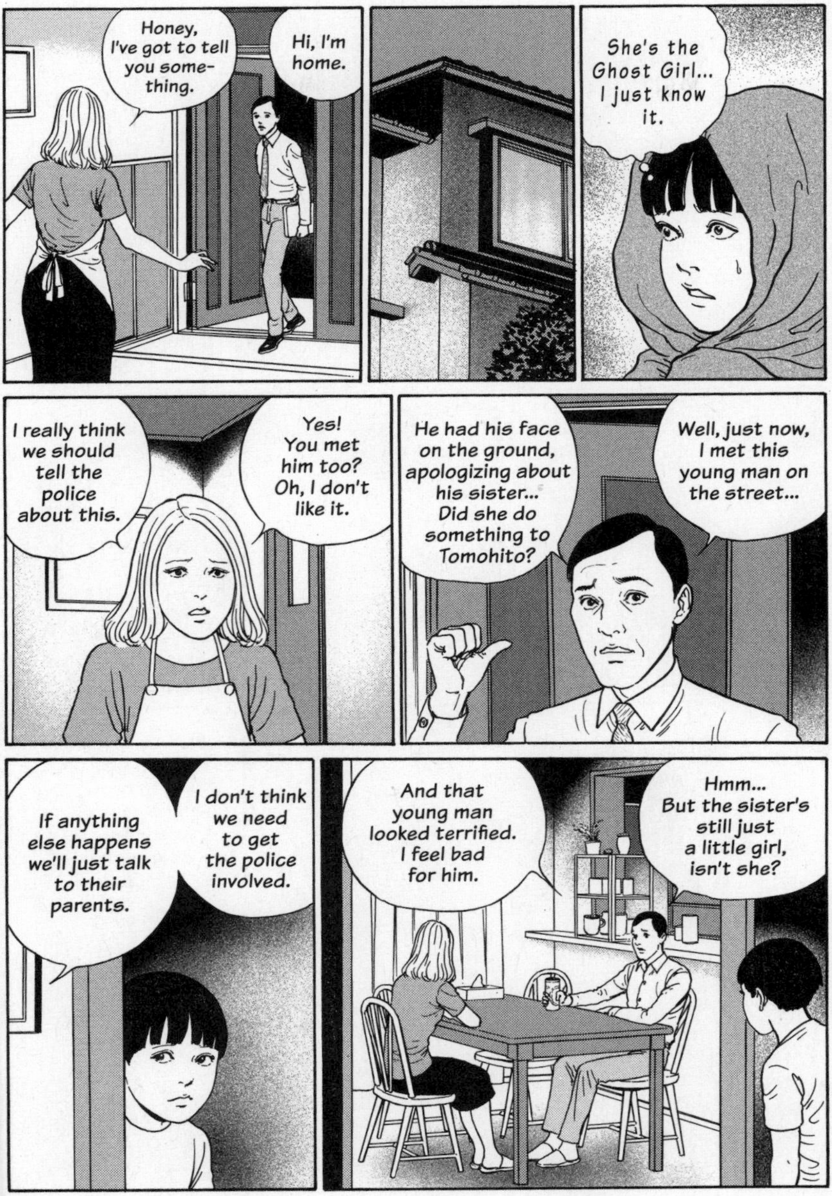
She's the Ghost Girl... I just know it.
Hi, I'm home.
Honey, I've got to tell you some-thing.
Well, just now, I met this young man on the street...
He had his face on the ground, apologizing about his sister... Did she do something to Tomohito?
Yes! You met him too? Oh, I don't like it.
I really think we should tell the police about this.
Hmm... But the sister's still just a little girl, isn't she?
And that young man looked terrified. I feel bad for him.
I don't think we need to get the police involved.
If anything else happens we'll just talk to their parents.

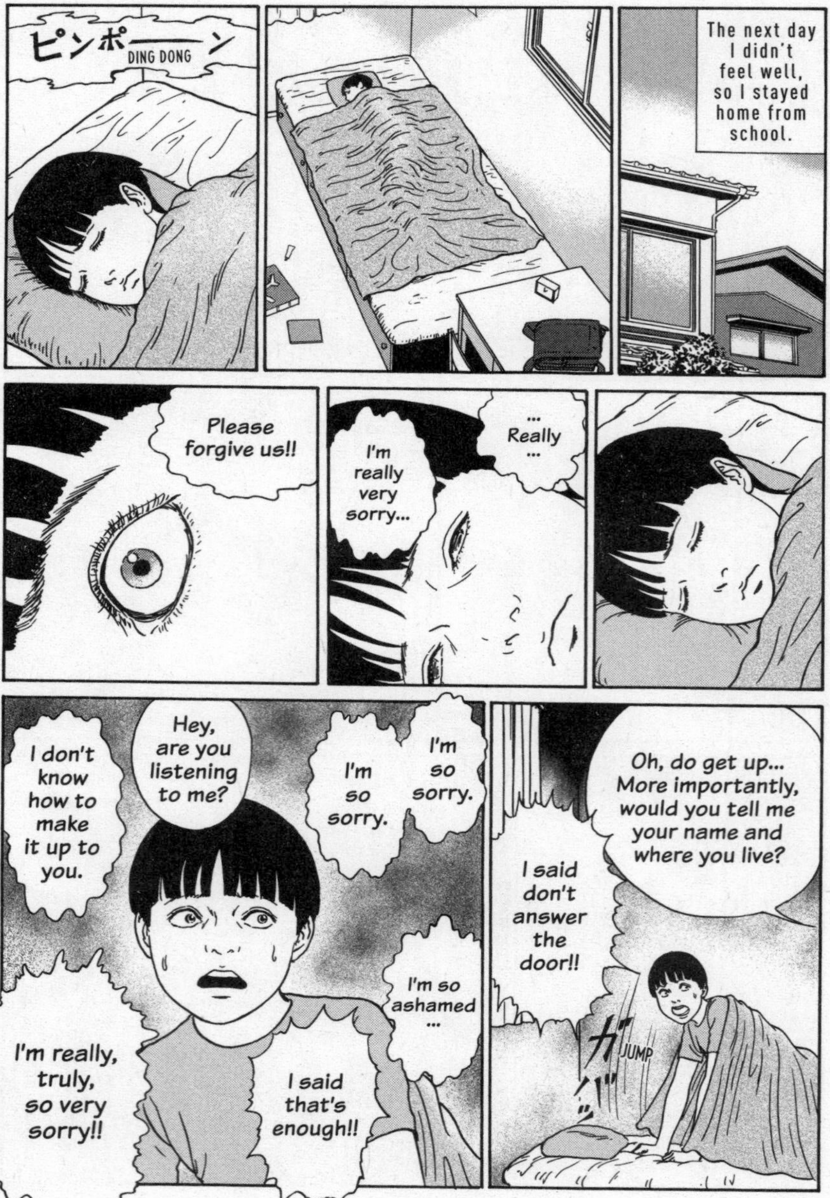
The next day I didn't feel well, so I stayed home from school.
ピンポーーン
DING DONG
... Really ...
I'm really very sorry...
Please forgive us!!
Oh, do get up... More importantly, would you tell me your name and where you live?
I said don't answer the door!!
ガ
JUMP
I'm so sorry.
I'm so sorry.
Hey, are you listening to me?
I don't know how to make it up to you.
I'm so ashamed ...
I said that's enough!!
I'm really, truly, so very sorry!!

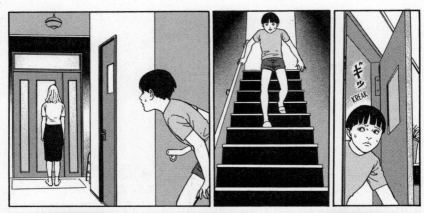

But... he is good-looking...

...?

Really... what a strange boy.

Mom...

Did he leave?

But he is good-looking.

That boy showed up on my way home again today. He's very odd.

Hm... Well, I guess. Ah ha ha ha ha!

Mom, Dad... Something's wrong.

Wh... what's happening...

TEE HEE HEE!

OOZE

HA HA HA.

OOZE

Just hold on!

I... I'm gonna call a doctor!

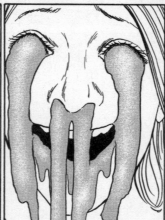

Ah!

I gotta—

I gotta hurry... or they'll die!

DASH

104

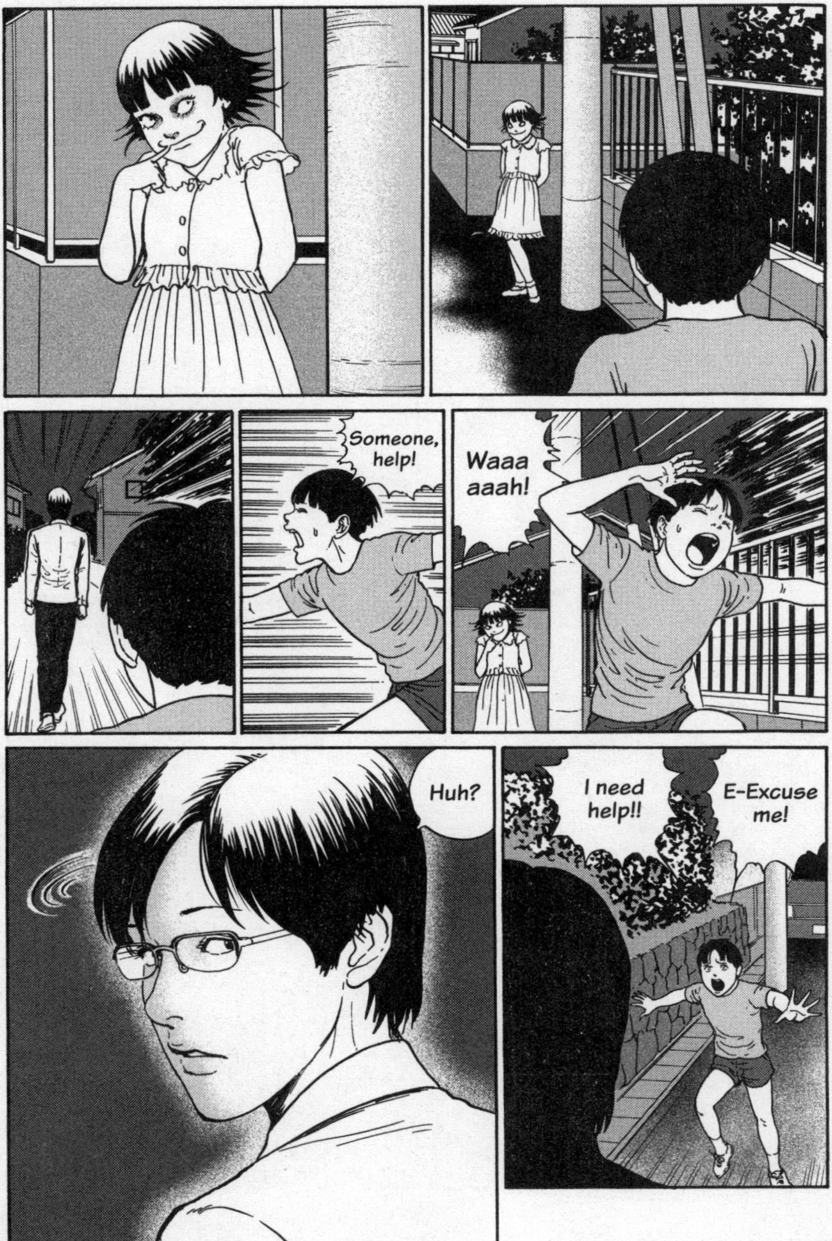
Waaa aaah!
Someone, help!
E-Excuse me!
I need help!!
Huh?

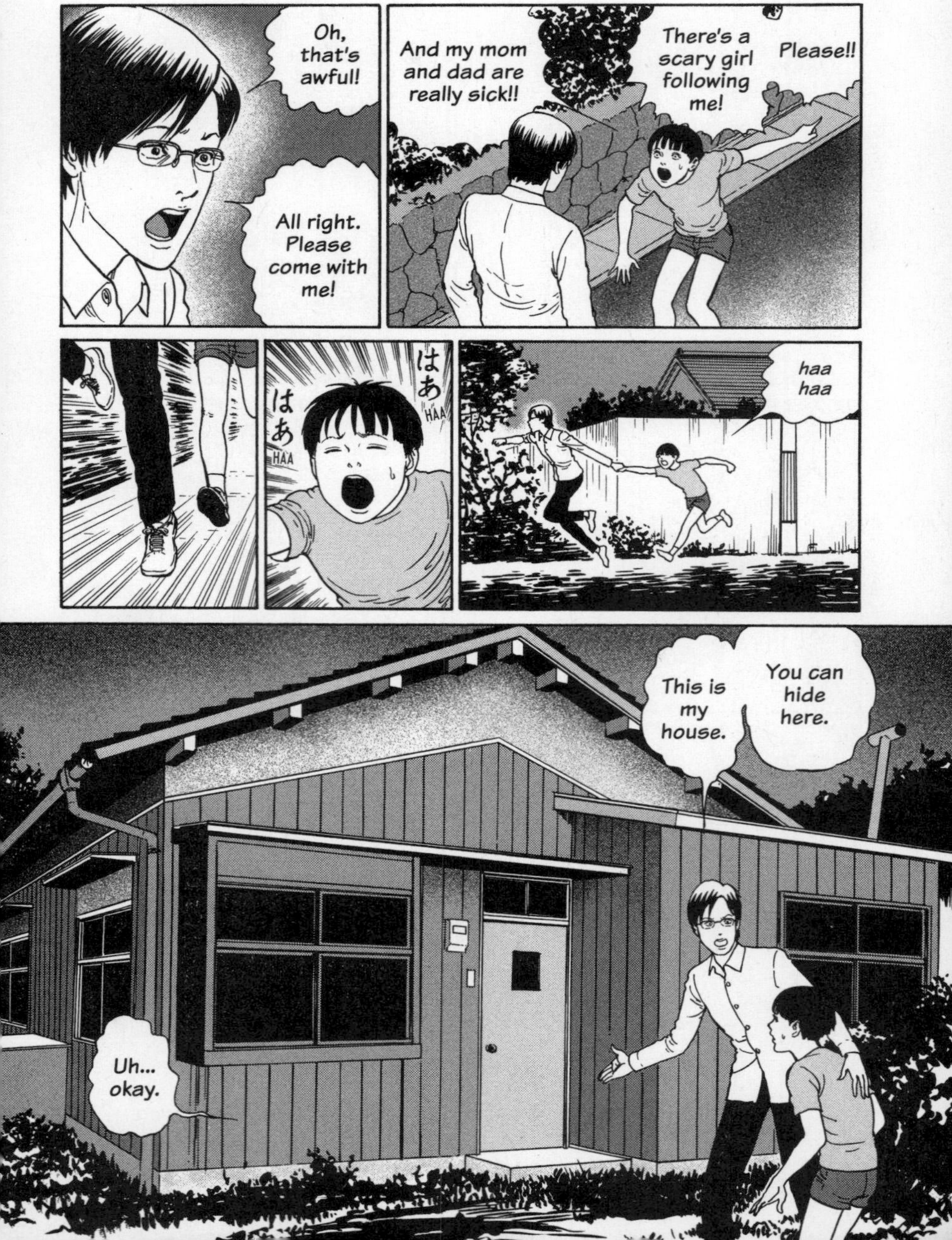
Please!!
There's a scary girl following me!
And my mom and dad are really sick!!
Oh, that's awful!
All right. Please come with me!
haa haa
はあ
HAA
はあ
HAA
You can hide here.
This is my house.
Uh... okay.

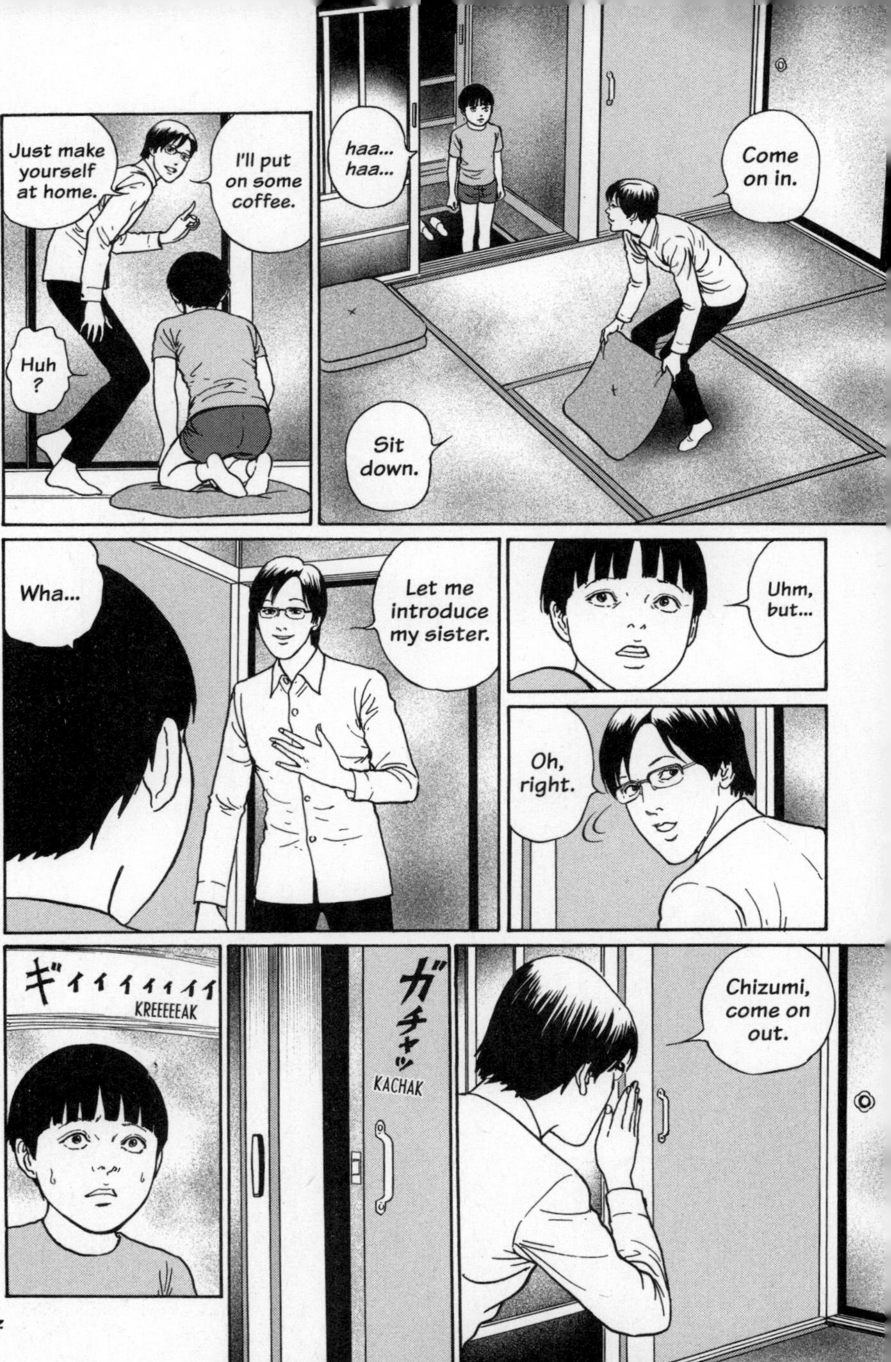
Come on in.
haa... haa...
Sit down.
I'll put on some coffee.
Just make yourself at home.
Huh ?
Uhm, but...
Oh, right.
Let me introduce my sister.
Wha...
Chizumi, come on out.
ガチャッ
KACHAK
ギイイイイイイイ
KREEEEEAK

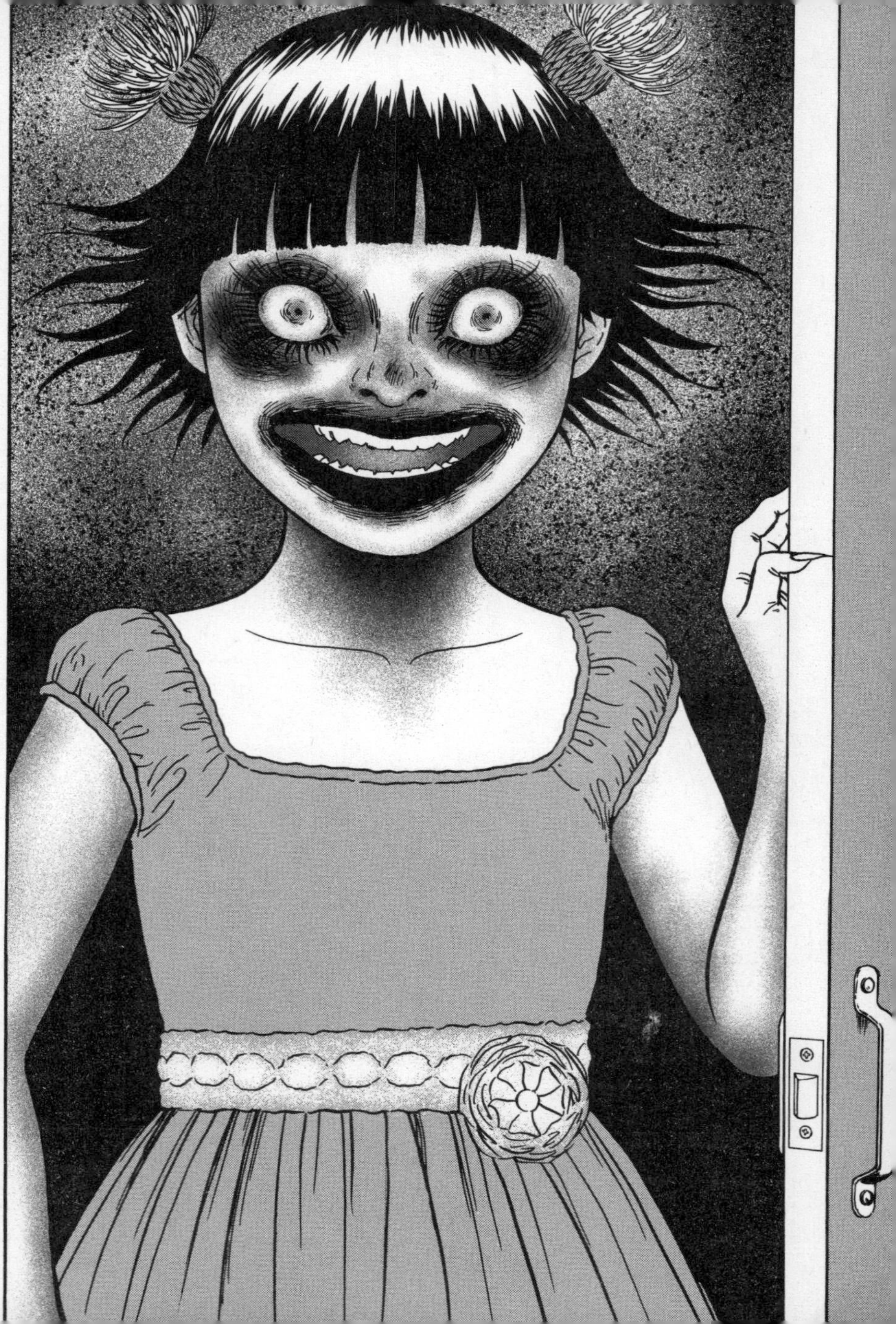

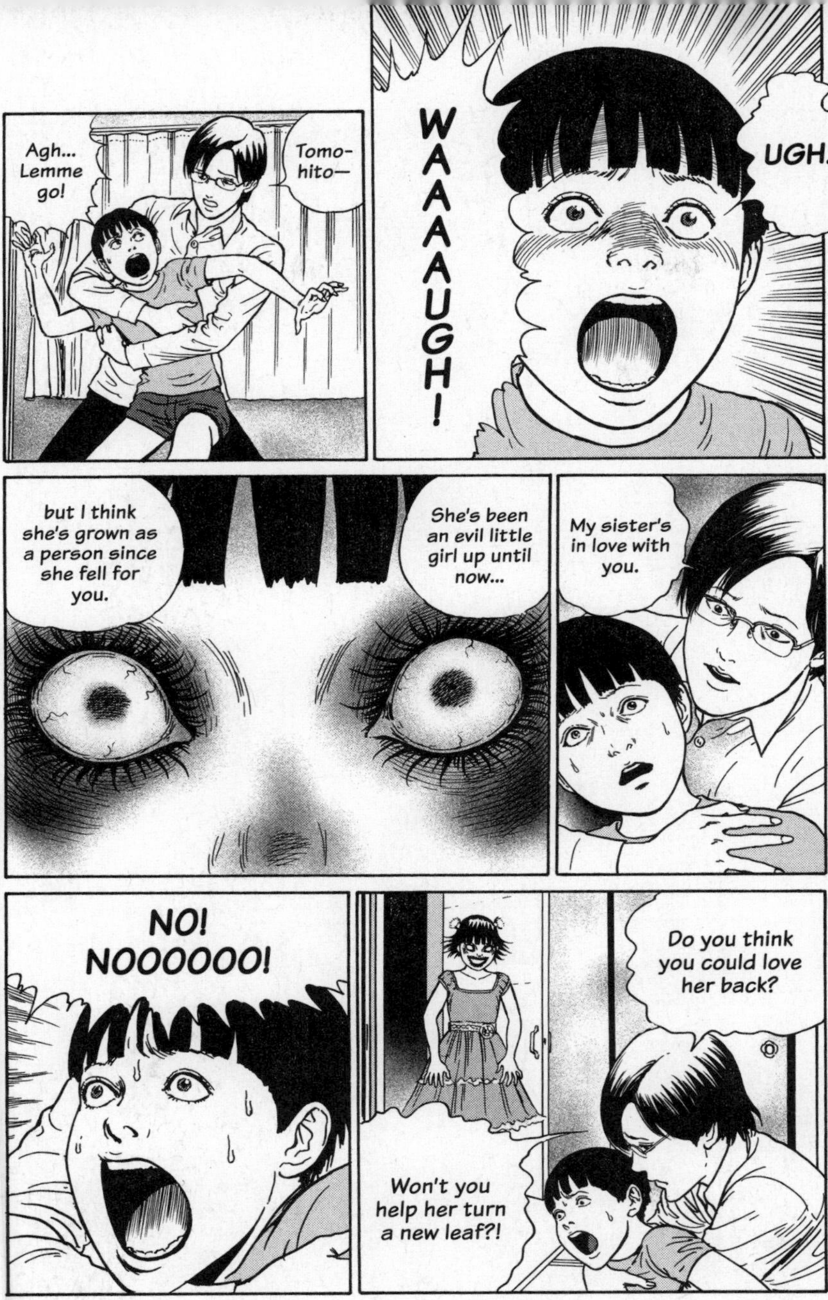
UGH...
WAAAAAUGH!
Tomo-hito—
Agh... Lemme go!
My sister's in love with you.
She's been an evil little girl up until now...
but I think she's grown as a person since she fell for you.
Do you think you could love her back?
Won't you help her turn a new leaf?!
NO! NOOOOOO!

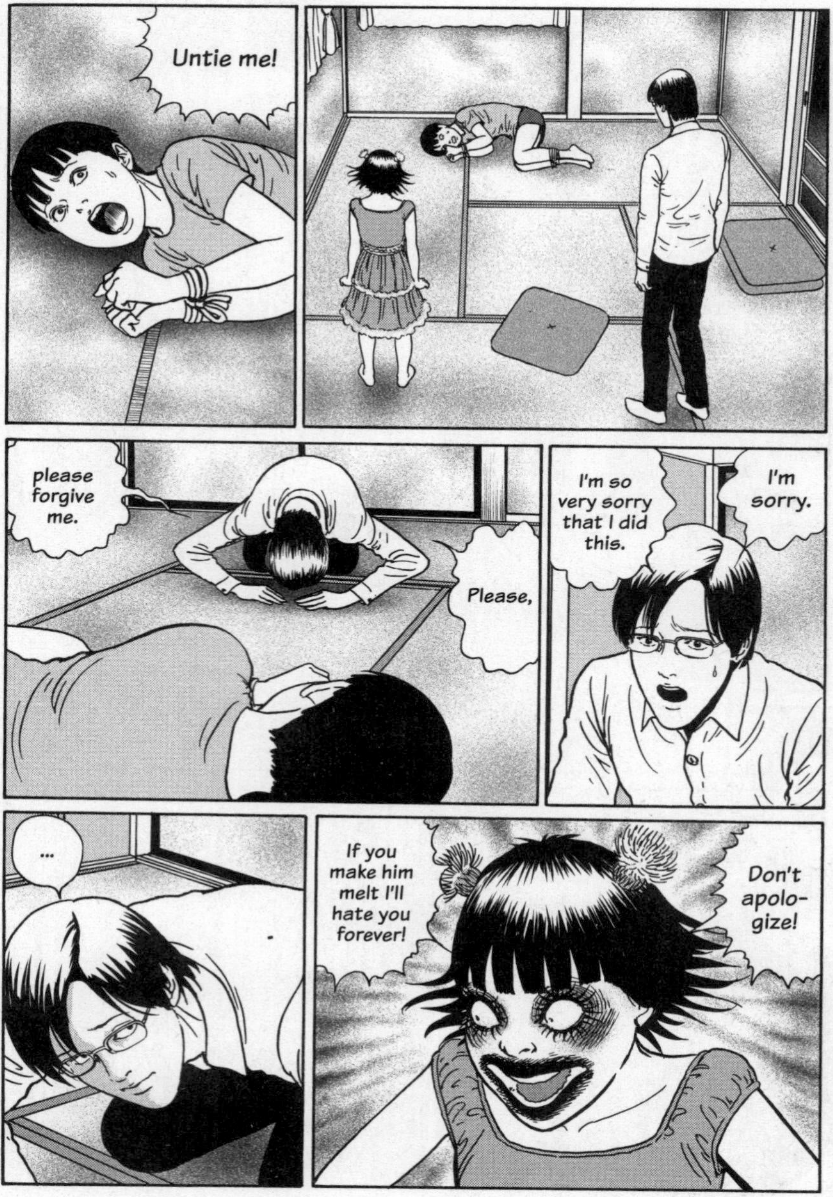
Untie me!
I'm sorry.
I'm so very sorry that I did this.
Please,
please forgive me.
Don't apolo-gize!
If you make him melt I'll hate you forever!
...

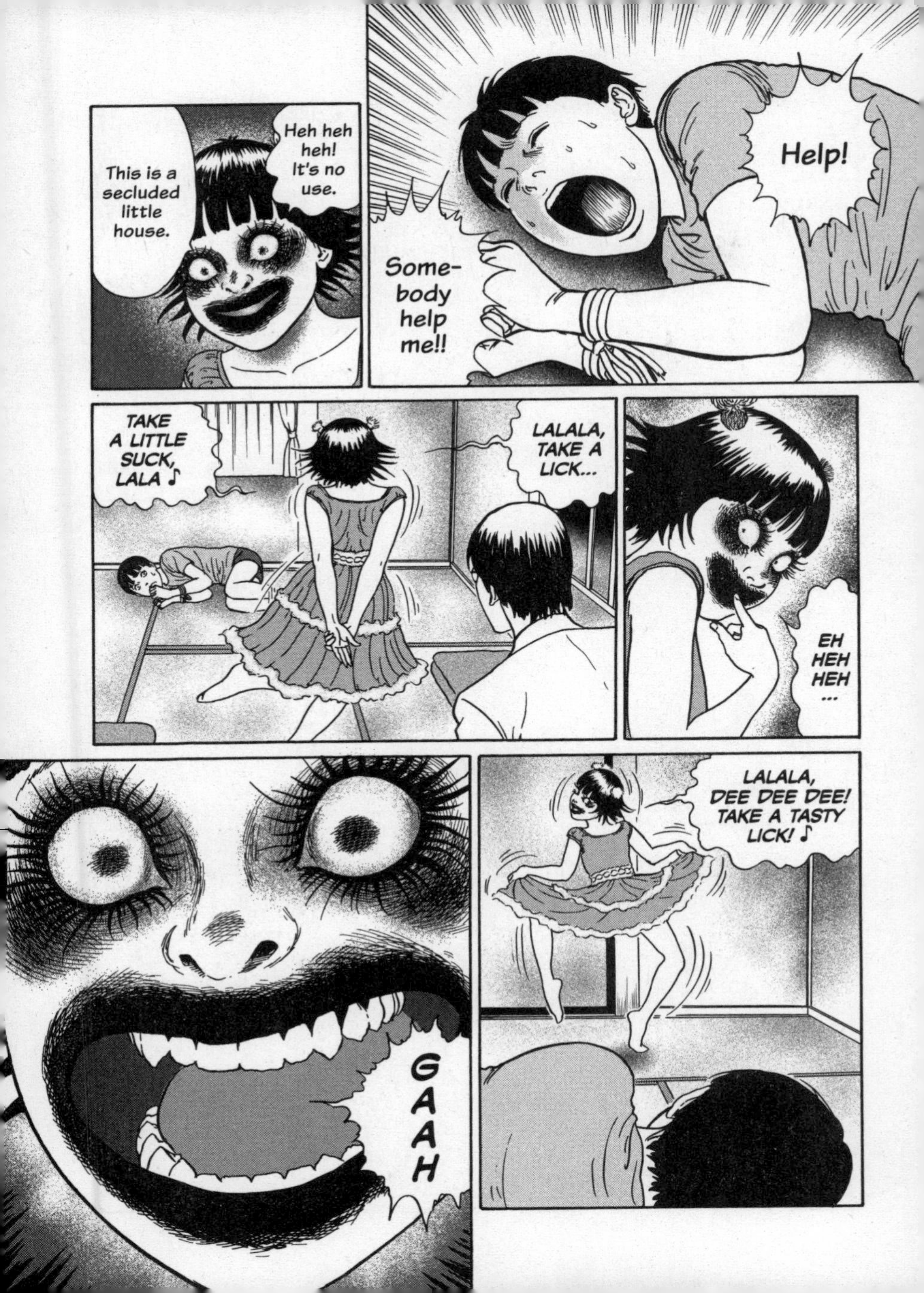
Help!
Some-body help me!!
Heh heh heh! It's no use.
This is a secluded little house.
EH HEH HEH ...
LALALA, TAKE A LICK...
TAKE A LITTLE SUCK, LALA ♪
LALALA, DEE DEE DEE! TAKE A TASTY LICK! ♪
GAAH

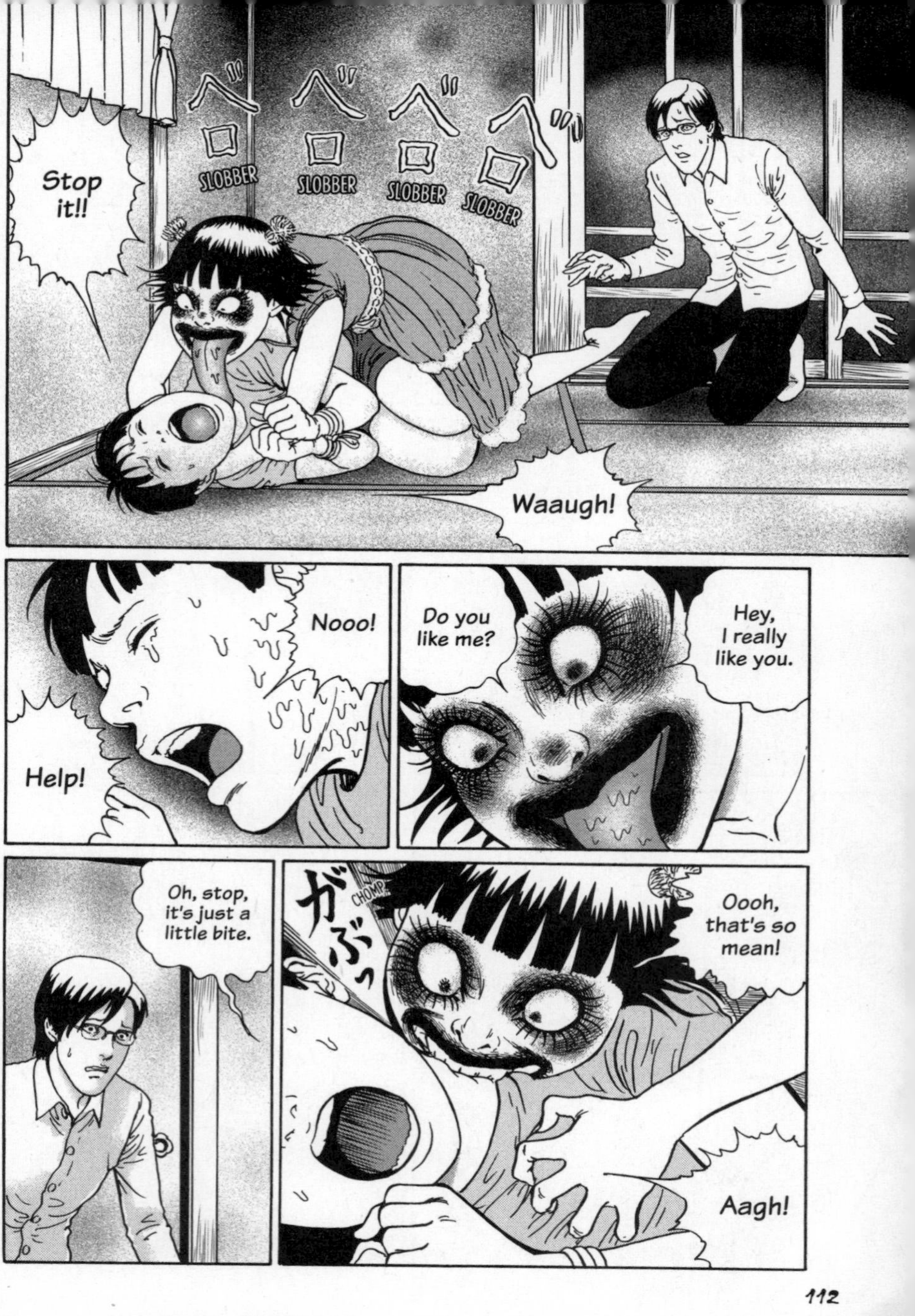
ベロ
SLOBBER
ベロ
SLOBBER
ベロ
SLOBBER
ベロ
SLOBBER
Stop it!!
Waaugh!
Hey, I really like you.
Do you like me?
Nooo!
Help!
Oooh, that's so mean!
がぶっ
CHOMP
Aagh!
Oh, stop, it's just a little bite.

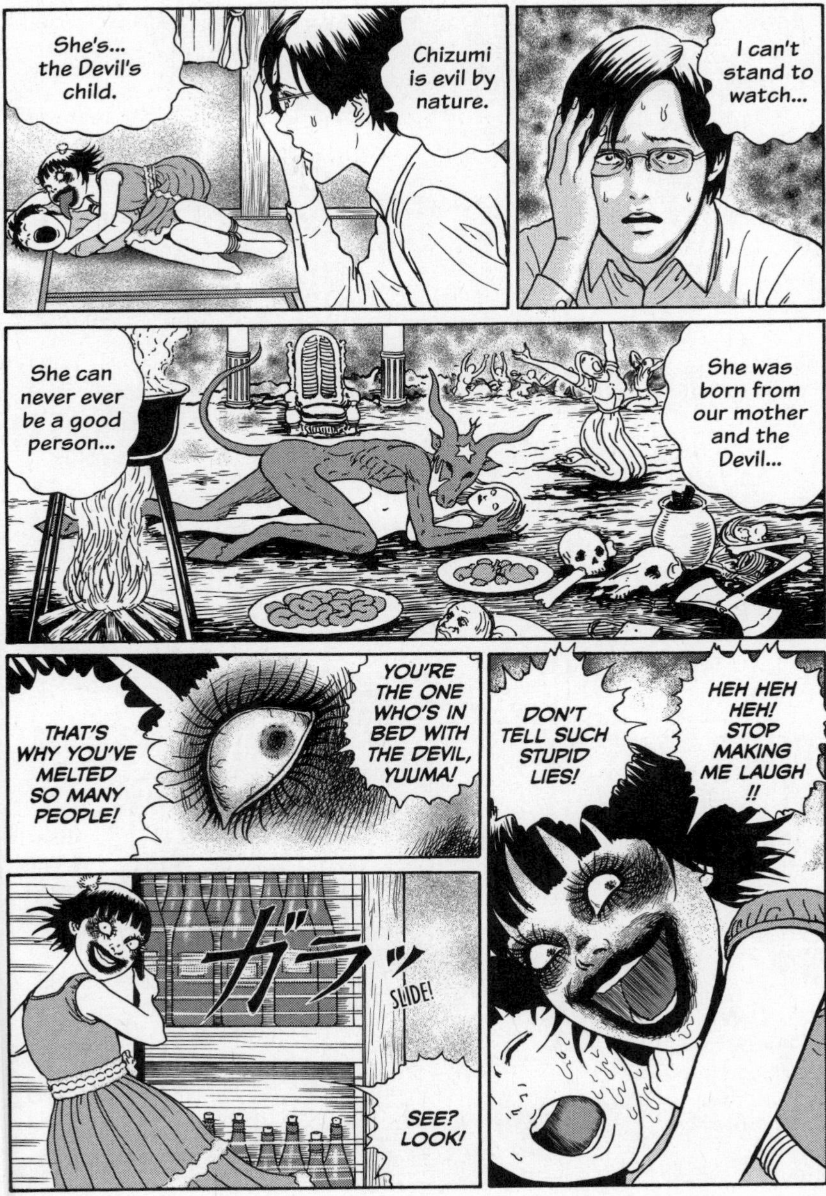
She's... the Devil's child.
Chizumi is evil by nature.
I can't stand to watch...
She can never ever be a good person...
She was born from our mother and the Devil...
THAT'S WHY YOU'VE MELTED SO MANY PEOPLE!
YOU'RE THE ONE WHO'S IN BED WITH THE DEVIL, YUUMA!
DON'T TELL SUCH STUPID LIES!
HEH HEH HEH! STOP MAKING ME LAUGH !!
ガラッ
SLIDE!
SEE? LOOK!

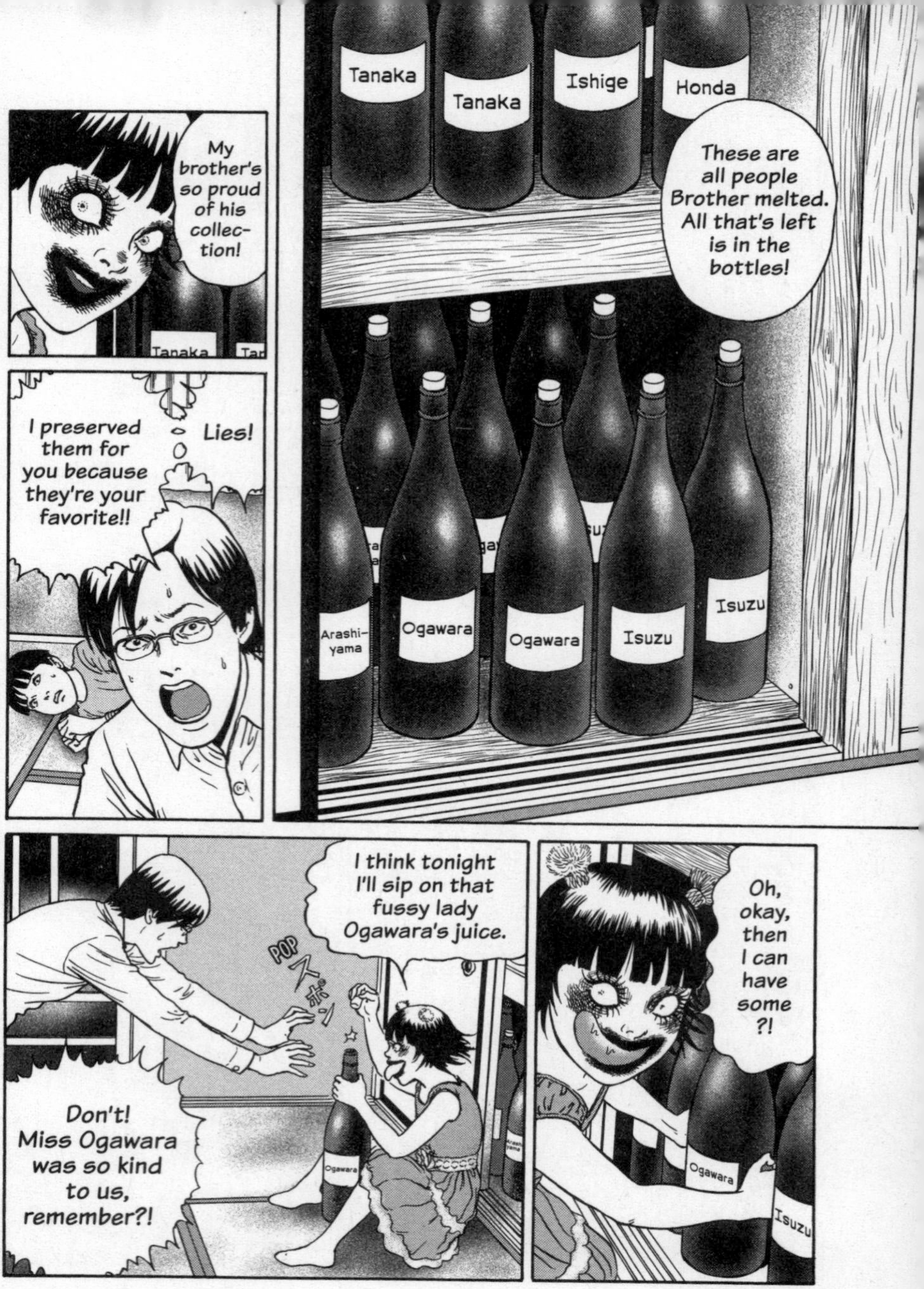
Tanaka
Tanaka
Ishige
Honda
These are all people Brother melted. All that's left is in the bottles!
Arashi-yama
Ogawara
Ogawara
Isuzu
Isuzu
My brother's so proud of his collection!
Tanaka
Lies!
I preserved them for you because they're your favorite!!
Oh, okay, then I can have some?!
Ogawara
Isuzu
I think tonight I'll sip on that fussy lady Ogawara's juice.
POP
Ogawara
Don't! Miss Ogawara was so kind to us, remember?!

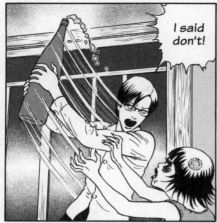

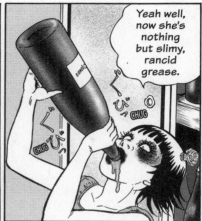

Yeah well, now she's nothing but slimy, rancid grease.
ぐびっ
CHUG
ぐびっ
CHUG
I said don't!
ビタ
SPLISH
ビタッ
SPLAT
ガクッ
SLUMP

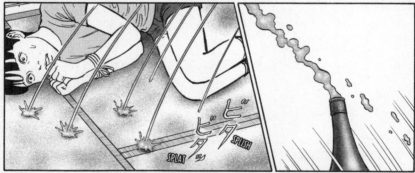

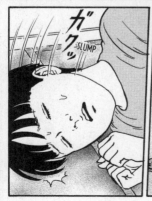

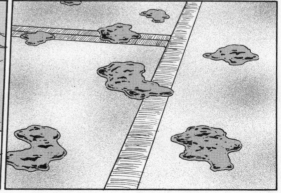

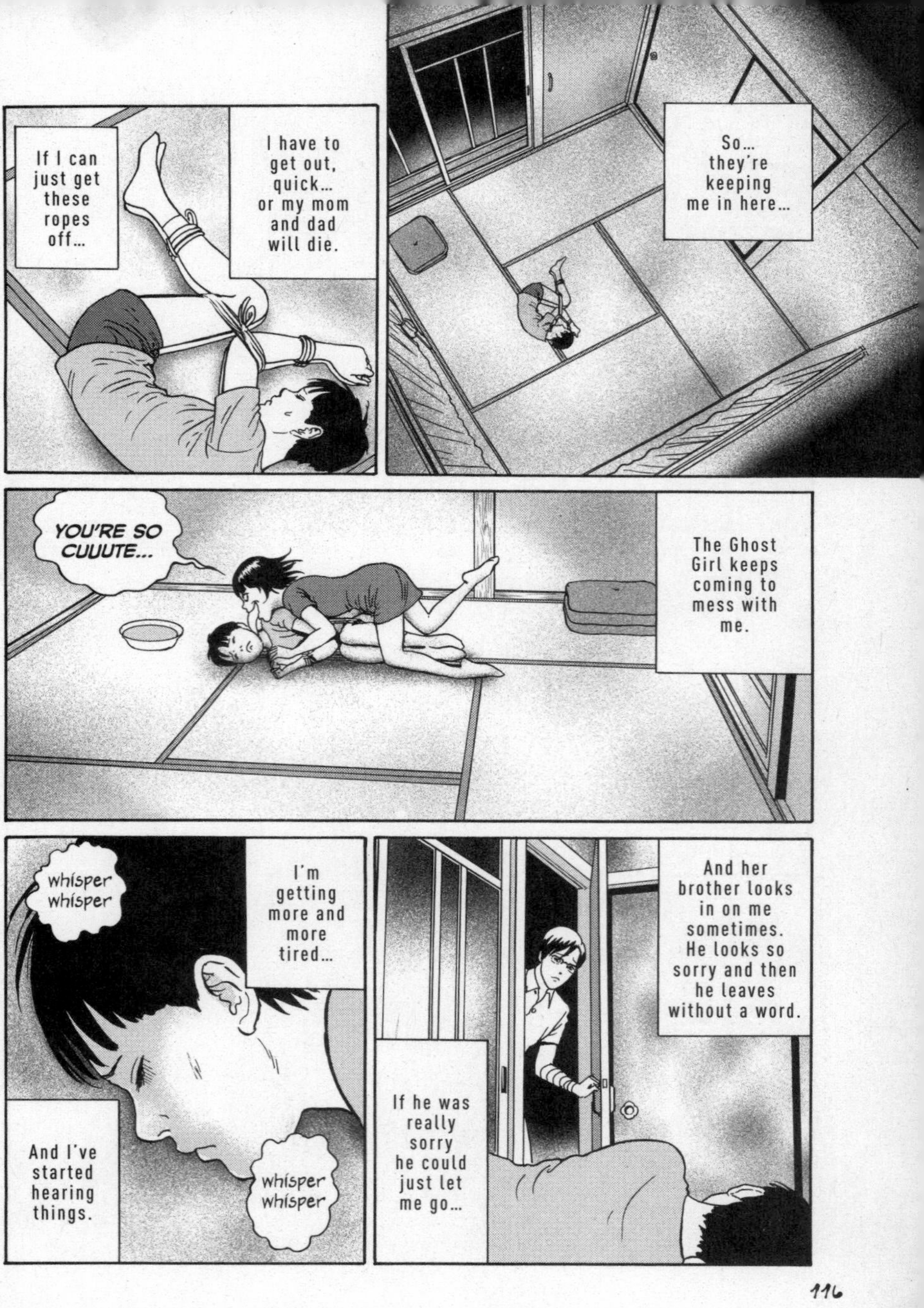
So… they're keeping me in here…
I have to get out, quick… or my mom and dad will die.
If I can just get these ropes off…
The Ghost Girl keeps coming to mess with me.
YOU'RE SO CUUUTE…
And her brother looks in on me sometimes. He looks so sorry and then he leaves without a word.
If he was really sorry he could just let me go…
I'm getting more and more tired…
whisper whisper
whisper whisper
And I've started hearing things.

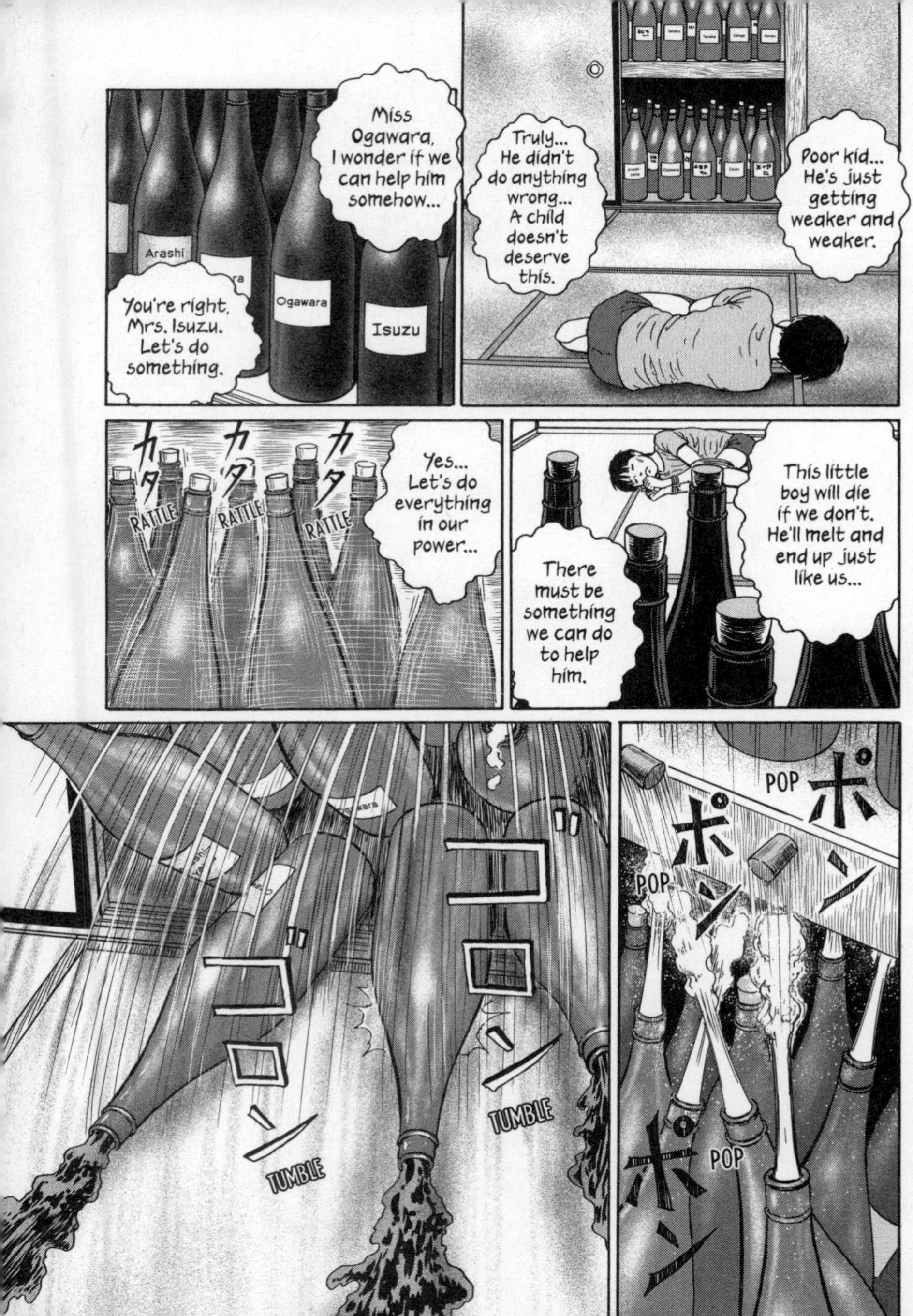
Poor kid... He's just getting weaker and weaker.
Truly... He didn't do anything wrong... A child doesn't deserve this.
Miss Ogawara, I wonder if we can help him somehow...
Arashi
Ogawara
Isuzu
You're right, Mrs. Isuzu. Let's do something.
This little boy will die if we don't. He'll melt and end up just like us...
There must be something we can do to help him.
Yes... Let's do everything in our power...
カタ
RATTLE
カタ
RATTLE
カタ
RATTLE
POP
ポ
ポ
POP
ポ
POP
TUMBLE
TUMBLE

Arashi-yama
ドロドロ ドロドロドロドロドロドロ
OOOOOOOZE...
OOOOOOOZE

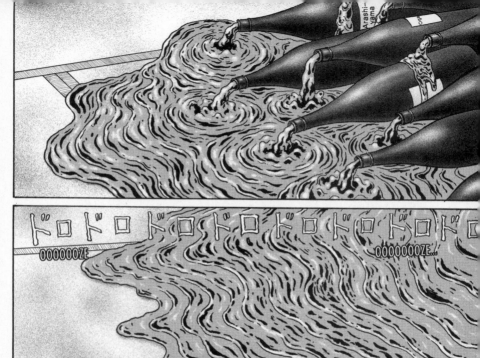

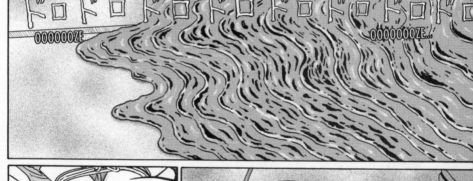

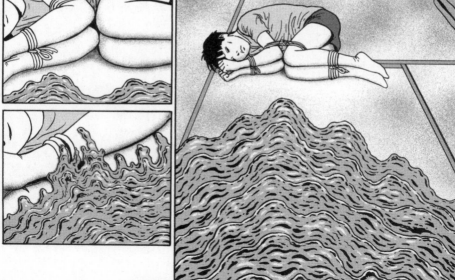

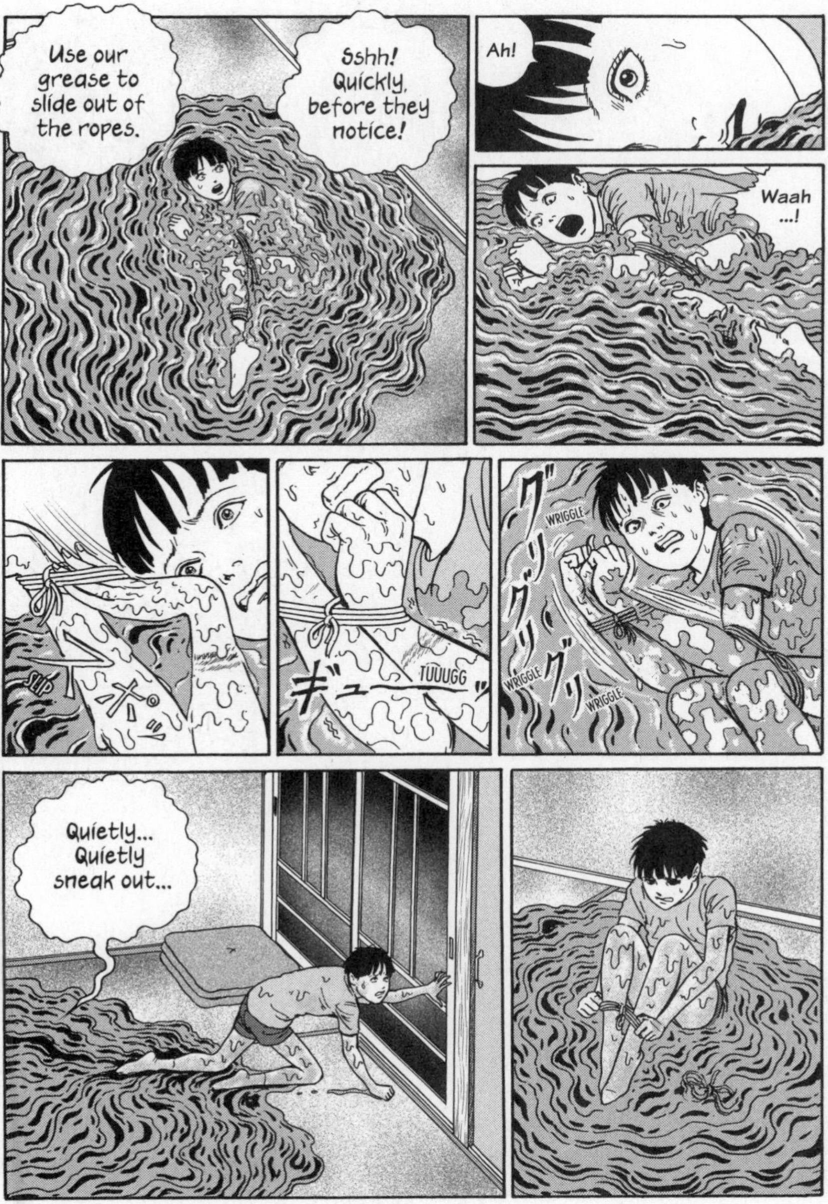
Ah!
Waah ...!
Sshh! Quickly, before they notice!
Use our grease to slide out of the ropes.
WRIGGLE
WRIGGLE
WRIGGLE
WRIGGLE
TUUUGG
SLIP
Quietly... Quietly sneak out...

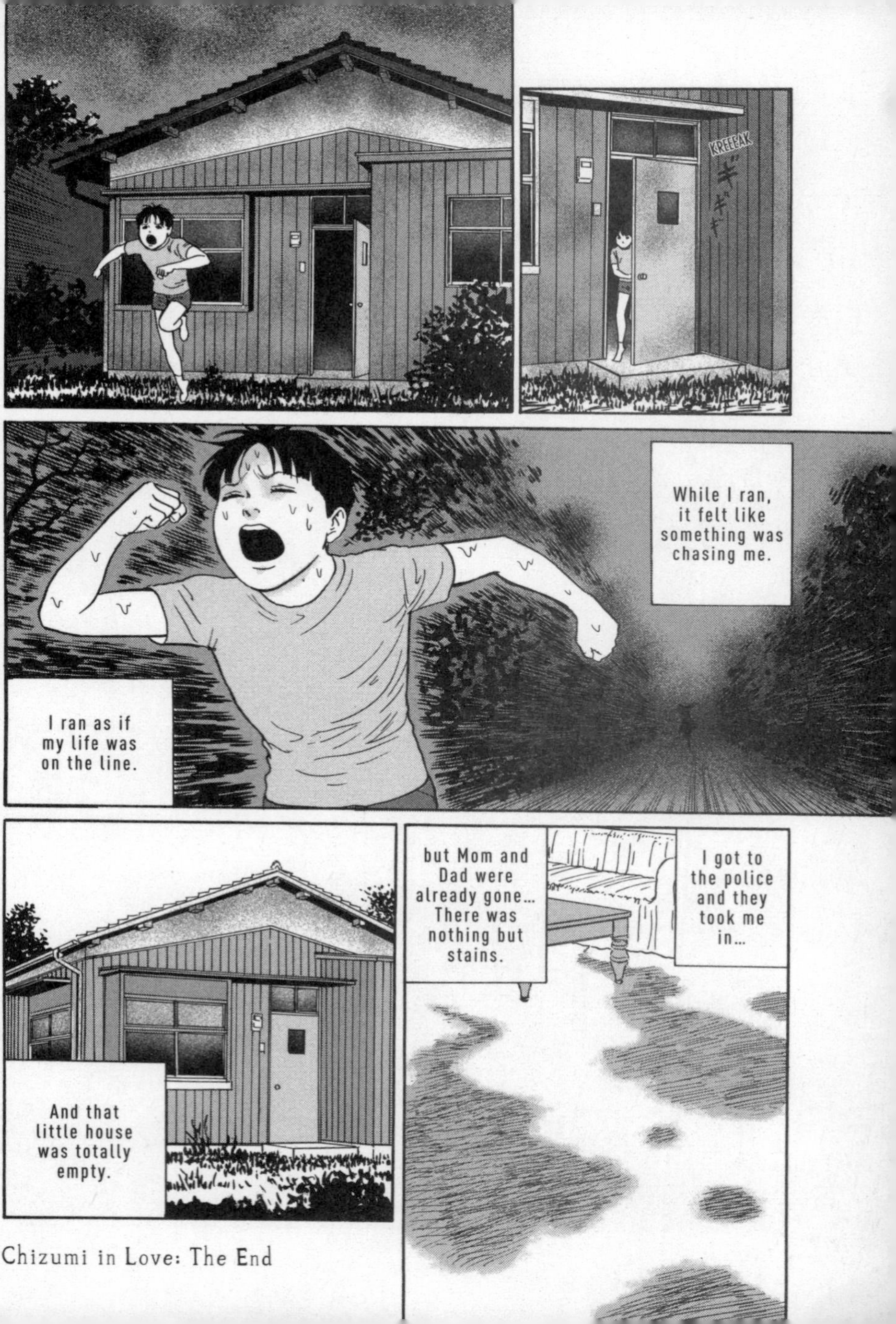
KREEEAK
ギギギ
While I ran, it felt like something was chasing me.
I ran as if my life was on the line.
I got to the police and they took me in...
but Mom and Dad were already gone... There was nothing but stains.
And that little house was totally empty.

Chizumi in Love: The End

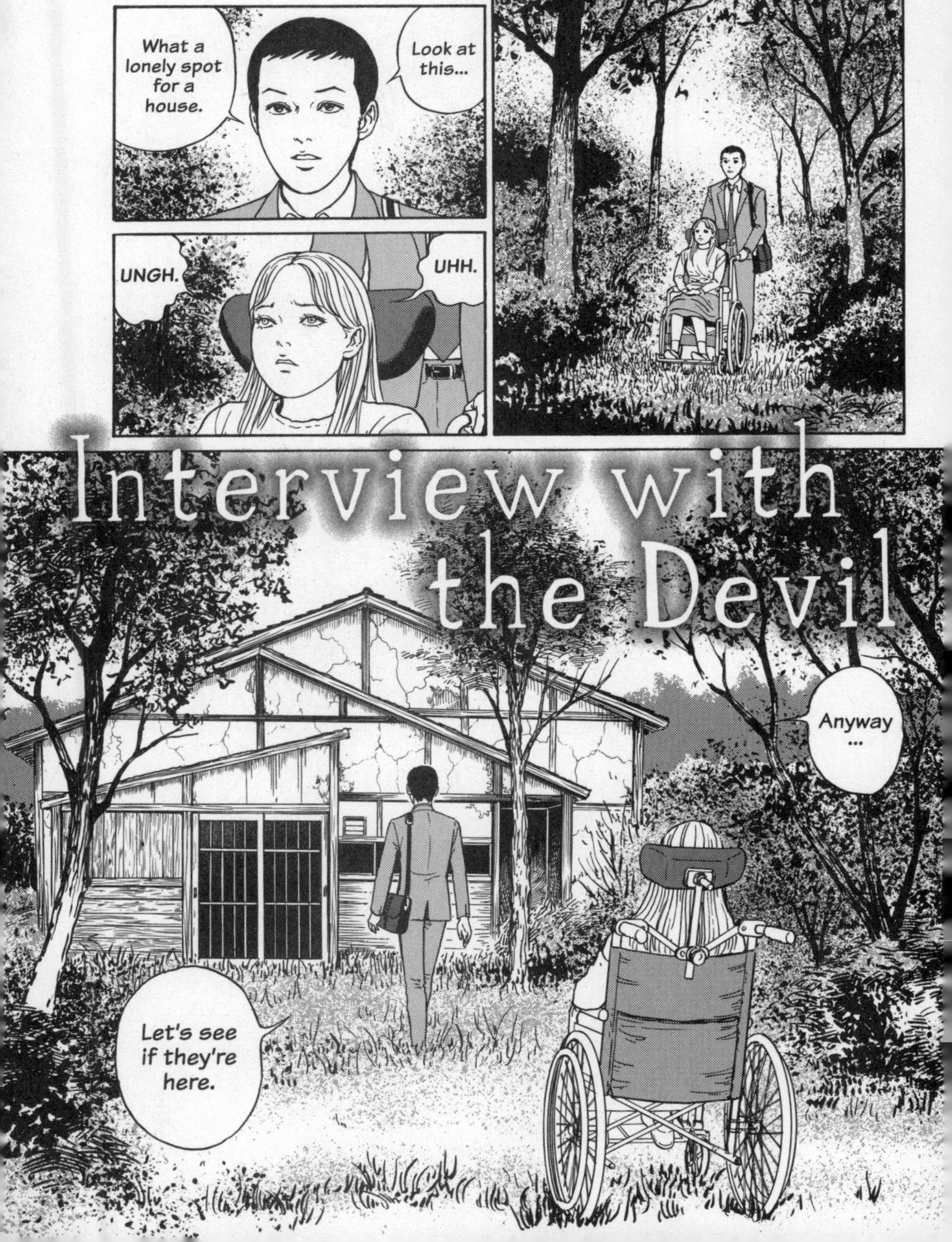
Look at this...
What a lonely spot for a house.
UHH.
UNGH.
Interview with the Devil
Anyway ...
Let's see if they're here.

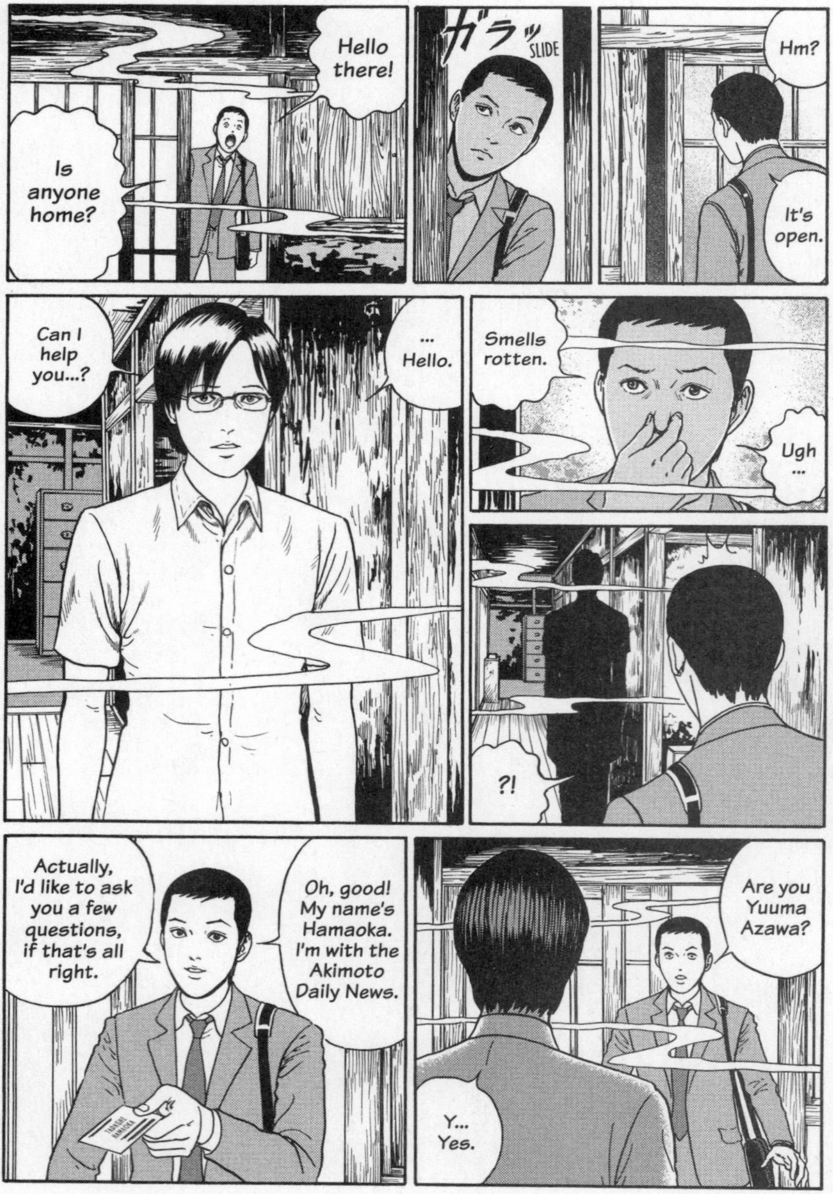
Hm?
It's open.
ガラッ
SLIDE
Hello there!
Is anyone home?
Smells rotten.
Ugh ...
?!
... Hello.
Can I help you...?
Are you Yuuma Azawa?
Y... Yes.
Oh, good! My name's Hamaoka. I'm with the Akimoto Daily News.
Actually, I'd like to ask you a few questions, if that's all right.

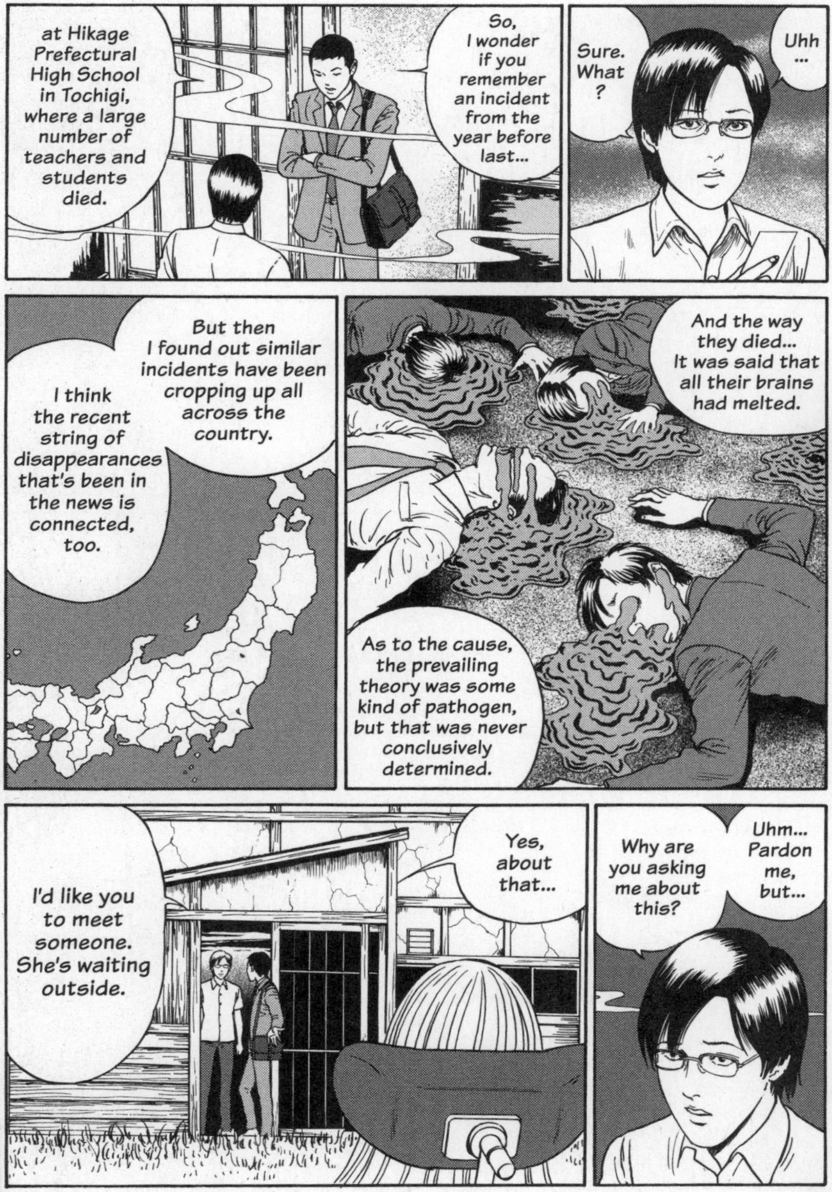
Uhh ...
Sure. What ?
So, I wonder if you remember an incident from the year before last...
at Hikage Prefectural High School in Tochigi, where a large number of teachers and students died.
And the way they died... It was said that all their brains had melted.
As to the cause, the prevailing theory was some kind of pathogen, but that was never conclusively determined.
But then I found out similar incidents have been cropping up all across the country.
I think the recent string of disappearances that's been in the news is connected, too.
Uhm... Pardon me, but...
Why are you asking me about this?
Yes, about that...
I'd like you to meet someone. She's waiting outside.

I think you know her, Yuuma?
...
Sorry, but who are you...?
Her name is Keiko Arisu. She's a survivor of the incident at Hikage High School...
She nearly lost her life, and her brain was badly damaged.
For a long time, she was unable to talk, but recently, she's been able to say a few words.

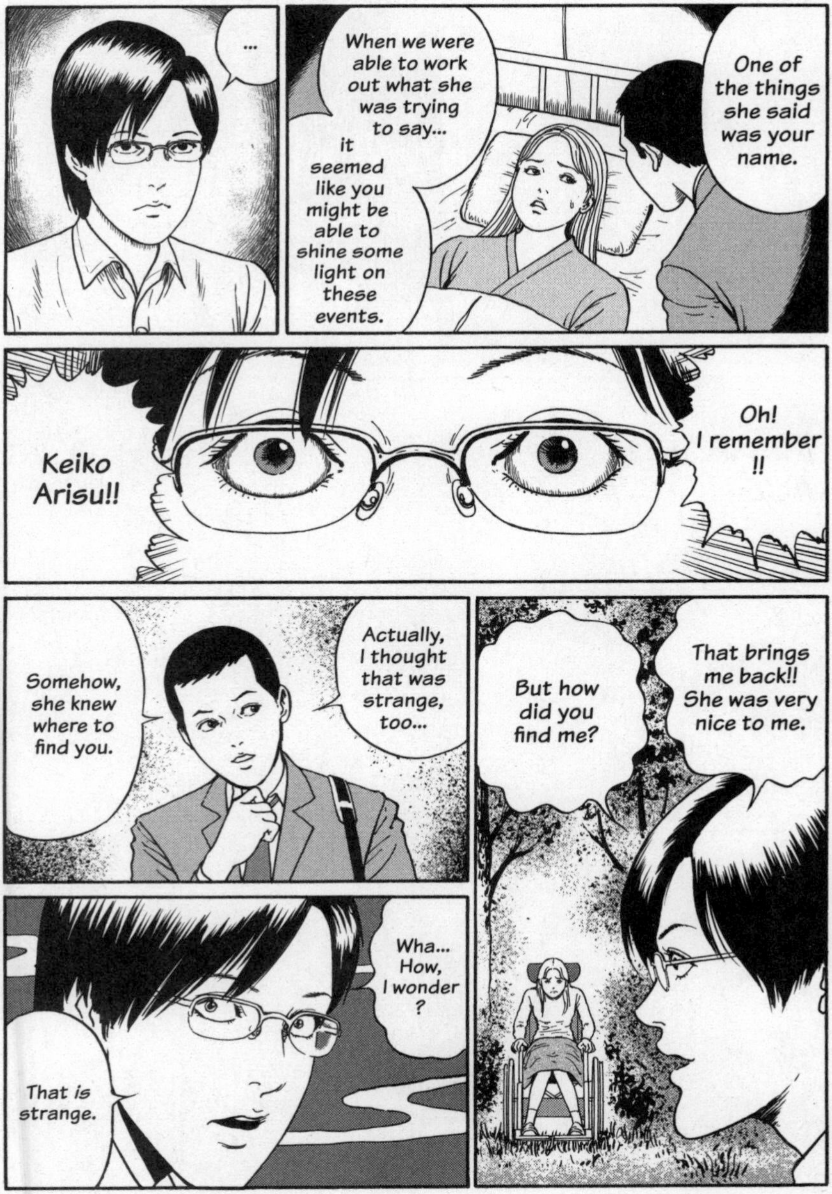
One of the things she said was your name.
When we were able to work out what she was trying to say...
it seemed like you might be able to shine some light on these events.
...
Oh! I remember !!
Keiko Arisu!!
That brings me back!! She was very nice to me.
But how did you find me?
Actually, I thought that was strange, too...
Somehow, she knew where to find you.
Wha... How, I wonder ?
That *is* strange.

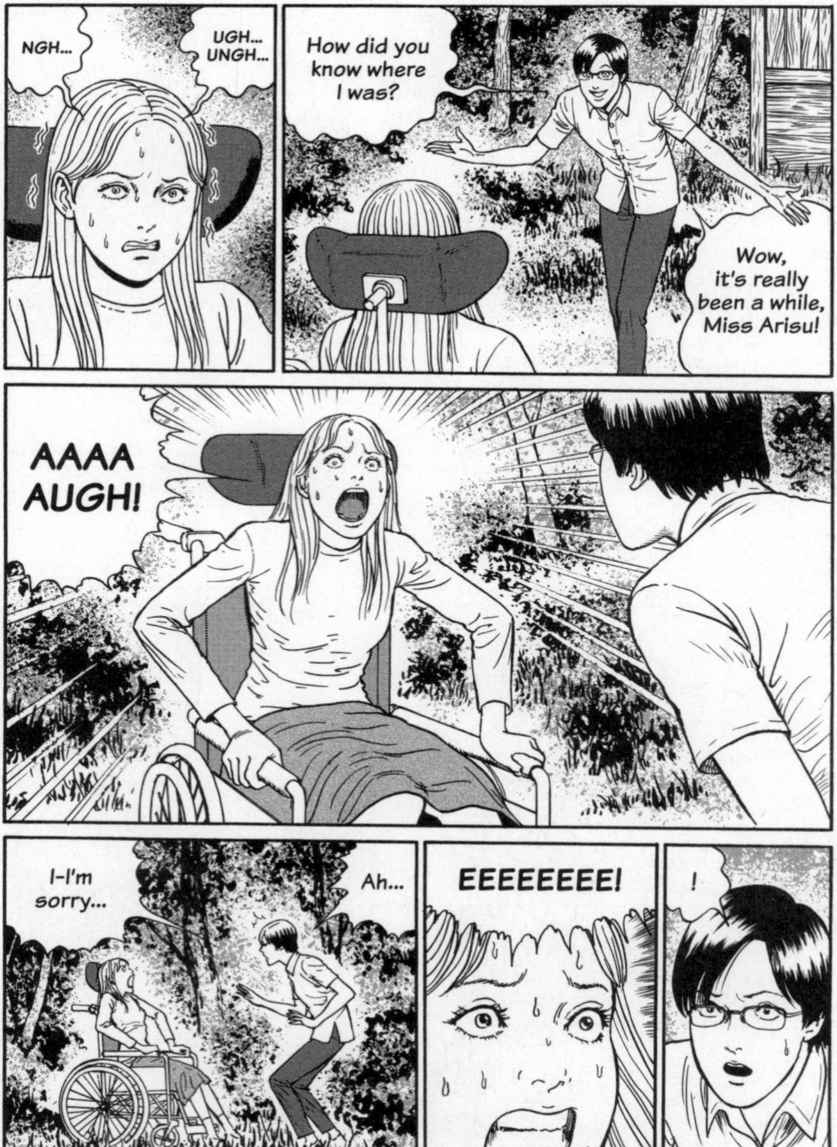
How did you know where I was?
Wow, it's really been a while, Miss Arisu!
UGH... UNGH...
NGH...
AAAA AUGH!
!
EEEEEEEE!
Ah...
I-I'm sorry...

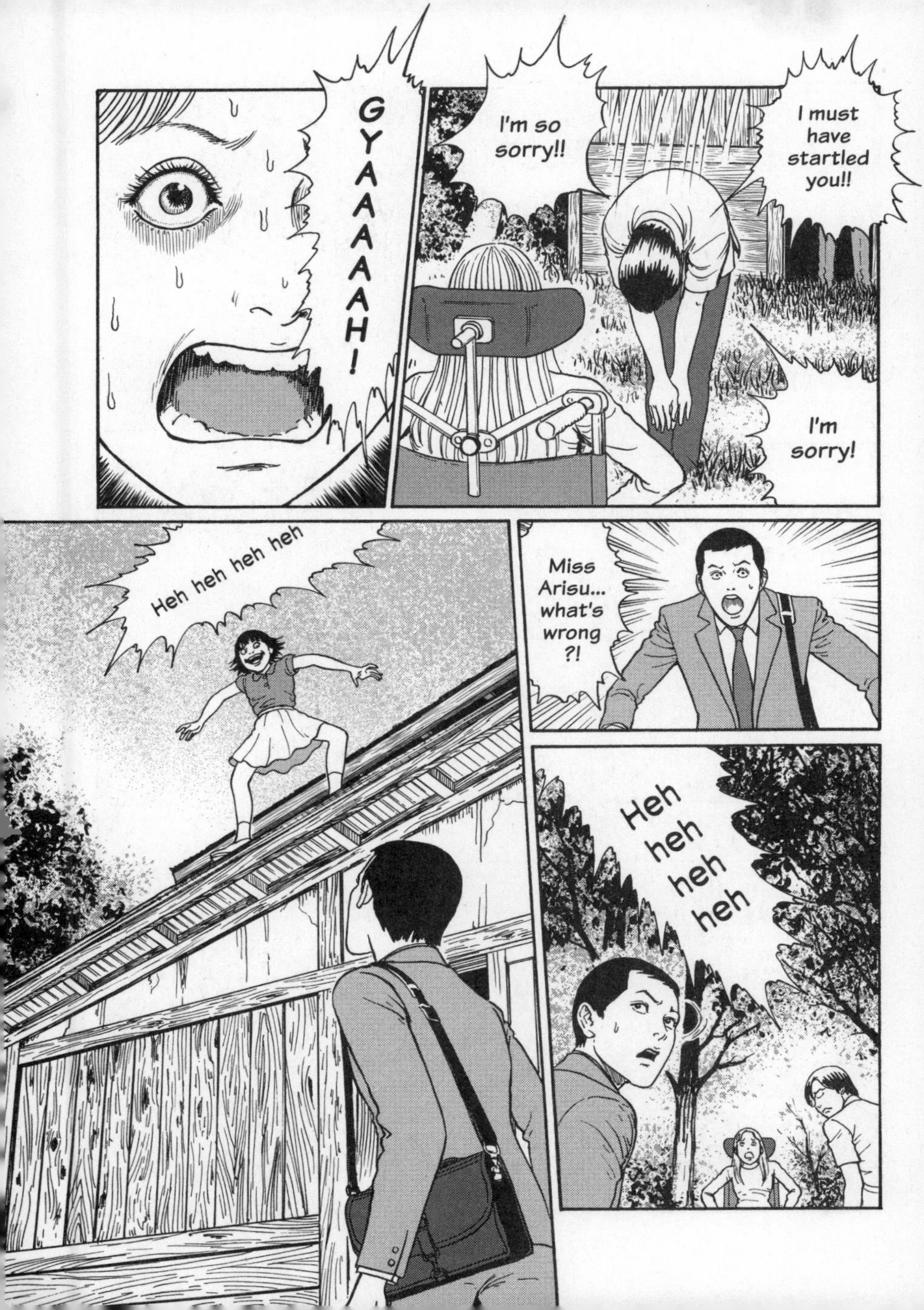
I must have startled you!!
I'm so sorry!!
I'm sorry!
GYAAAAAH!
Miss Arisu... what's wrong ?!
Heh heh heh heh
Heh heh heh heh

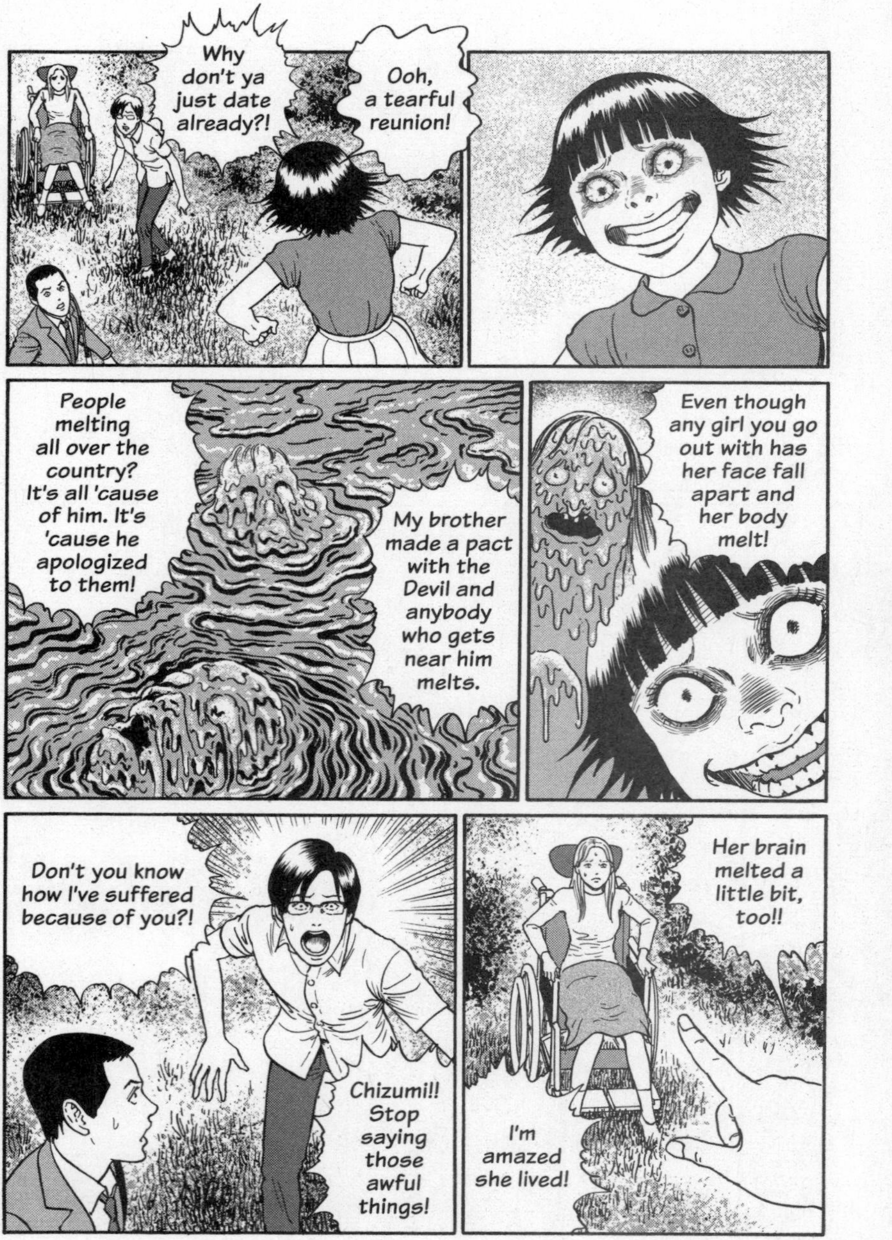
Ooh, a tearful reunion!
Why don't ya just date already?!
Even though any girl you go out with has her face fall apart and her body melt!
My brother made a pact with the Devil and anybody who gets near him melts.
People melting all over the country? It's all 'cause of him. It's 'cause he apologized to them!
Her brain melted a little bit, too!!
I'm amazed she lived!
Don't you know how I've suffered because of you?!
Chizumi!! Stop saying those awful things!

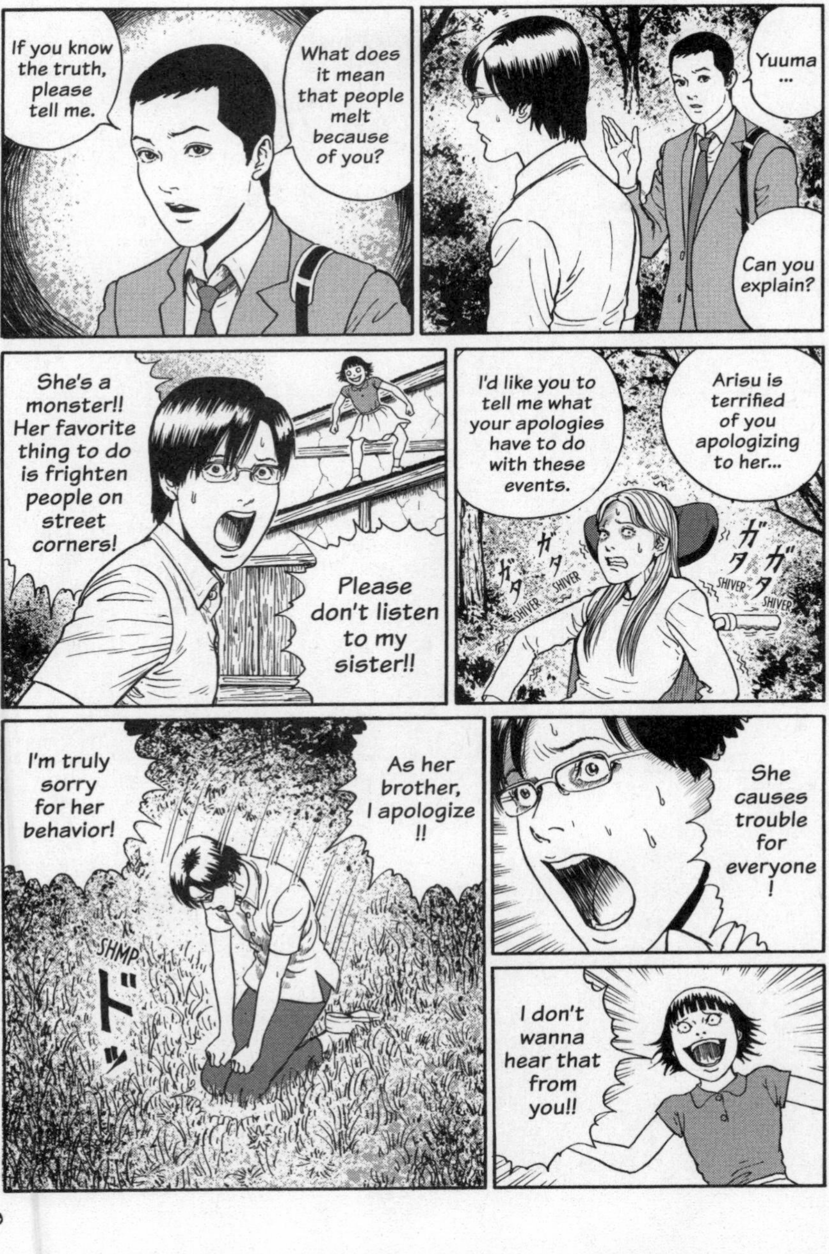
Yuuma ...
Can you explain?
What does it mean that people melt because of you?
If you know the truth, please tell me.
Arisu is terrified of you apologizing to her...
I'd like you to tell me what your apologies have to do with these events.
ガタ SHIVER
ガタ SHIVER
ガタ SHIVER
ガタ SHIVER
She's a monster!! Her favorite thing to do is frighten people on street corners!
Please don't listen to my sister!!
She causes trouble for everyone!
I don't wanna hear that from you!!
As her brother, I apologize!!
I'm truly sorry for her behavior!
SHMP
ドッ

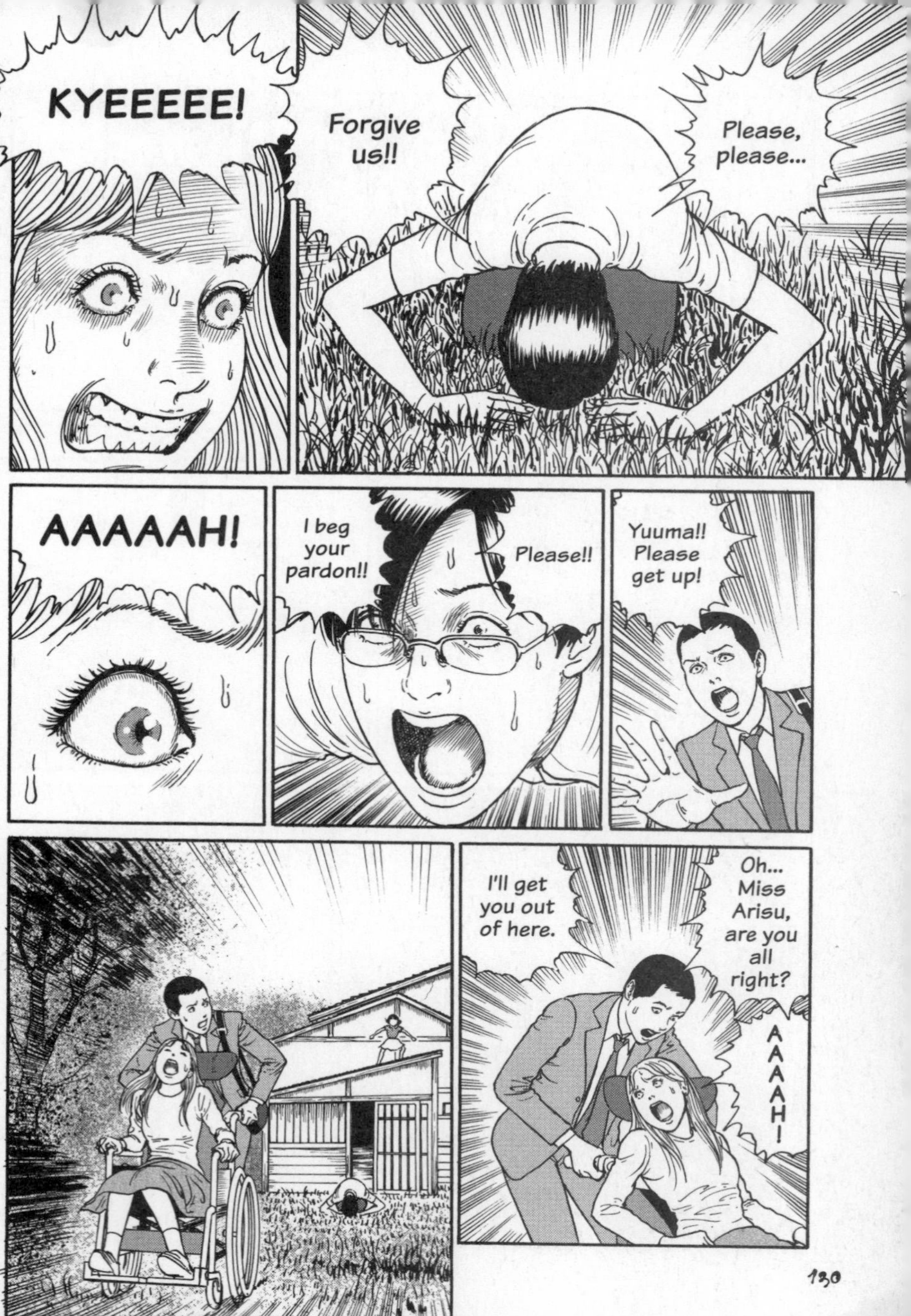
Please, please...
Forgive us!!
KYEEEEE!
Yuuma!! Please get up!
Please!!
I beg your pardon!!
AAAAAH!
Oh... Miss Arisu, are you all right?
I'll get you out of here.
AAAAH!

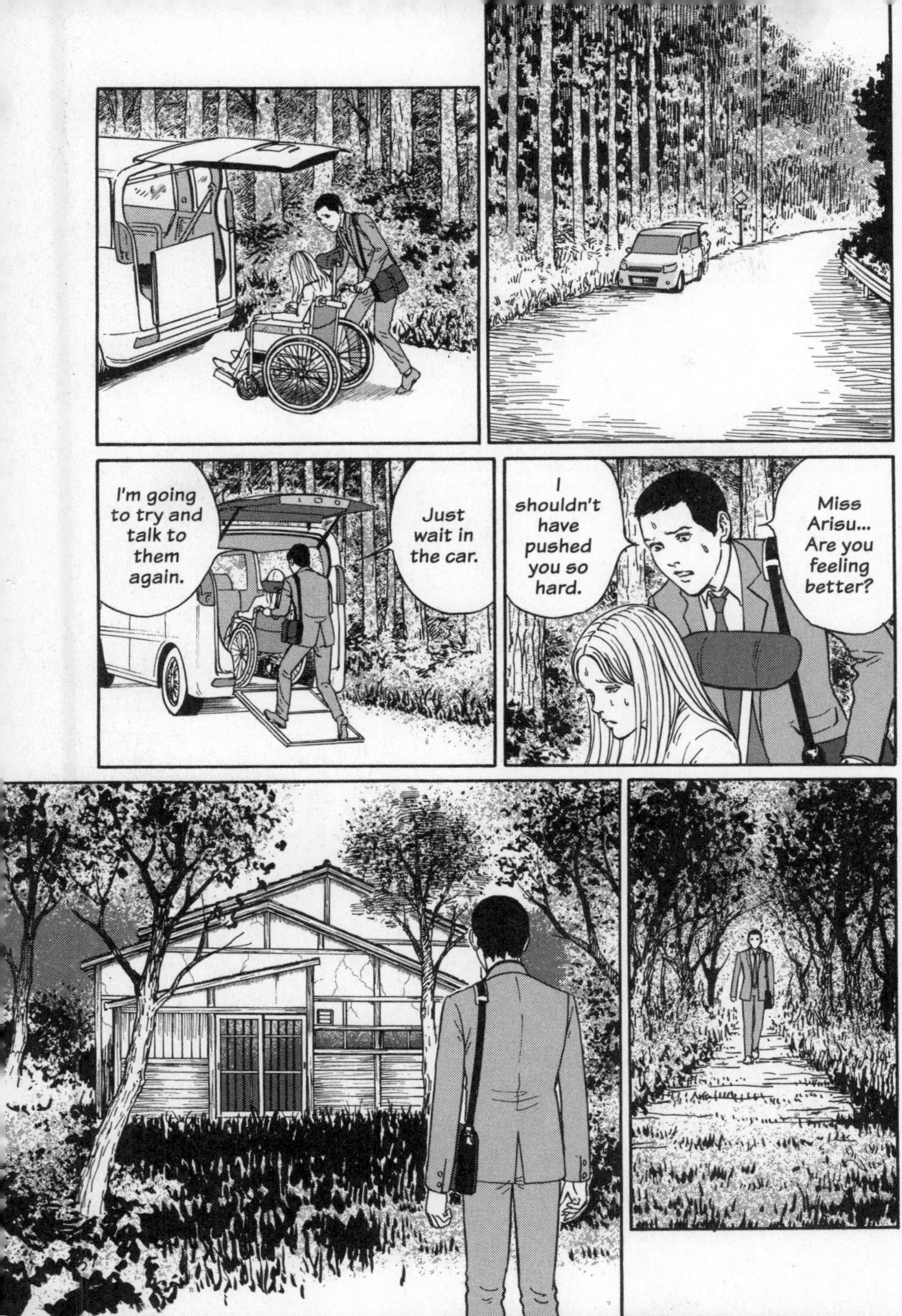
Miss Arisu... Are you feeling better?
I shouldn't have pushed you so hard.
Just wait in the car.
I'm going to try and talk to them again.

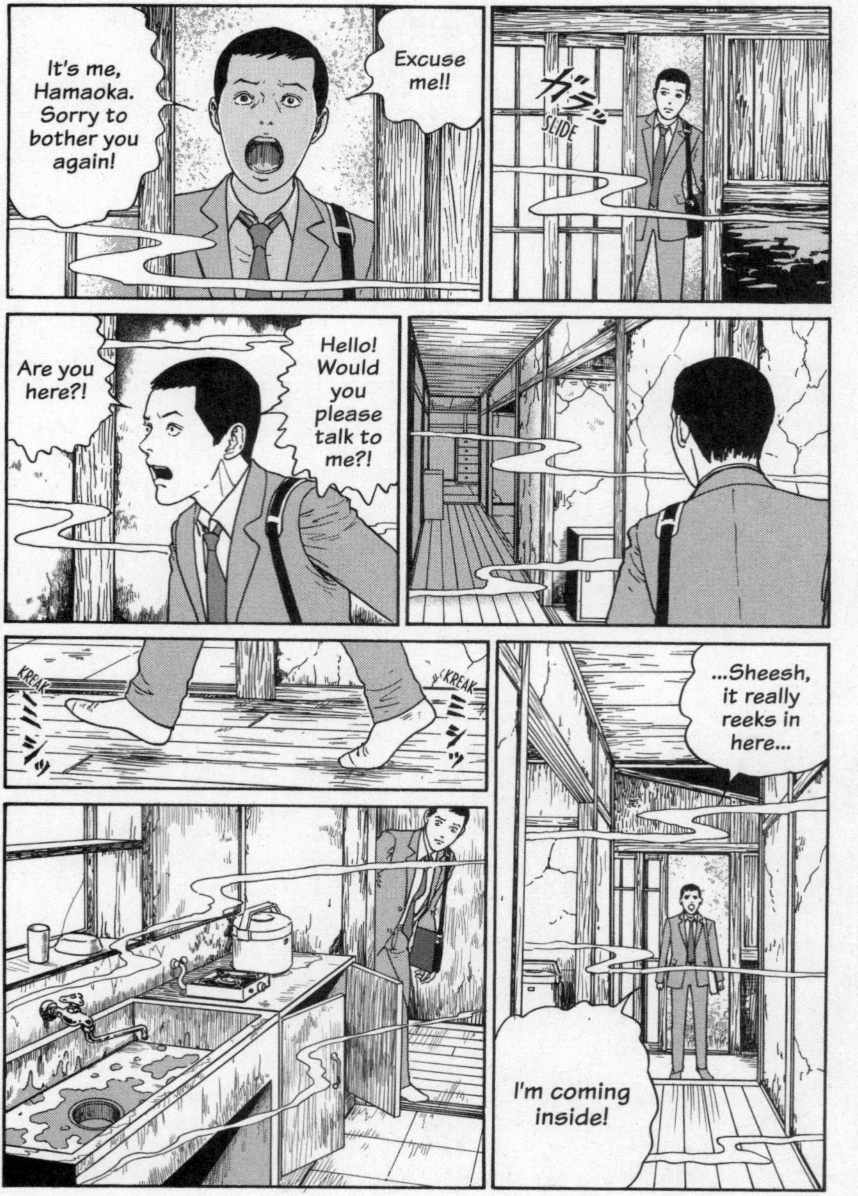
ガラッ
SLIDE
Excuse me!!
It's me, Hamaoka. Sorry to bother you again!
Hello! Would you please talk to me?!
Are you here?!
...Sheesh, it really reeks in here...
I'm coming inside!
KREAK
ミシッ
KREAK
ミシッ

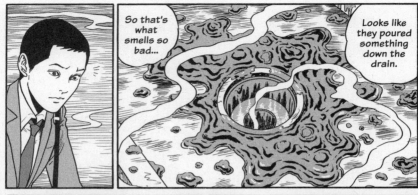

Looks like they poured something down the drain.
So that's what smells so bad...
Tana
Yuuma, are we moving again?
Hurry up, Chizumi!

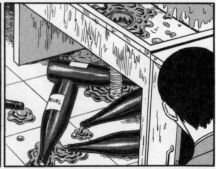

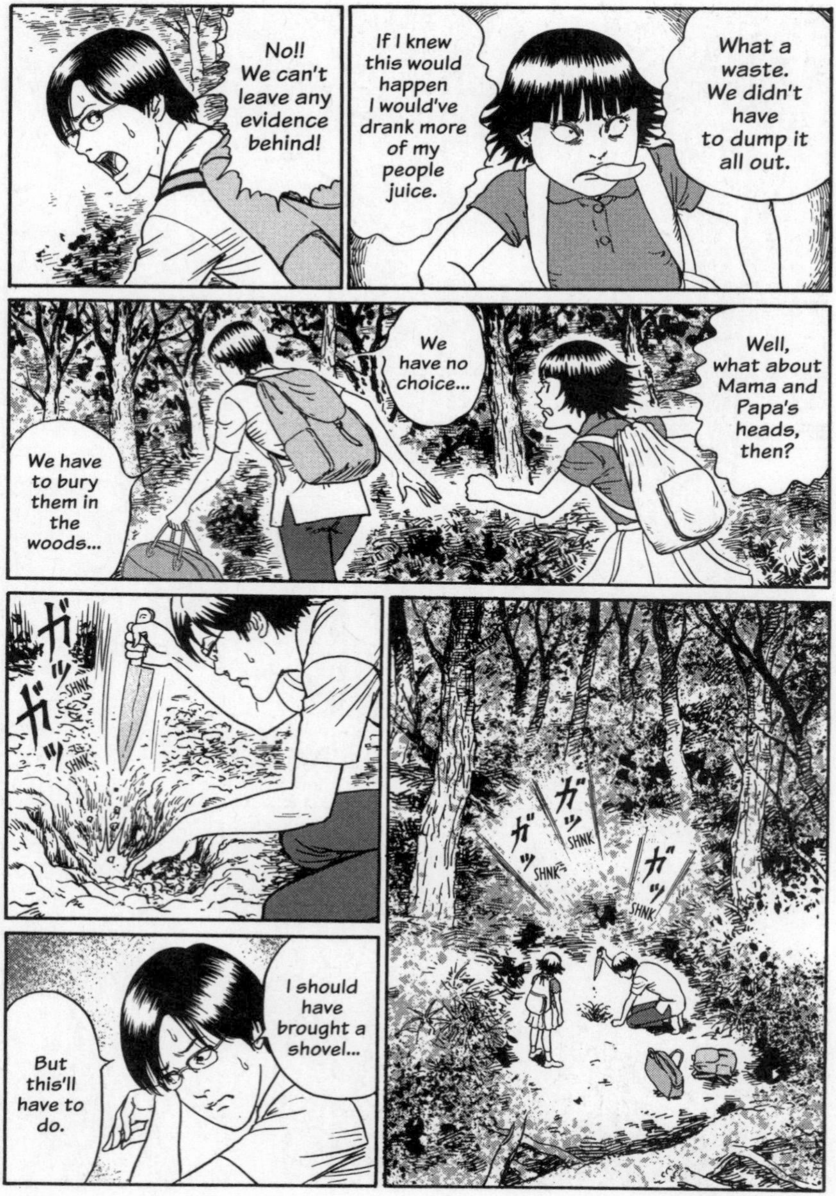
What a waste. We didn't have to dump it all out.
If I knew this would happen I would've drank more of my people juice.
No!! We can't leave any evidence behind!
Well, what about Mama and Papa's heads, then?
We have no choice...
We have to bury them in the woods...
ガッ
SHNK
ガッ
SHNK
ガッ
SHNK
ガッ
SHNK
ガッ
SHNK
I should have brought a shovel...
But this'll have to do.

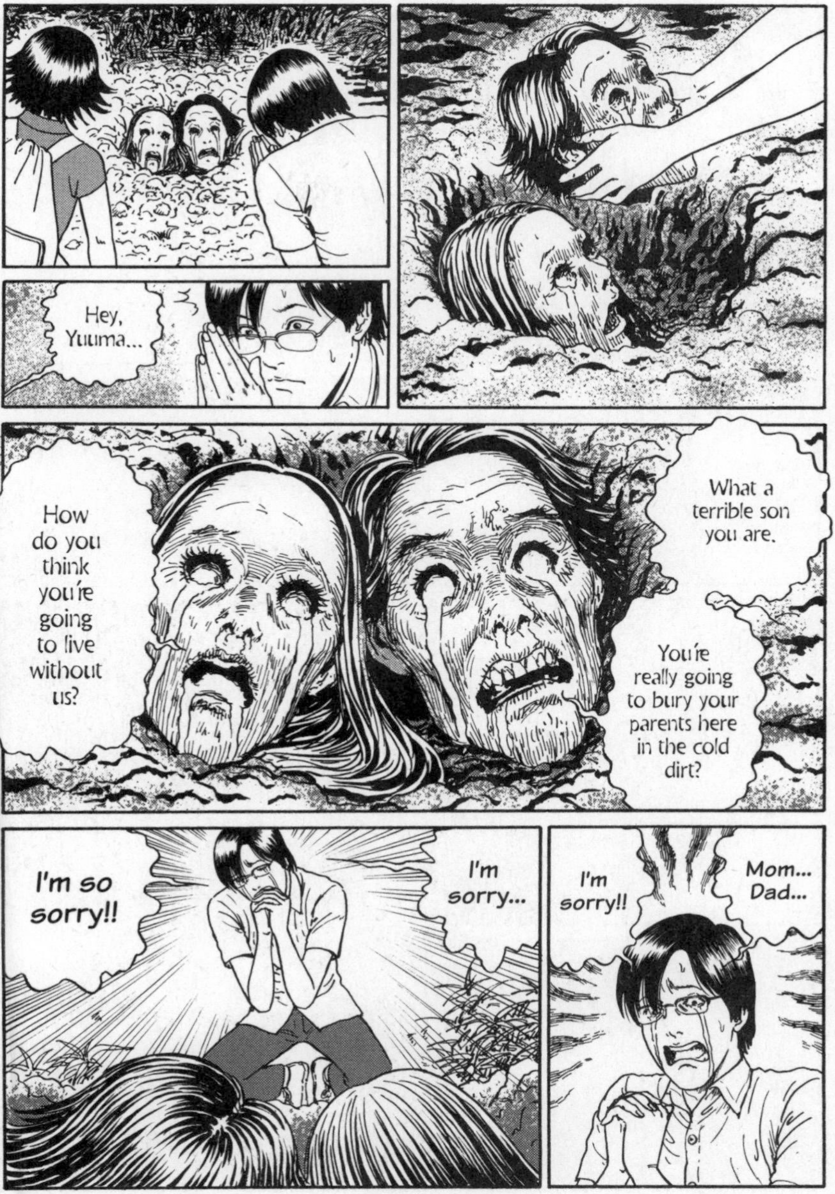
Hey, Yuuma...
What a terrible son you are.
You're really going to bury your parents here in the cold dirt?
How do you think you're going to live without us?
Mom... Dad...
I'm sorry!!
I'm sorry...
I'm so sorry!!

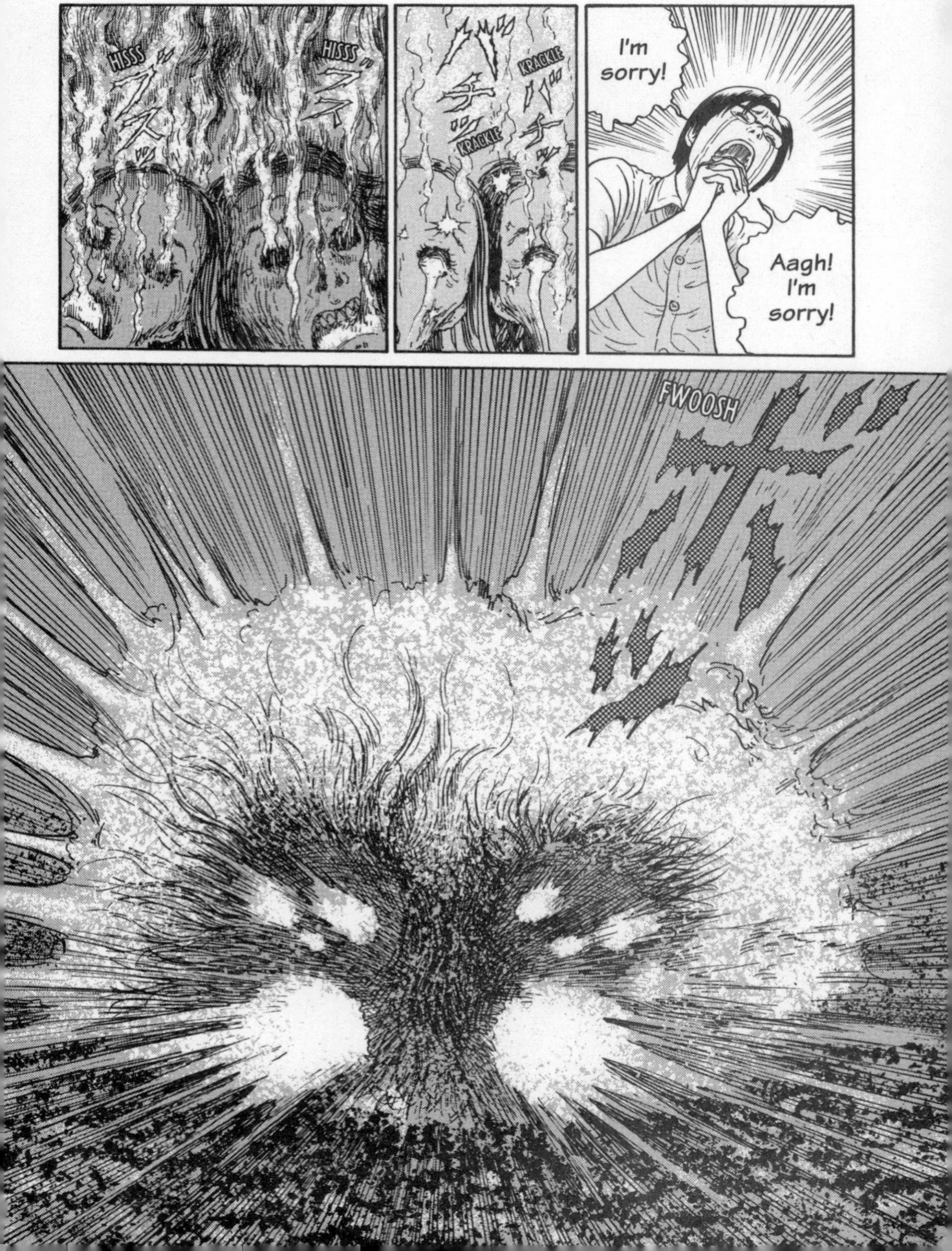
I'm sorry!
Aagh! I'm sorry!
KRACKLE
KRACKLE
HISSS
HISSS
FWOOSH

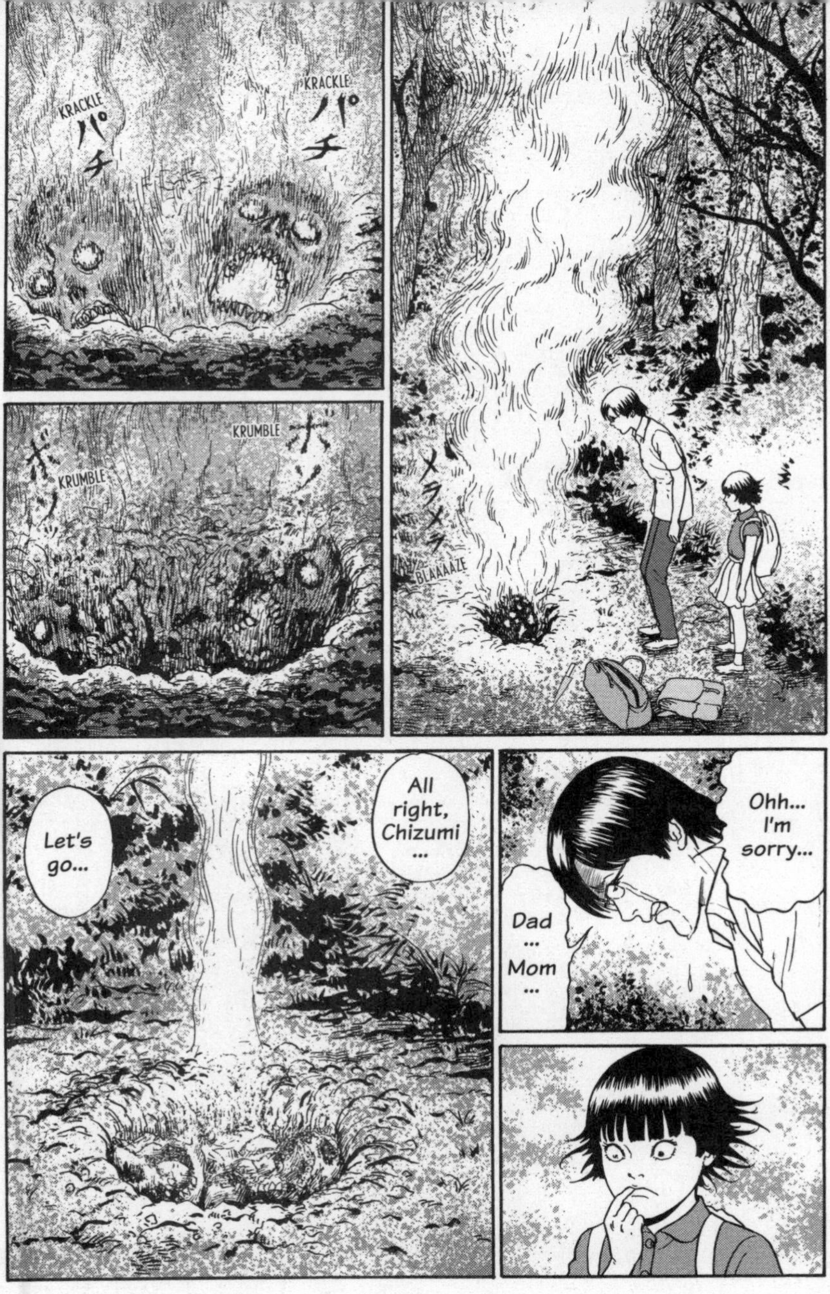
メラメラ
BLAAAZE
KRACKLE
パチ
KRACKLE
パチ
KRUMBLE
ボソ
KRUMBLE
ボソ
Ohh... I'm sorry...
Dad ... Mom ...
All right, Chizumi ...
Let's go...

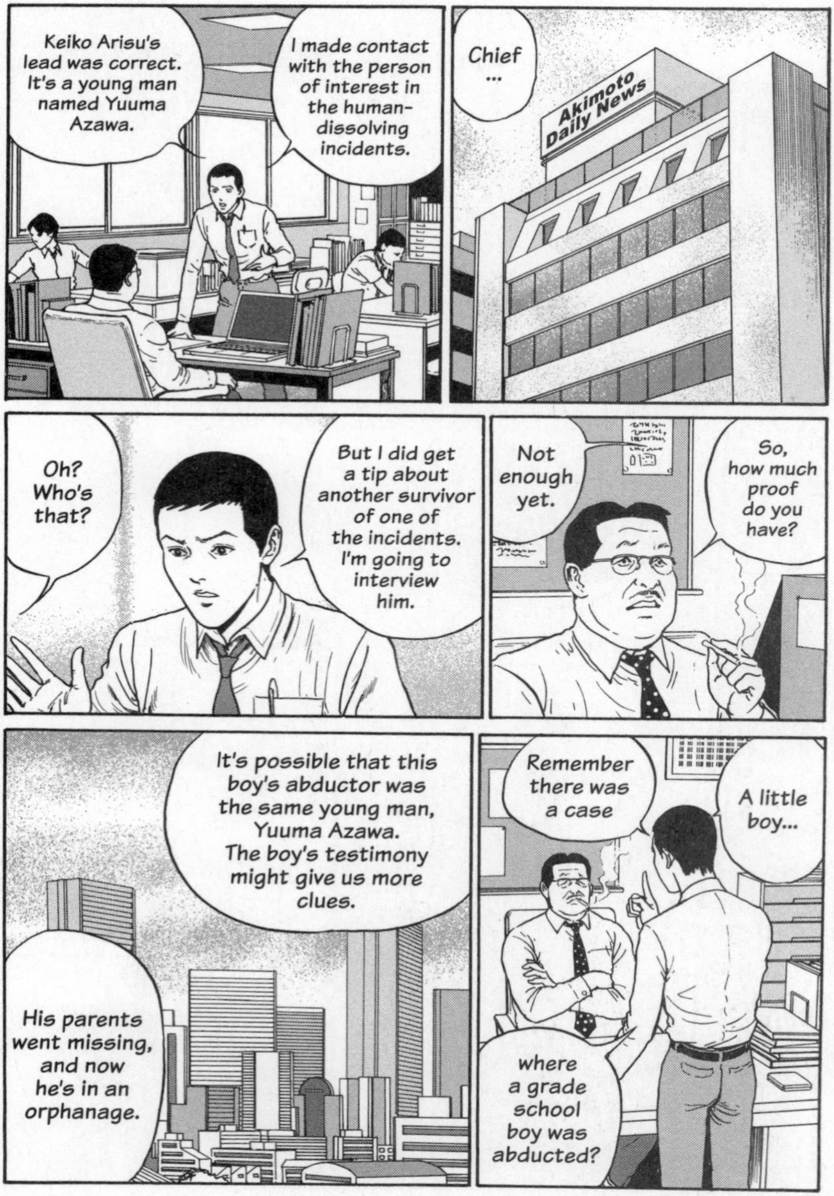
Chief ...
Akimoto Daily News
I made contact with the person of interest in the human-dissolving incidents.
Keiko Arisu's lead was correct. It's a young man named Yuuma Azawa.
So, how much proof do you have?
Not enough yet.
But I did get a tip about another survivor of one of the incidents. I'm going to interview him.
Oh? Who's that?
A little boy...
Remember there was a case
where a grade school boy was abducted?
It's possible that this boy's abductor was the same young man, Yuuma Azawa. The boy's testimony might give us more clues.
His parents went missing, and now he's in an orphanage.

It's Tomohito—!

What's wrong?!

Ma'am, come quick!

Social Welfare Services
Morning Glory House

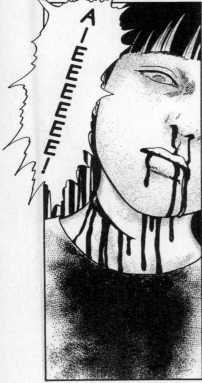

AIEEEEEE!

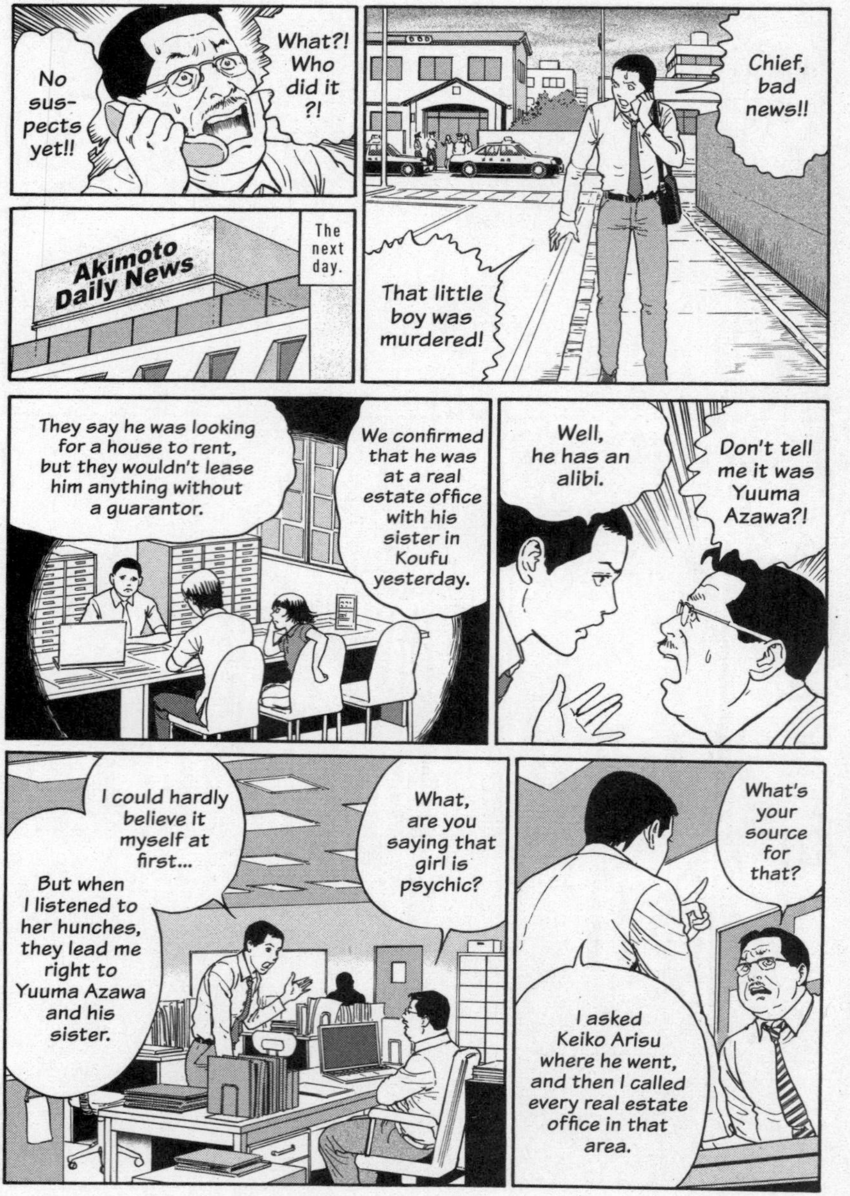
Chief, bad news!!
That little boy was murdered!
What?! Who did it?!
No sus-pects yet!!
The next day.
Akimoto Daily News
Don't tell me it was Yuuma Azawa?!
Well, he has an alibi.
We confirmed that he was at a real estate office with his sister in Koufu yesterday.
They say he was looking for a house to rent, but they wouldn't lease him anything without a guarantor.
What's your source for that?
I asked Keiko Arisu where he went, and then I called every real estate office in that area.
What, are you saying that girl is psychic?
I could hardly believe it myself at first...
But when I listened to her hunches, they lead me right to Yuuma Azawa and his sister.

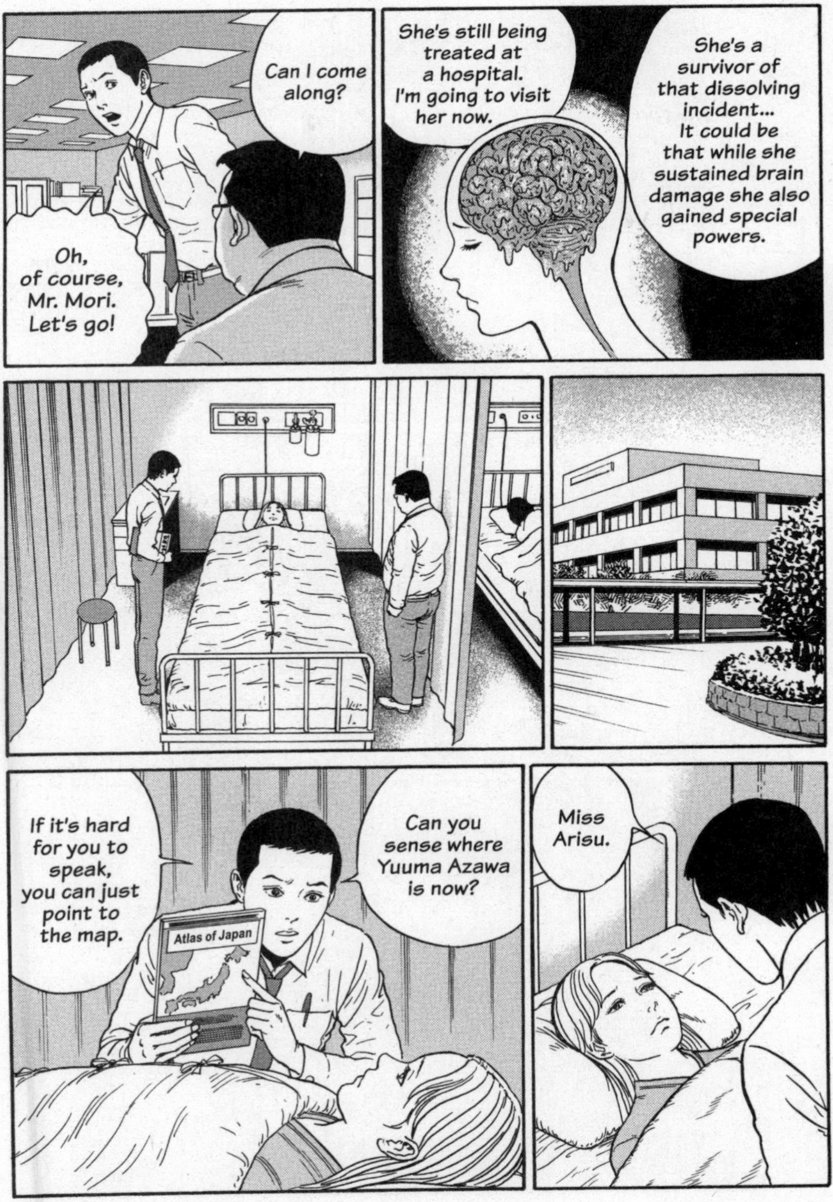
She's a survivor of that dissolving incident... It could be that while she sustained brain damage she also gained special powers.
She's still being treated at a hospital. I'm going to visit her now.
Can I come along?
Oh, of course, Mr. Mori. Let's go!
Miss Arisu.
Can you sense where Yuuma Azawa is now?
If it's hard for you to speak, you can just point to the map.
Atlas of Japan

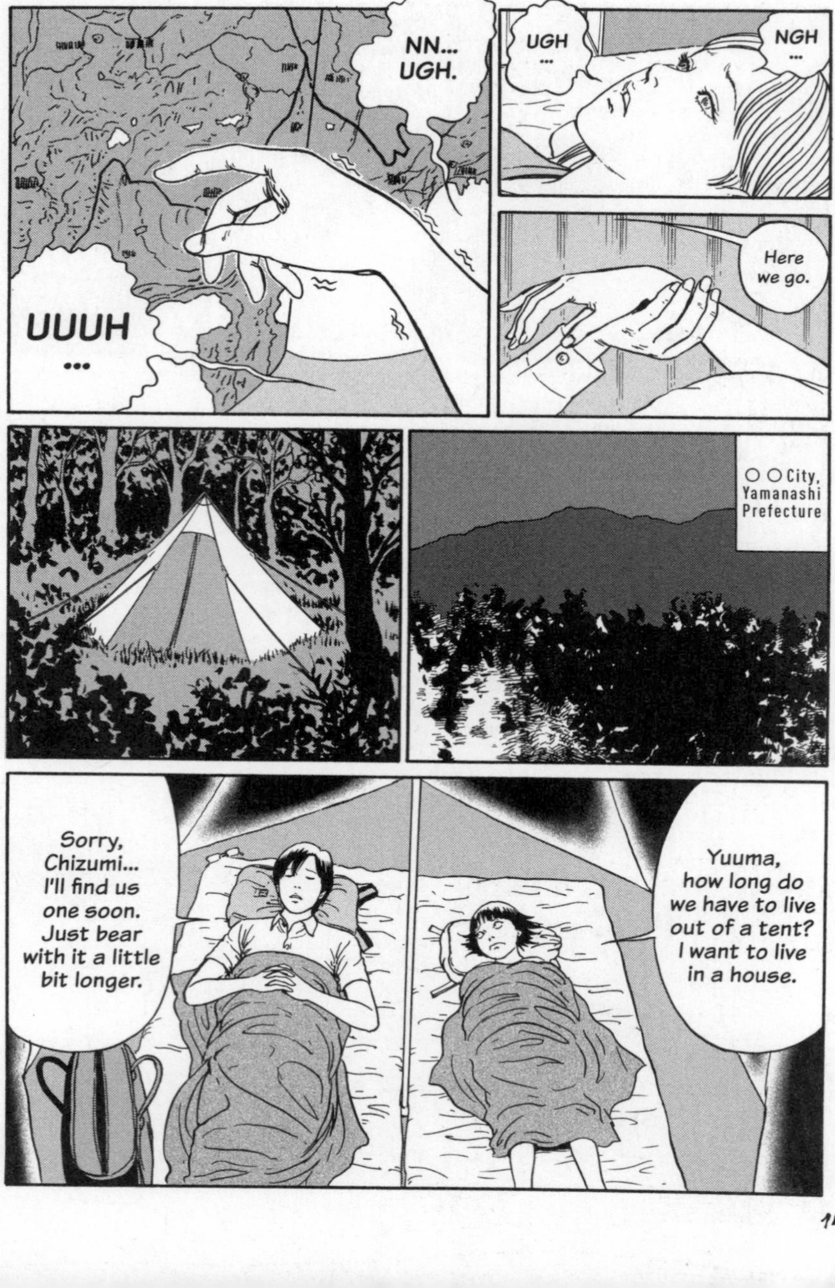
NGH ...
UGH ...
Here we go.
NN... UGH.
UUUH ...
○○City, Yamanashi Prefecture
Yuuma, how long do we have to live out of a tent? I want to live in a house.
Sorry, Chizumi... I'll find us one soon. Just bear with it a little bit longer.

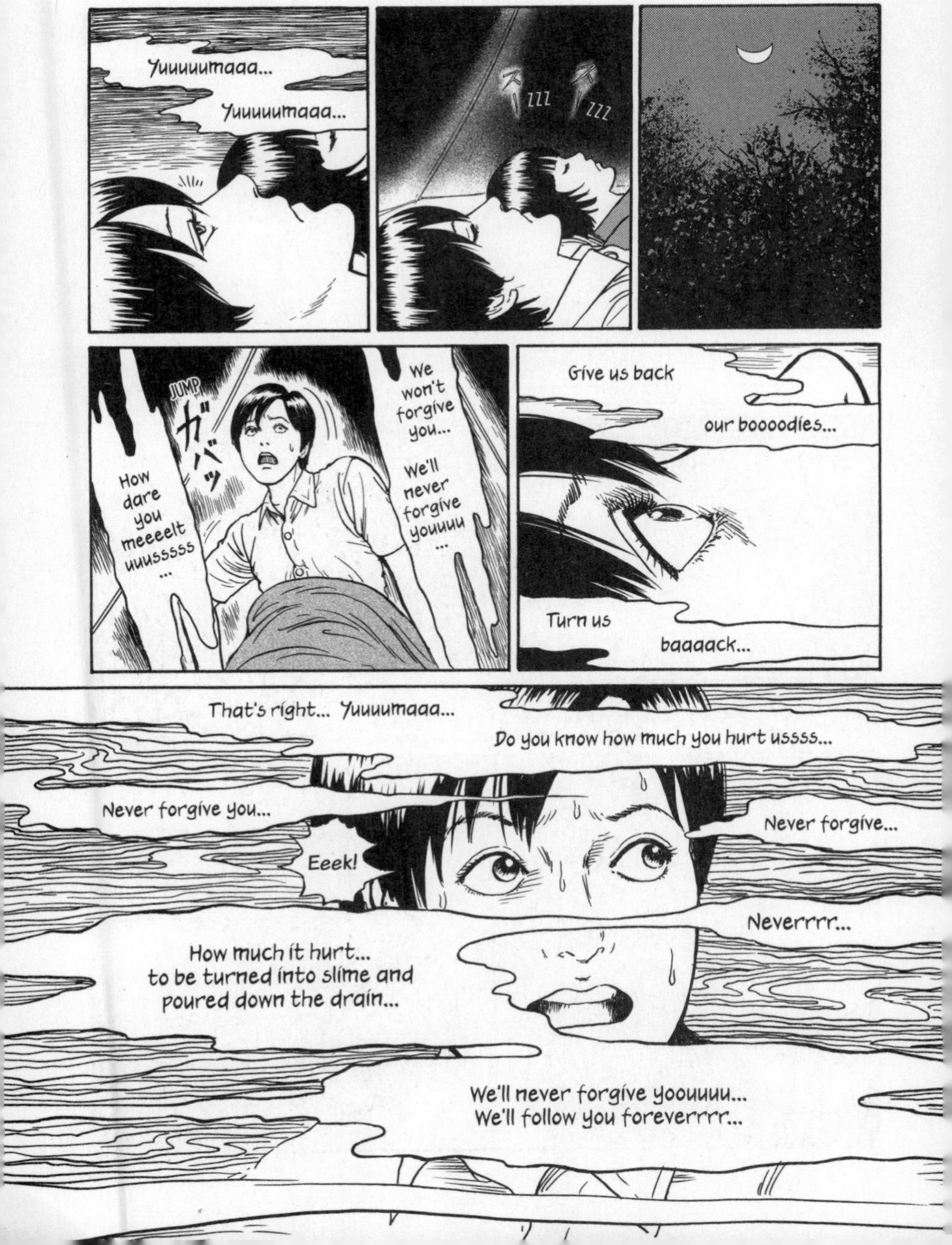
ス zzz
ス zzz
Yuuuumaaa...
Yuuuumaaa...
Give us back
our booodies...
Turn us
baaaack...
We won't forgive you...
We'll never forgive youuuu...
JUMP
ガバッ
How dare you meeeelt uuussss...
That's right... Yuuuumaaa...
Do you know how much you hurt ussss...
Never forgive...
Never forgive you...
Eeek!
Neverrrr...
How much it hurt... to be turned into slime and poured down the drain...
We'll never forgive yoouuuu...
We'll follow you foreverrrr...

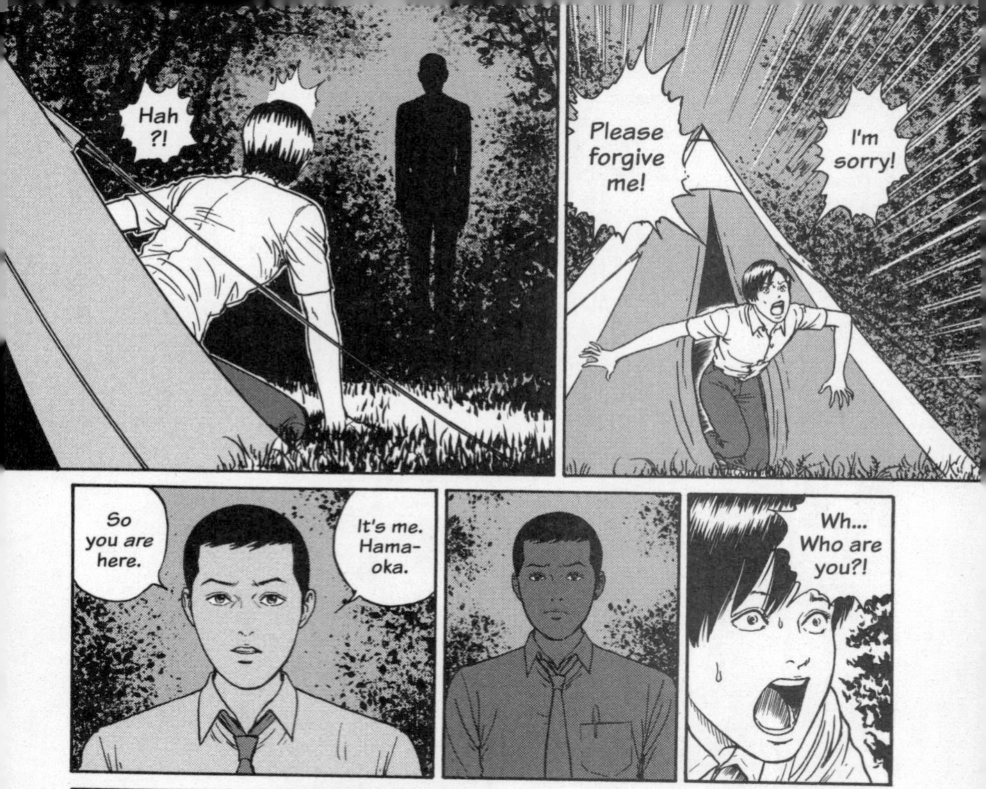
I'm sorry!
Please forgive me!
Hah ?!
Wh... Who are you?!
It's me. Hama-oka.
So you are here.
Wh... What... are you doing here?!
I just want to talk to you. That's all.
The other day a little boy was murdered at an orphanage. That boy could have given us an important testimony...
And I've tracked down other people who said they know you all around the country... But, strangely...
in the last few days, I've lost contact with every one of them.

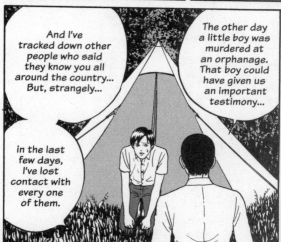

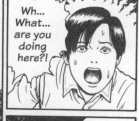

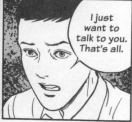

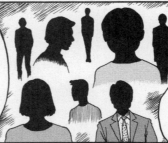

When I looked into it, it turned out they'd all died under various circumstances, or disappeared...
Of course, I'm not saying all of this was your doing.
But I can say this: The only step forward in pursuing the truth behind these human-dissolving and disappearance incidents that are shaking up the country...
is to hear you explain it yourself! There's no other way!!
People are starting to panic. They want to know who's behind these incidents.
And I intend to publish a scoop about you in the news soon!
If you won't talk to me, public opinion will take on a life of its own... So if you're innocent, just come out and tell me.
I— I don't know... I don't know anything...

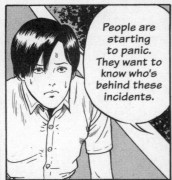

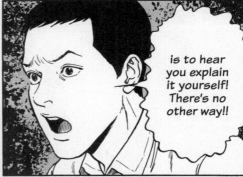

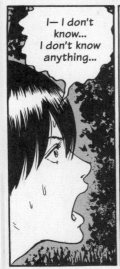

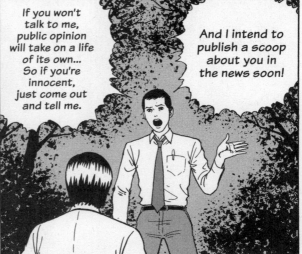

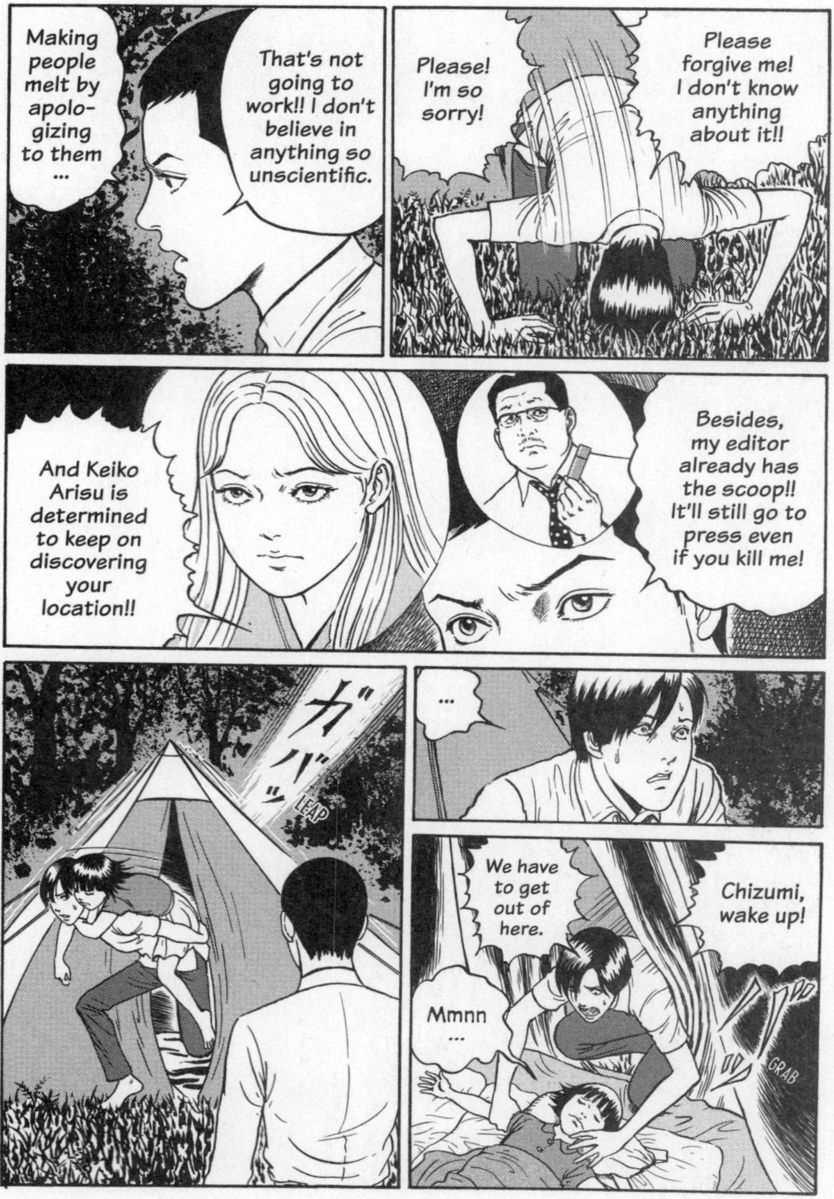
Please forgive me! I don't know anything about it!!
Please! I'm so sorry!
That's not going to work!! I don't believe in anything so unscientific.
Making people melt by apologizing to them ...
Besides, my editor already has the scoop!! It'll still go to press even if you kill me!
And Keiko Arisu is determined to keep on discovering your location!!
...
Chizumi, wake up!
We have to get out of here.
GRAB
Mmnn ...
ガバッ
LEAP

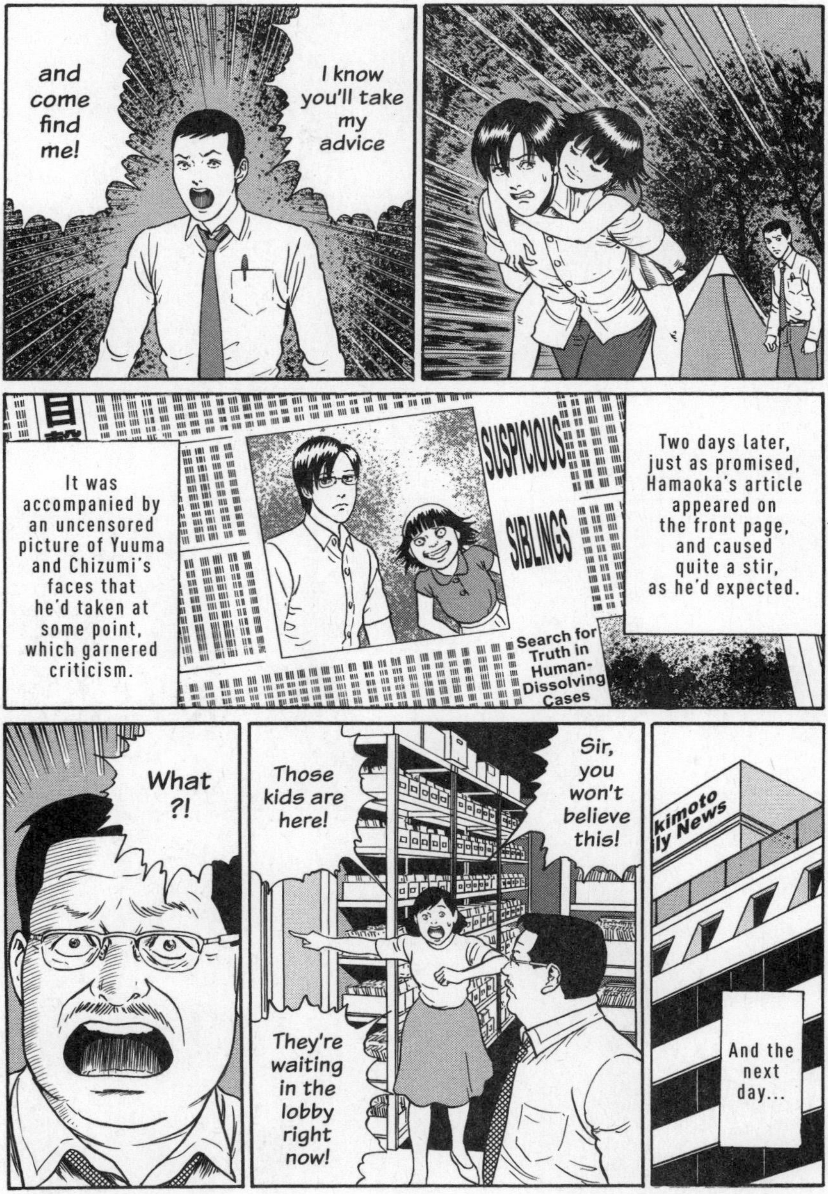
I know you'll take my advice
and come find me!
Two days later, just as promised, Hamaoka's article appeared on the front page, and caused quite a stir, as he'd expected.
SUSPICIOUS SIBLINGS
Search for Truth in Human-Dissolving Cases
It was accompanied by an uncensored picture of Yuuma and Chizumi's faces that he'd taken at some point, which garnered criticism.
And the next day...
Sir, you won't believe this!
Those kids are here!
They're waiting in the lobby right now!
What?!

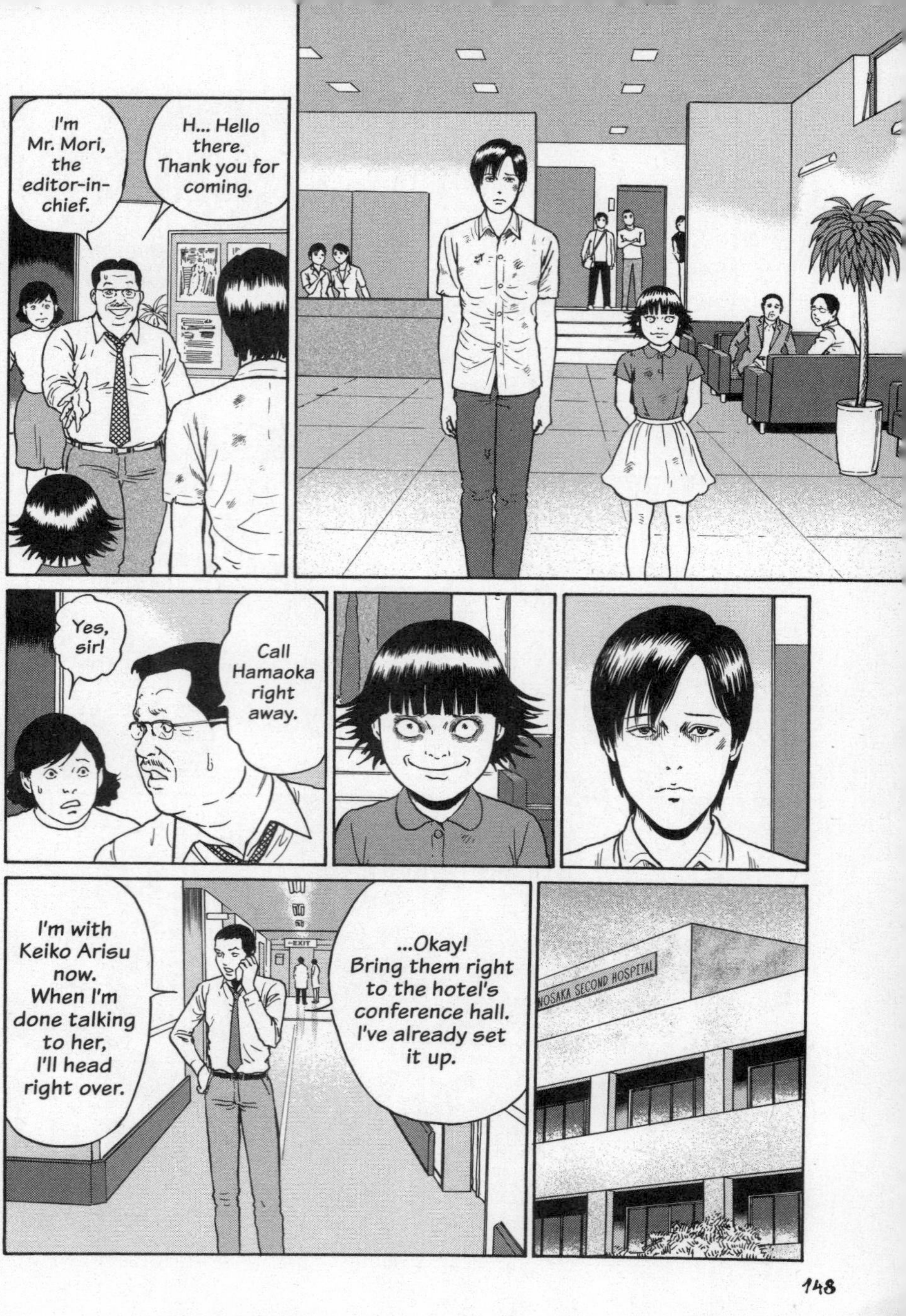
H... Hello there. Thank you for coming.
I'm Mr. Mori, the editor-in-chief.
Call Hamaoka right away.
Yes, sir!
NOSAKA SECOND HOSPITAL
...Okay! Bring them right to the hotel's conference hall. I've already set it up.
EXIT
I'm with Keiko Arisu now. When I'm done talking to her, I'll head right over.

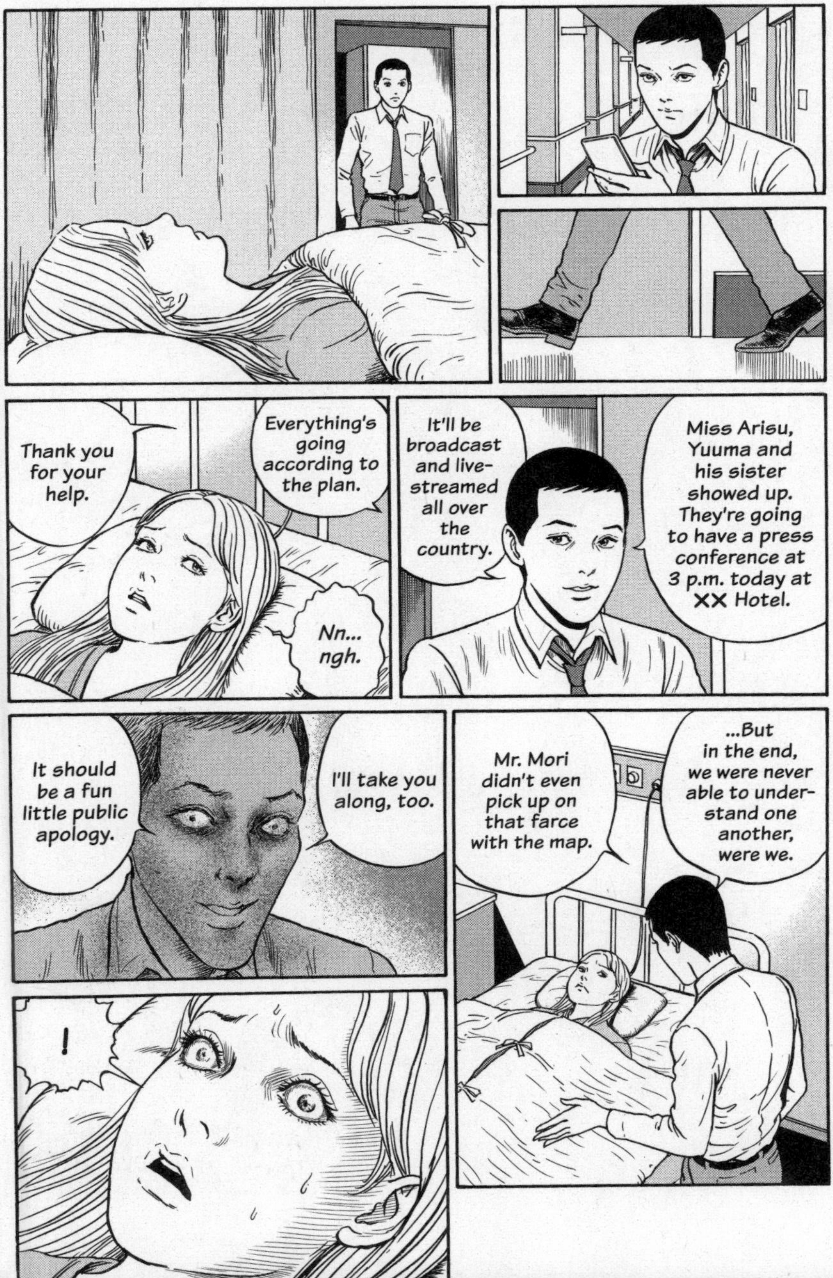
Miss Arisu, Yuuma and his sister showed up. They're going to have a press conference at 3 p.m. today at XX Hotel.
It'll be broadcast and live-streamed all over the country.
Everything's going according to the plan.
Thank you for your help.
Nn... ngh.
...But in the end, we were never able to understand one another, were we.
Mr. Mori didn't even pick up on that farce with the map.
I'll take you along, too.
It should be a fun little public apology.
!

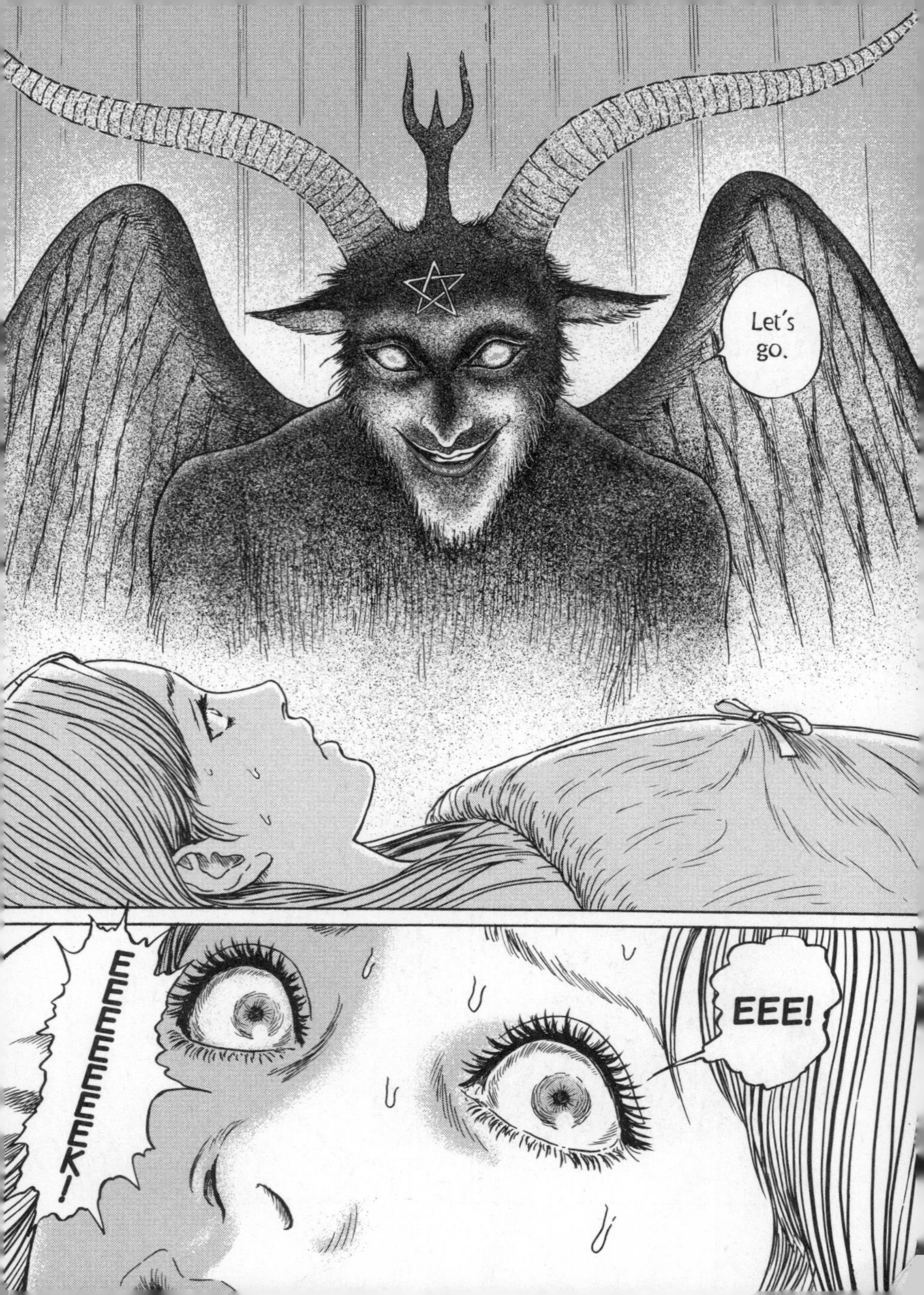
Let's go.
EEE!
EEEEEEEEEK!

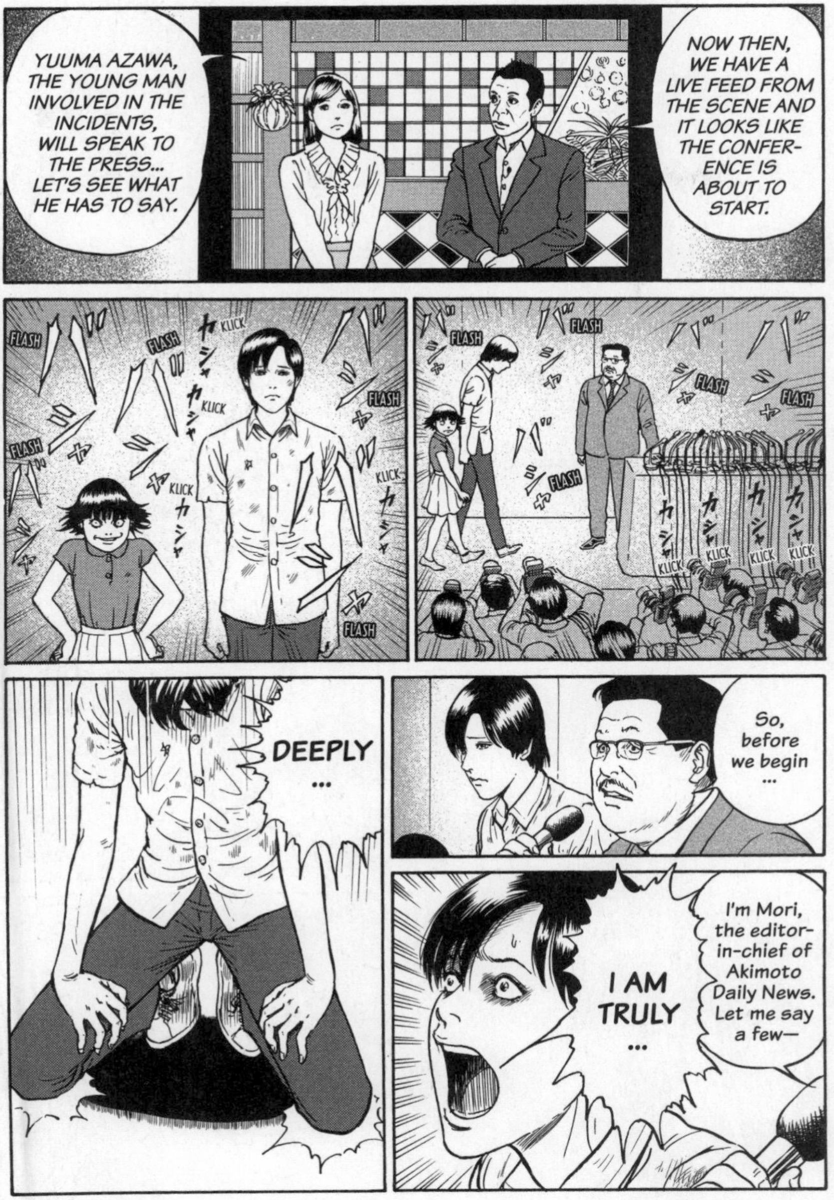
NOW THEN, WE HAVE A LIVE FEED FROM THE SCENE AND IT LOOKS LIKE THE CONFERENCE IS ABOUT TO START.
YUUMA AZAWA, THE YOUNG MAN INVOLVED IN THE INCIDENTS, WILL SPEAK TO THE PRESS... LET'S SEE WHAT HE HAS TO SAY.
FLASH
FLASH
FLASH
FLASH
FLASH
KLICK
KLICK
KLICK
KLICK
FLASH
FLASH
FLASH
FLASH
KLICK
KLICK
KLICK
KLICK
So, before we begin ...
I'm Mori, the editor-in-chief of Akimoto Daily News. Let me say a few—
I AM TRULY ...
DEEPLY ...

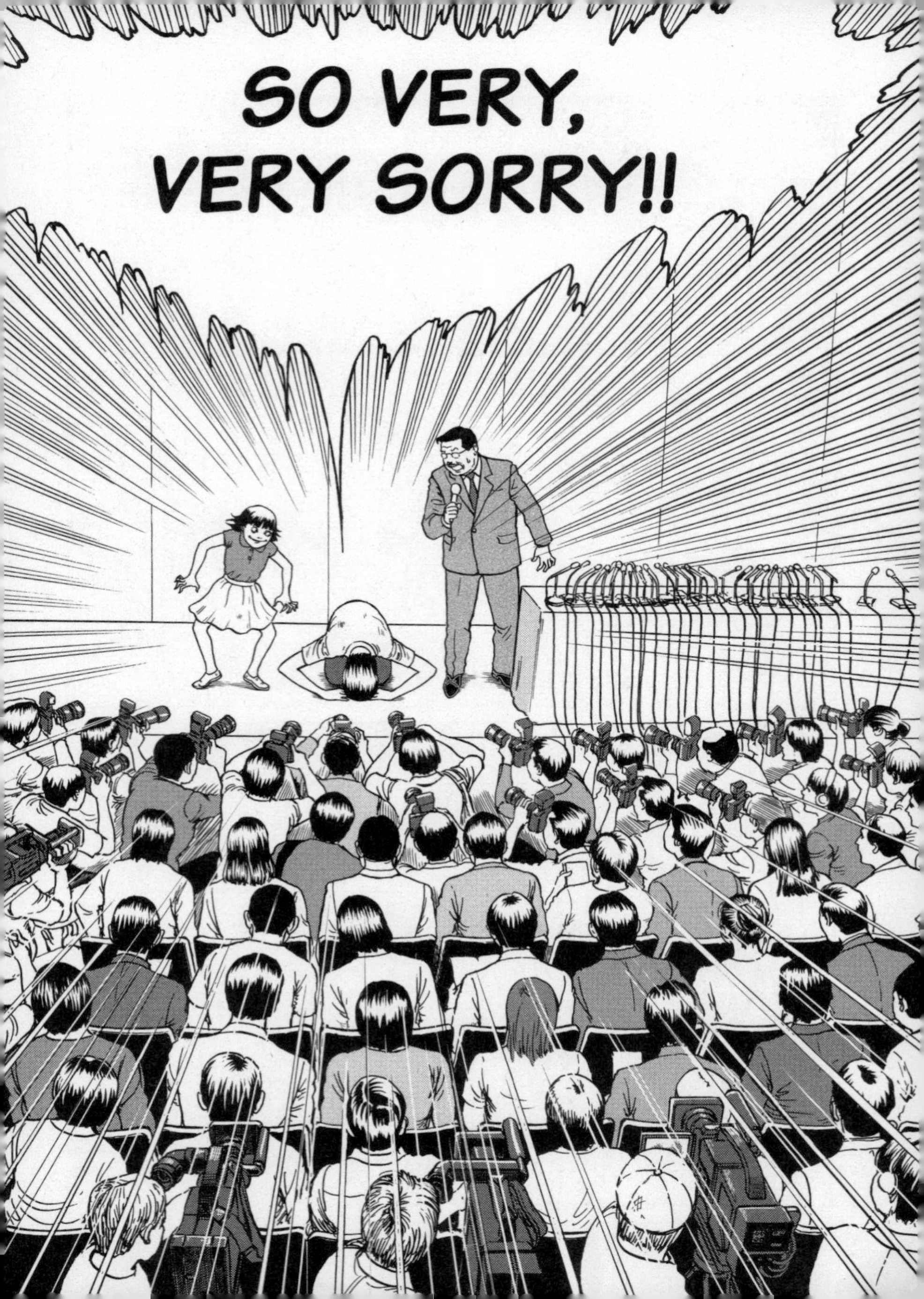
SO VERY, VERY SORRY!!

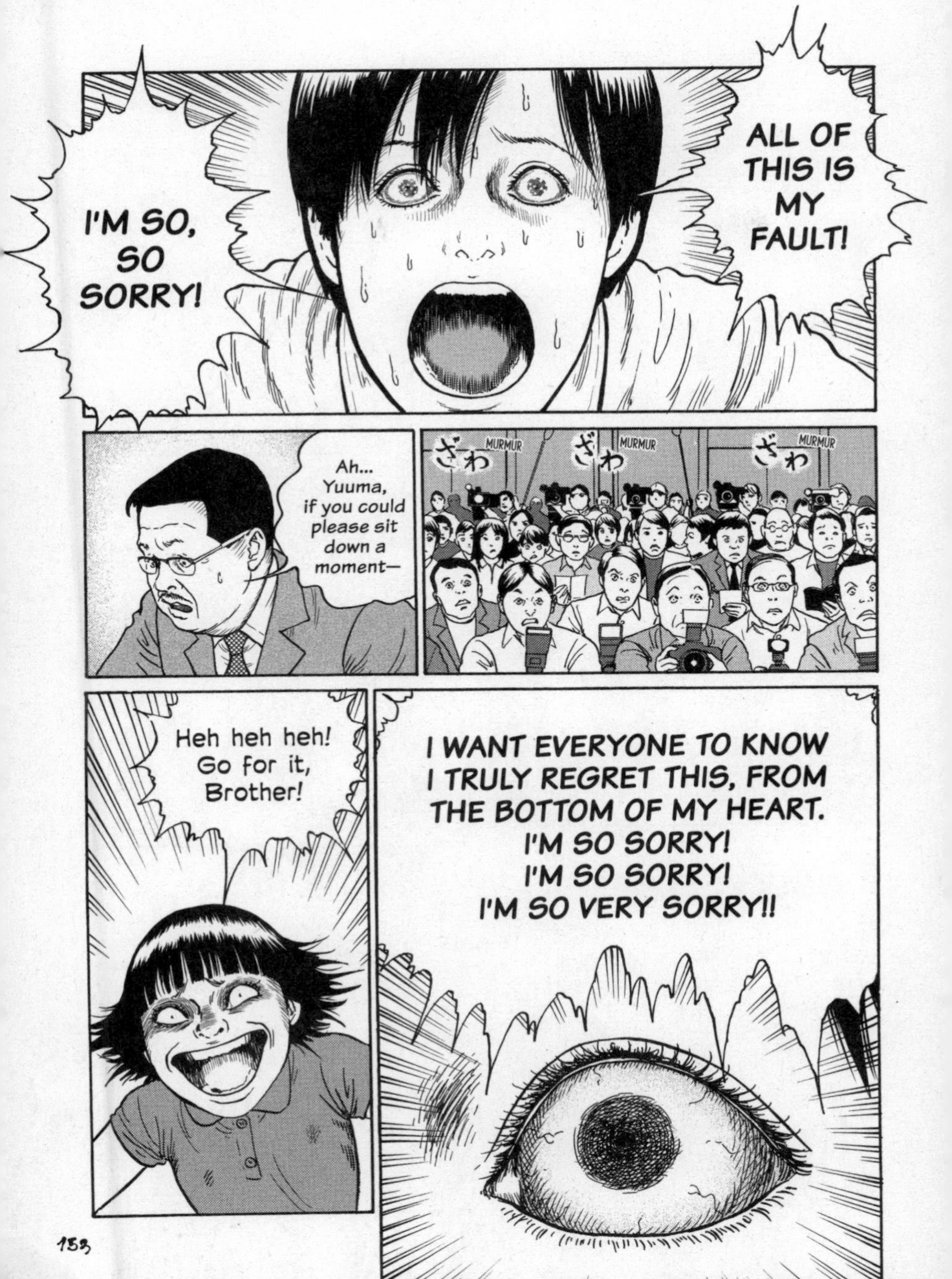
ALL OF THIS IS MY FAULT!
I'M SO, SO SORRY!
ざわ
MURMUR
ざわ
MURMUR
ざわ
MURMUR
Ah... Yuuma, if you could please sit down a moment—
I WANT EVERYONE TO KNOW I TRULY REGRET THIS, FROM THE BOTTOM OF MY HEART. I'M SO SORRY! I'M SO SORRY! I'M SO VERY SORRY!!
Heh heh heh! Go for it, Brother!

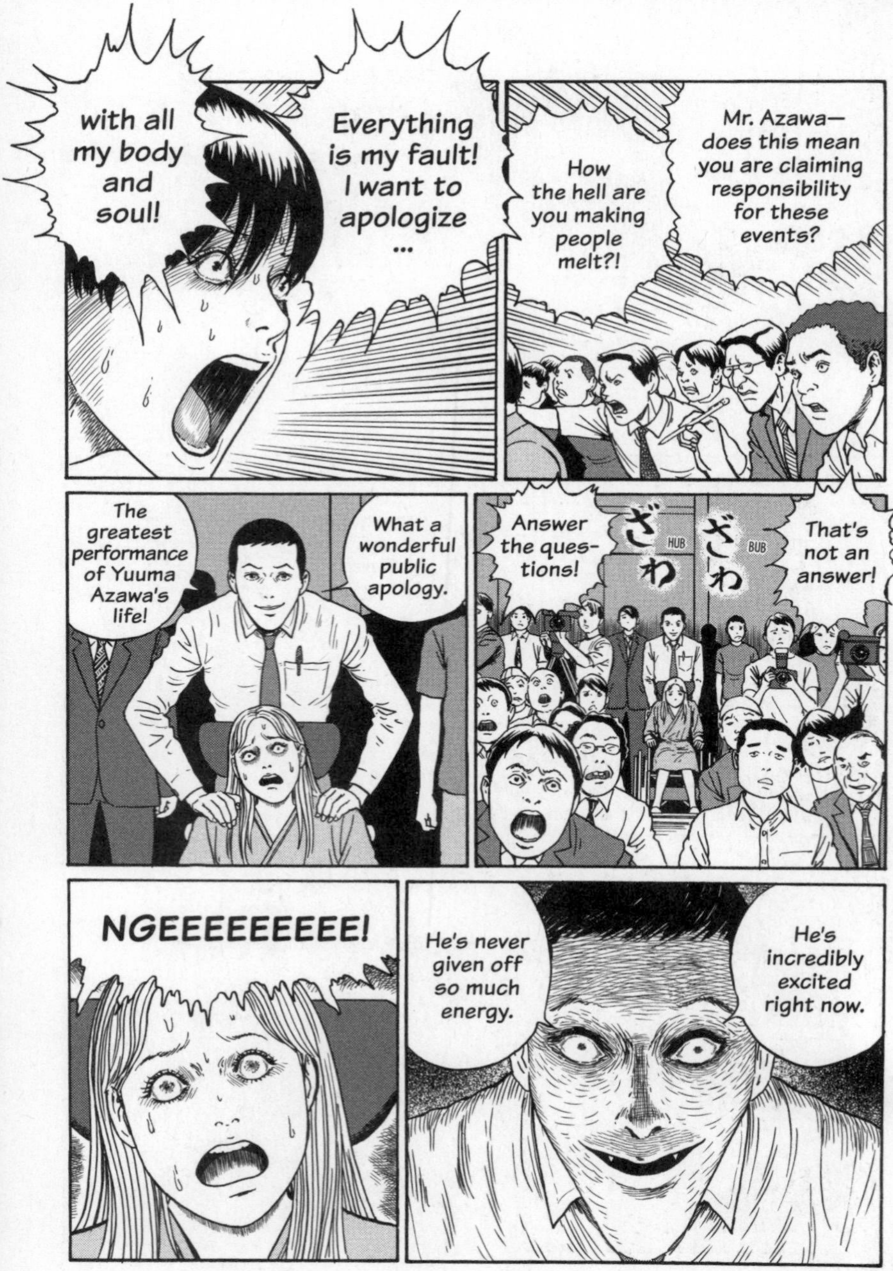
Mr. Azawa—does this mean you are claiming responsibility for these events?
How the hell are you making people melt?!
Everything is my fault! I want to apologize ...
with all my body and soul!
That's not an answer!
ざわ
BUB
ざわ
HUB
Answer the ques-tions!
What a wonderful public apology.
The greatest performance of Yuuma Azawa's life!
He's incredibly excited right now.
He's never given off so much energy.
NGEEEEEEEEE!

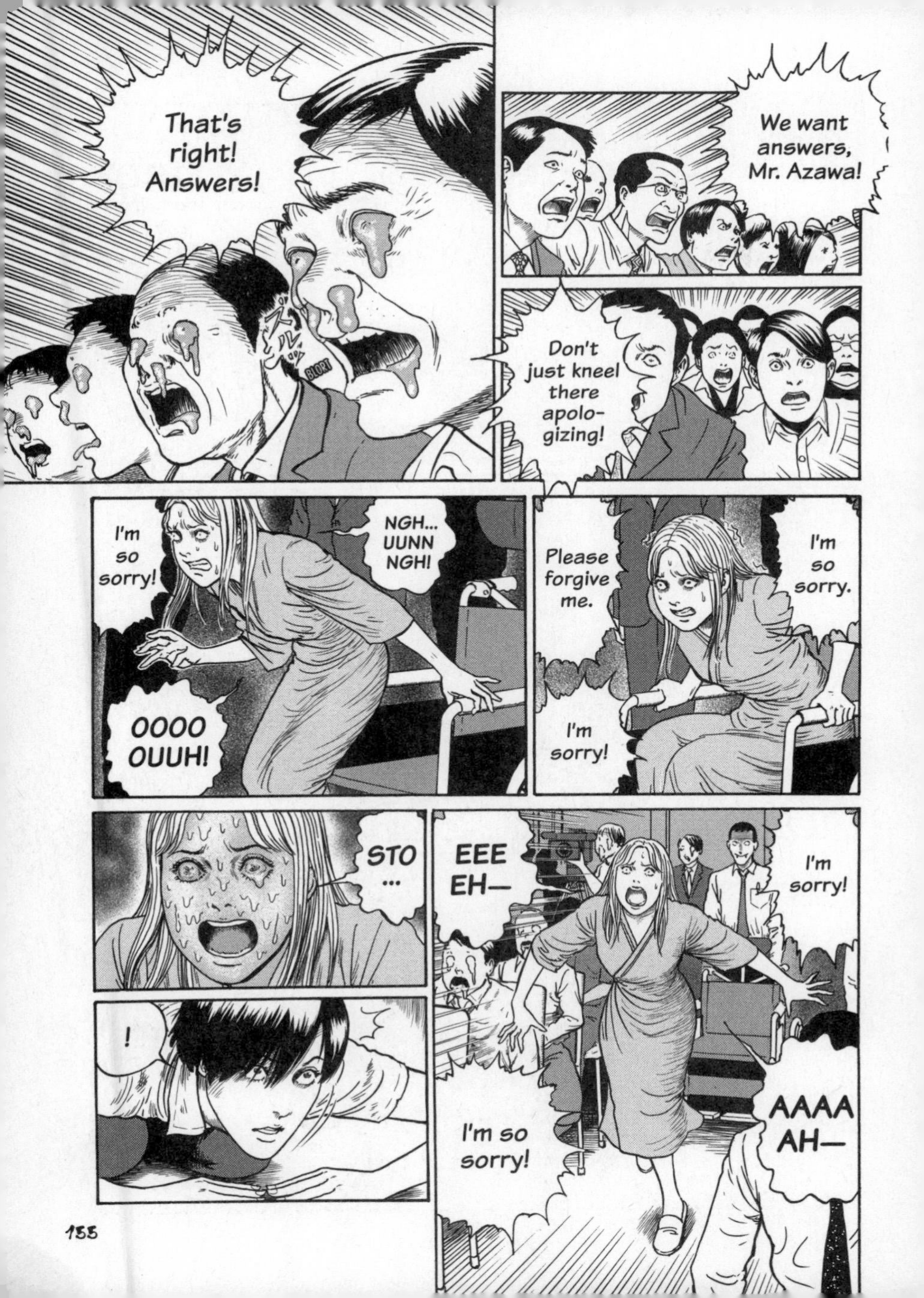

We want answers, Mr. Azawa!
Don't just kneel there apologizing!
That's right! Answers!
BLORT
I'm so sorry.
Please forgive me.
I'm sorry!
NGH... UUNN NGH!
I'm so sorry!
OOOO OUUH!
I'm sorry!
EEE EH—
AAAA AH—
I'm so sorry!
STO ...
!

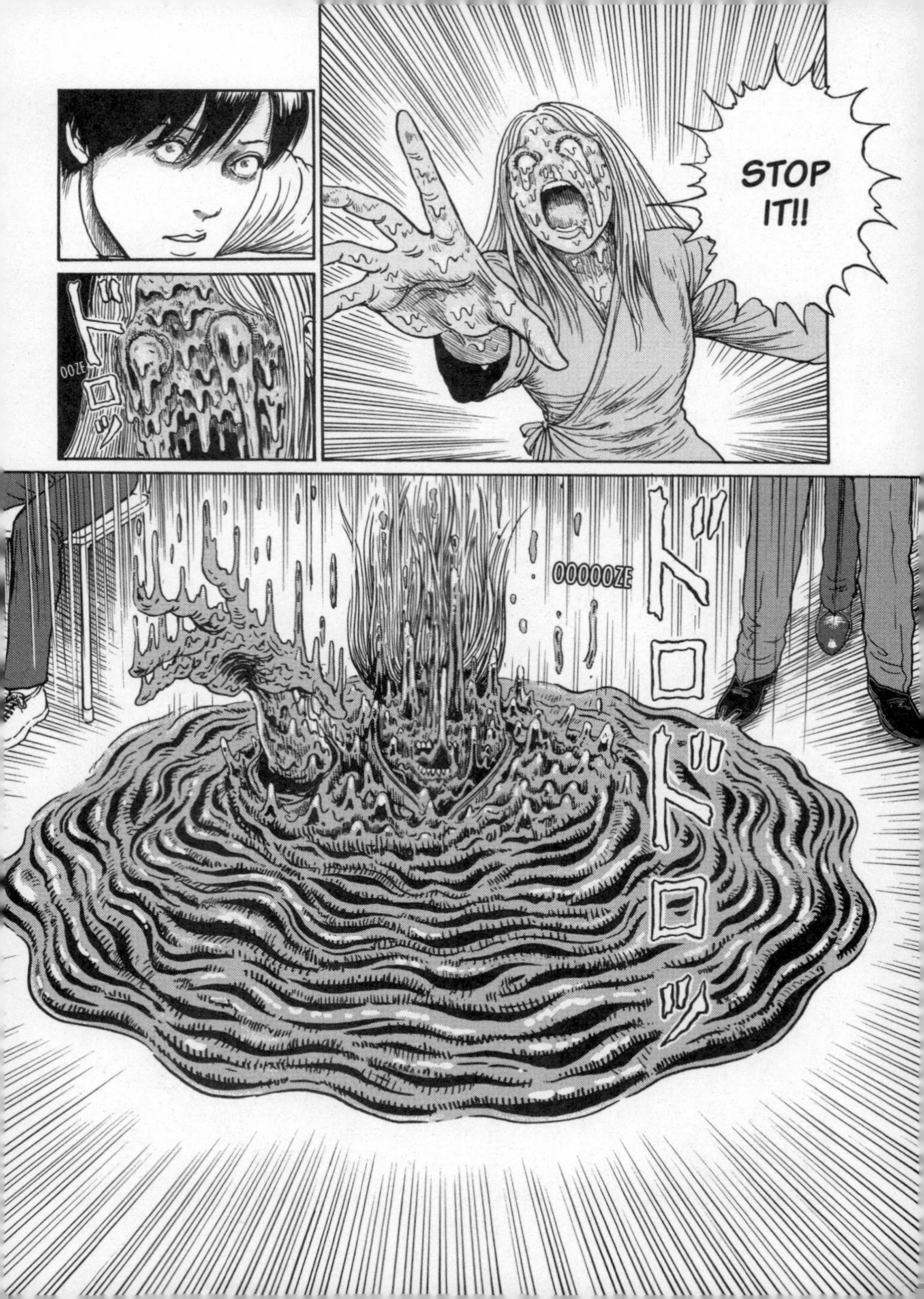
STOP IT!!
ドロッ
OOZE
ドロドロッ
OOOOOZE

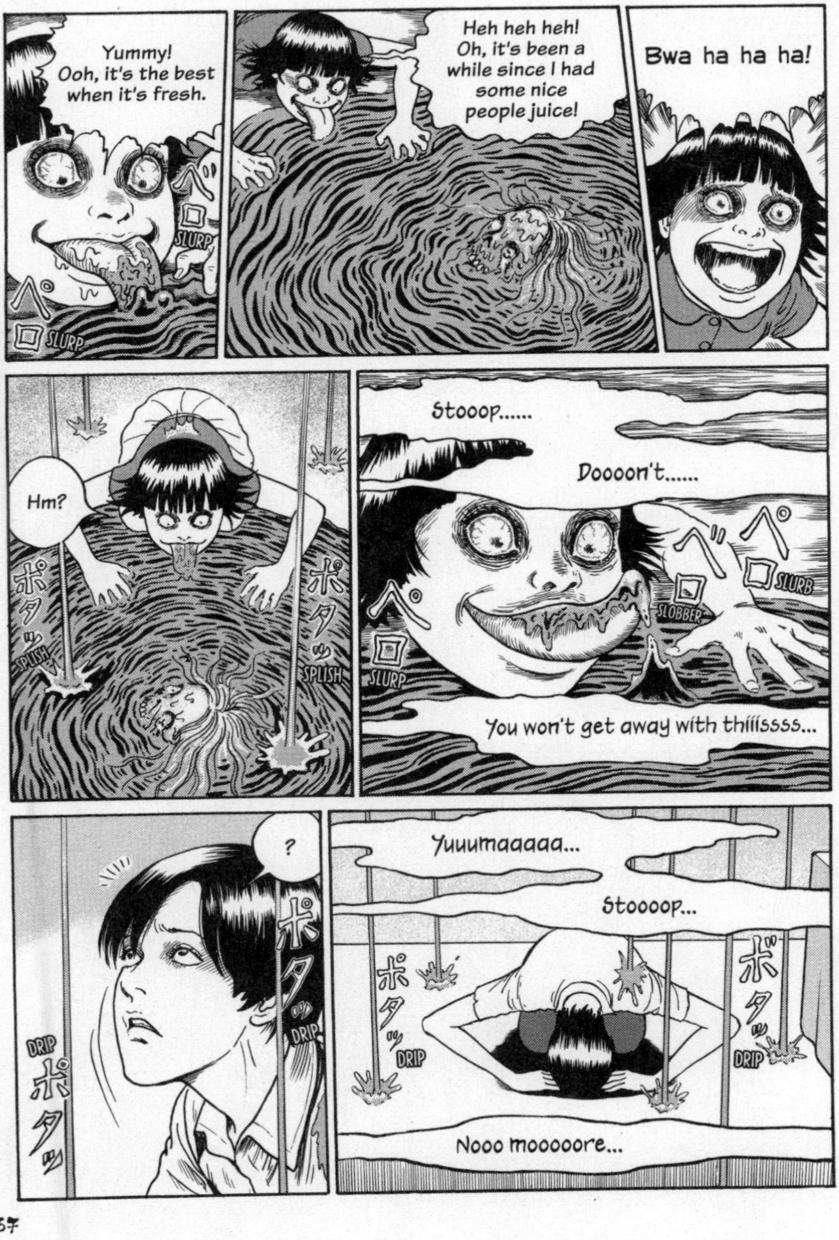
Bwa ha ha ha!
Heh heh heh! Oh, it's been a while since I had some nice people juice!
Yummy! Ooh, it's the best when it's fresh.
ペロ SLURP
ペロ SLURP
Stooop......
Doooon't......
ペロ SLURB
ベロ SLOBBER
ペロ SLURP
You won't get away with thiiissss...
Hm?
ポタッ SPLISH
ポタッ SPLISH
Yuuumaaaaa...
Stoooop...
ポタッ DRIP
ポタッ DRIP
Nooo mooooore...
?
ポタッ DRIP
ポタッ DRIP

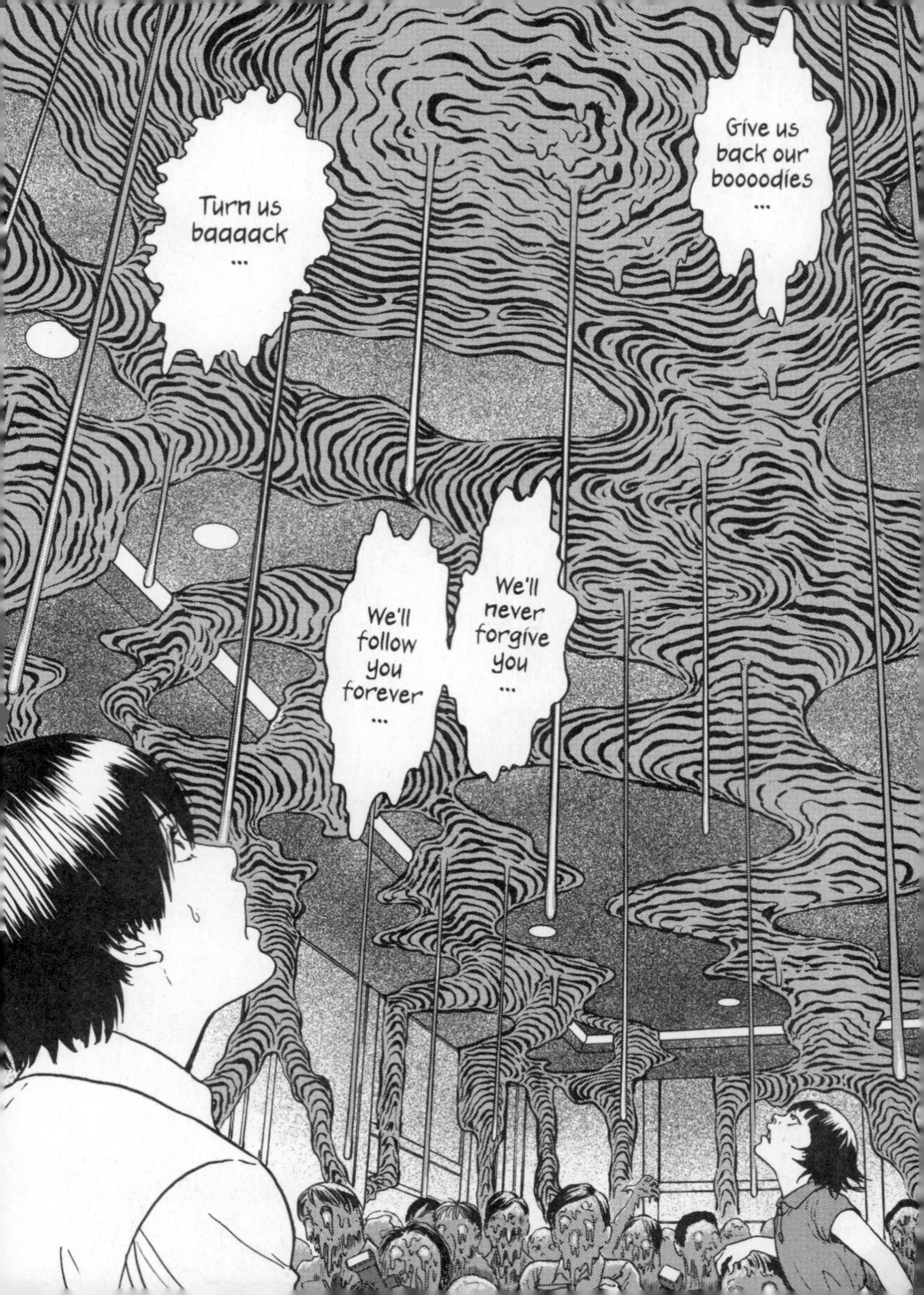
Give us back our booooodies ...
Turn us baaaack ...
We'll never forgive you ...
We'll follow you forever ...

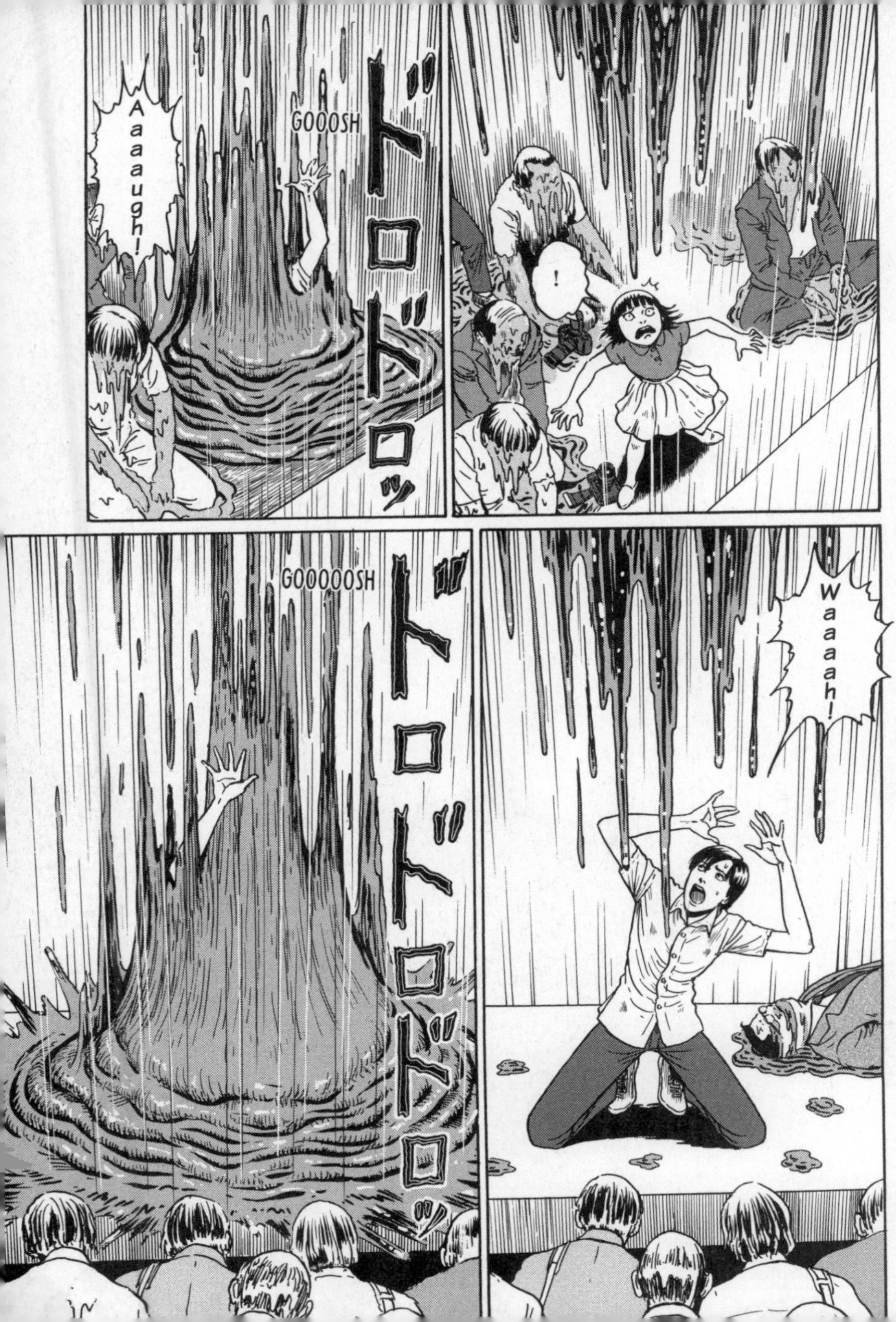
!
GOOOSH
ドロドロッ
Aaaaaugh!
Waaaaah!
GOOOOOSH
ドロドロドロッ

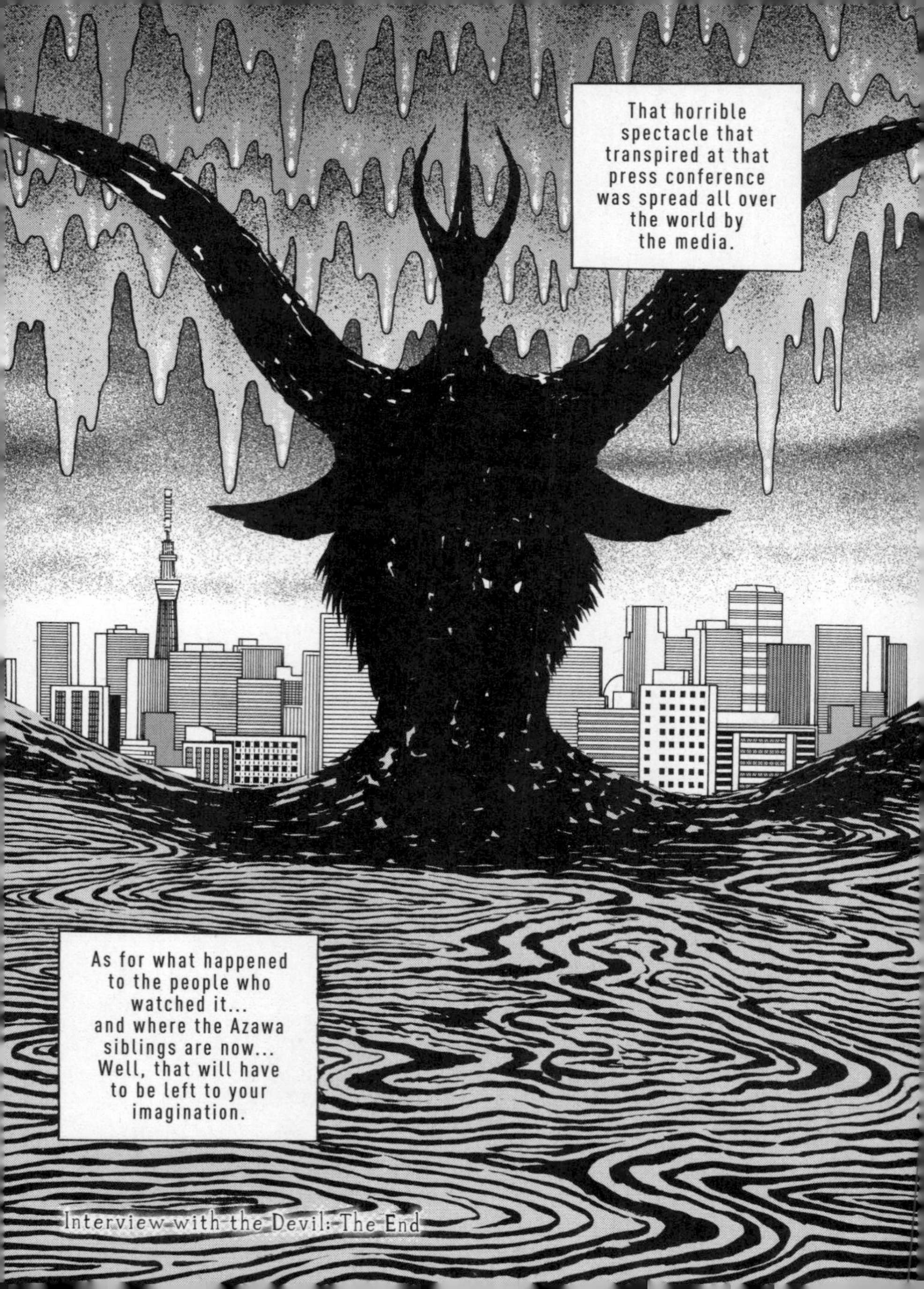
That horrible spectacle that transpired at that press conference was spread all over the world by the media.
As for what happened to the people who watched it... and where the Azawa siblings are now... Well, that will have to be left to your imagination.
Interview with the Devil: The End

Dissolving

✧

Classroom

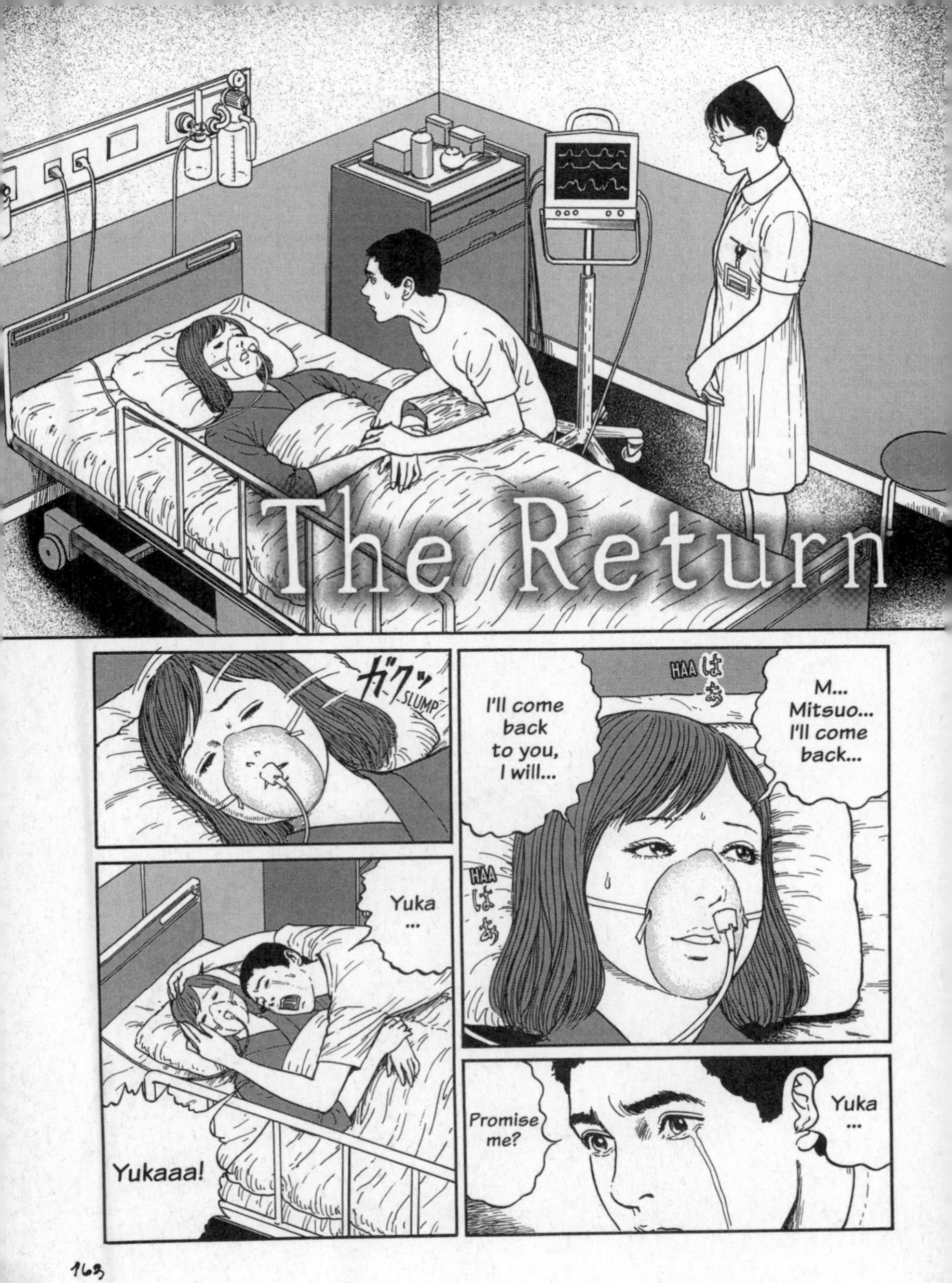
The Return
M... Mitsuo... I'll come back...
I'll come back to you, I will...
HAA はあ
HAA はあ
Yuka ...
Promise me?
ガクッ SLUMP
Yuka ...
Yukaaa!

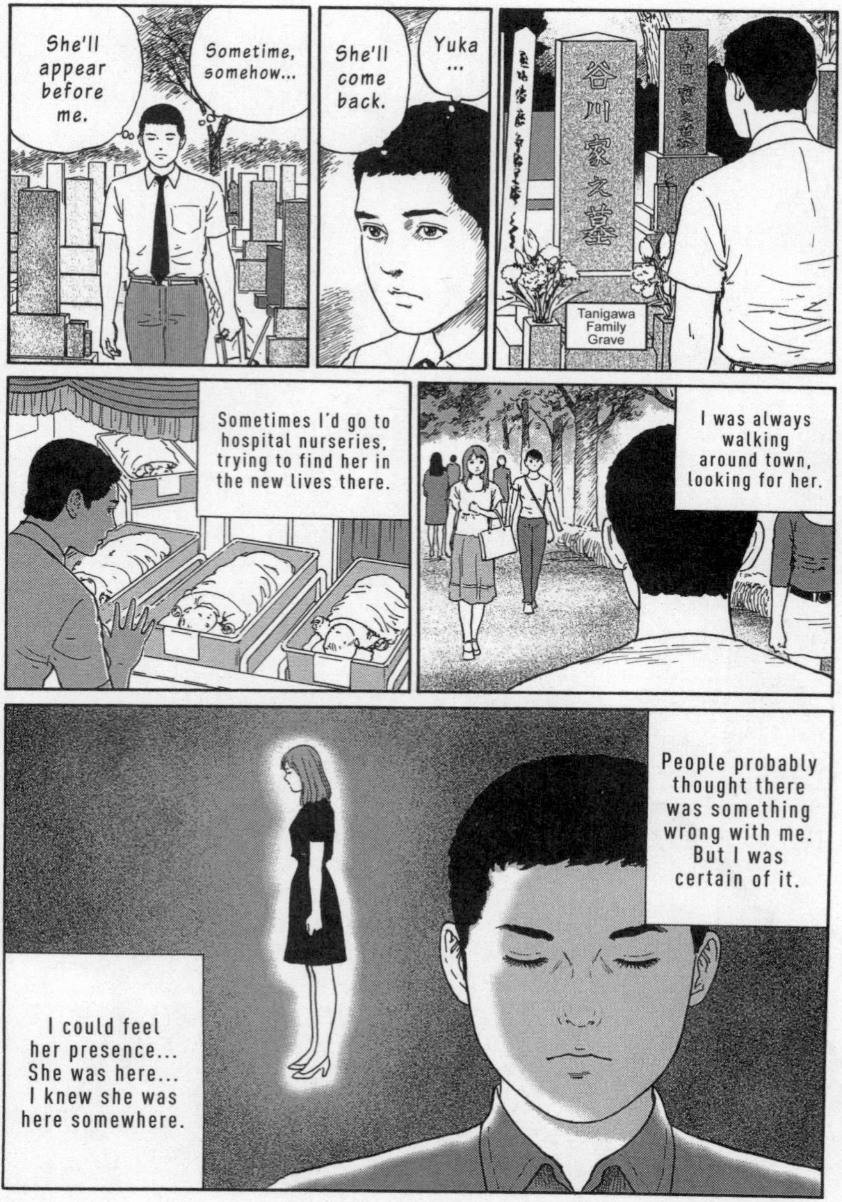
谷川家之墓
Tanigawa Family Grave
Yuka ...
She'll come back.
Sometime, somehow...
She'll appear before me.
I was always walking around town, looking for her.
Sometimes I'd go to hospital nurseries, trying to find her in the new lives there.
People probably thought there was something wrong with me. But I was certain of it.
I could feel her presence... She was here... I knew she was here somewhere.

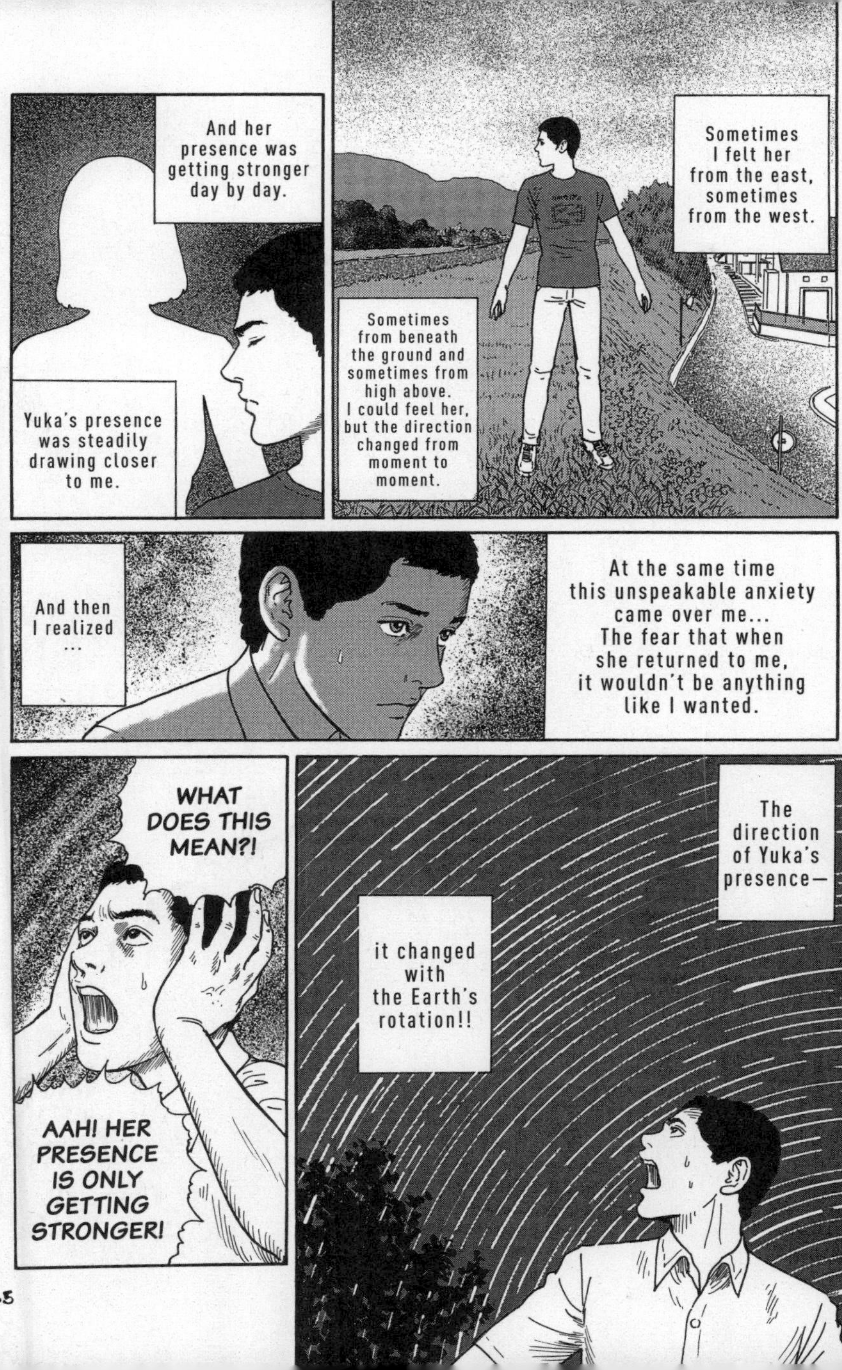
Sometimes I felt her from the east, sometimes from the west.
Sometimes from beneath the ground and sometimes from high above. I could feel her, but the direction changed from moment to moment.
And her presence was getting stronger day by day.
Yuka's presence was steadily drawing closer to me.
At the same time this unspeakable anxiety came over me... The fear that when she returned to me, it wouldn't be anything like I wanted.
And then I realized ...
The direction of Yuka's presence—
it changed with the Earth's rotation!!
WHAT DOES THIS MEAN?!
AAH! HER PRESENCE IS ONLY GETTING STRONGER!

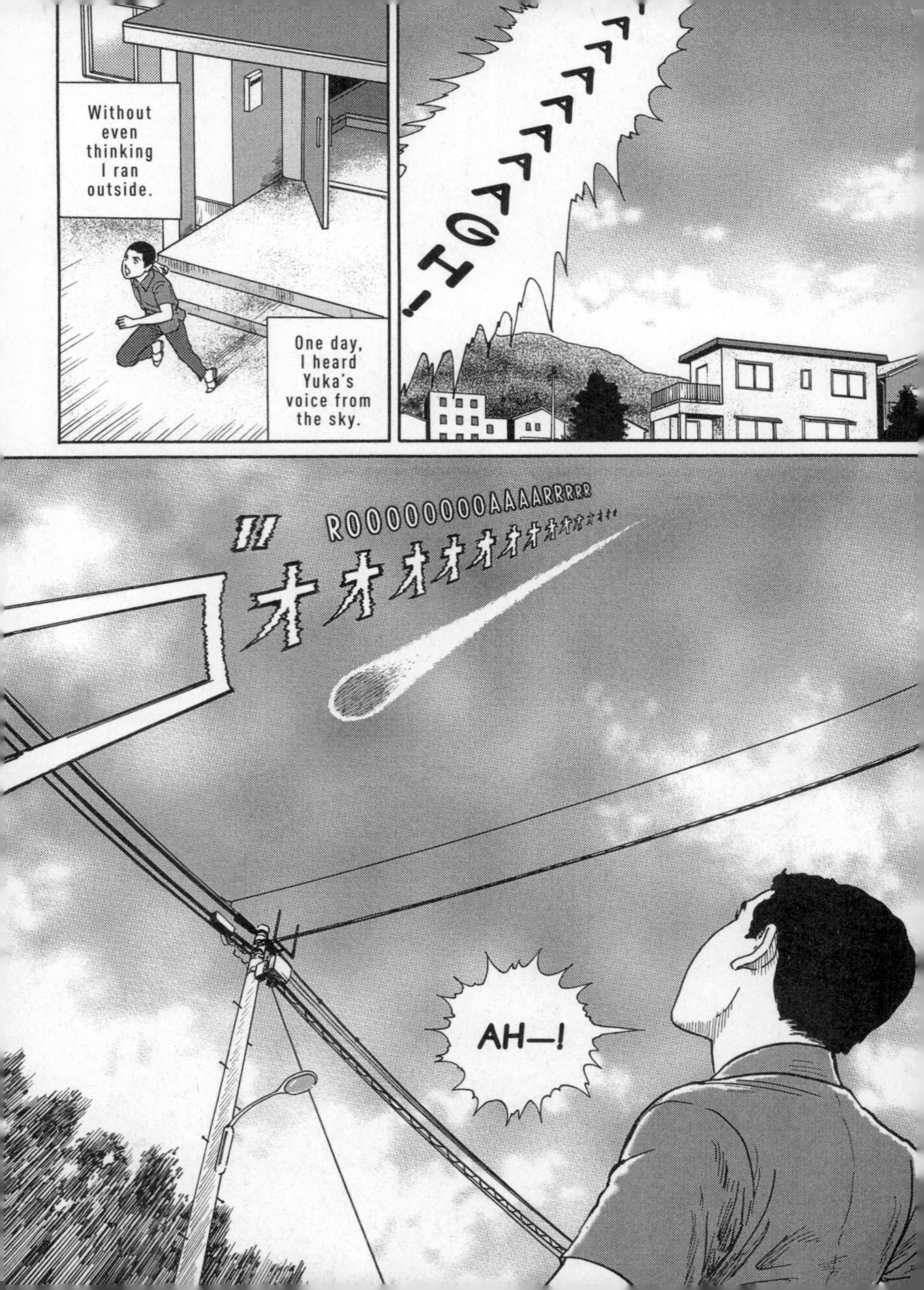

AAAAAAAGH!
One day, I heard Yuka's voice from the sky.
Without even thinking I ran outside.
ROOOOOOOOOAAAARRRR
オオオオオオオオオオオオオ
AH—!

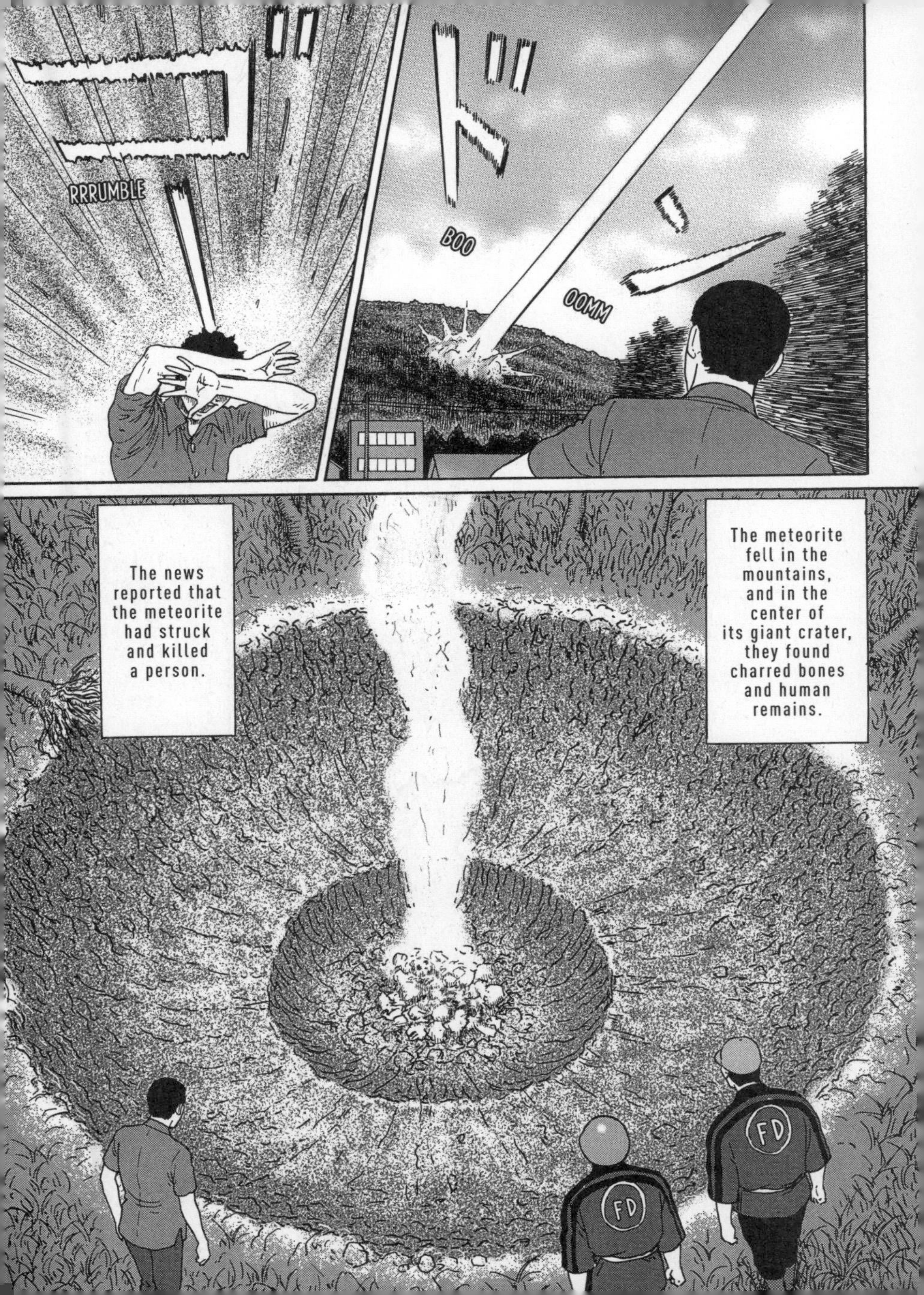
BOO
OOMM
RRRUMBLE
The meteorite fell in the mountains, and in the center of its giant crater, they found charred bones and human remains.
The news reported that the meteorite had struck and killed a person.

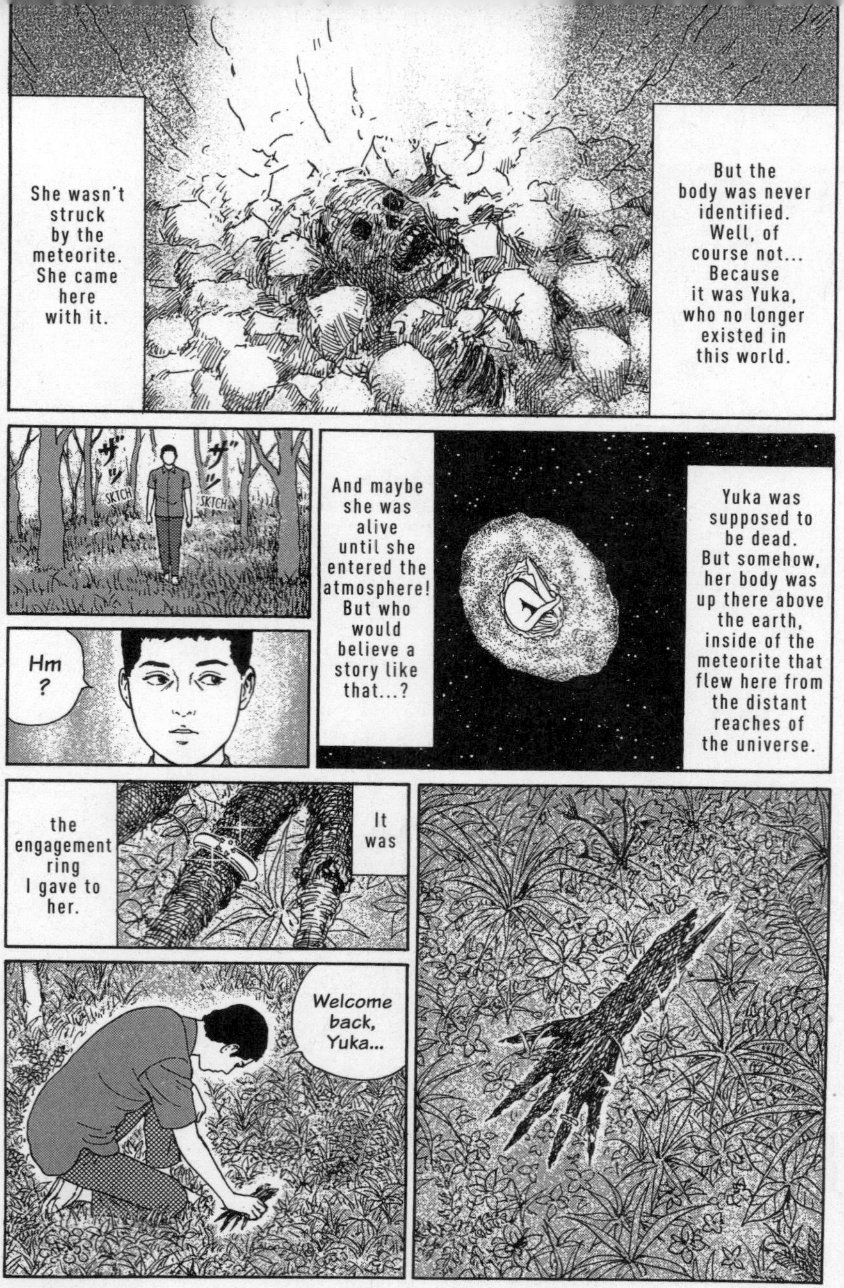
But the body was never identified. Well, of course not... Because it was Yuka, who no longer existed in this world.
She wasn't struck by the meteorite. She came here with it.
Yuka was supposed to be dead. But somehow, her body was up there above the earth, inside of the meteorite that flew here from the distant reaches of the universe.
And maybe she was alive until she entered the atmosphere! But who would believe a story like that...?
SKTCH
SKTCH
Hm ?
It was
the engagement ring I gave to her.
Welcome back, Yuka...

The Return: The End

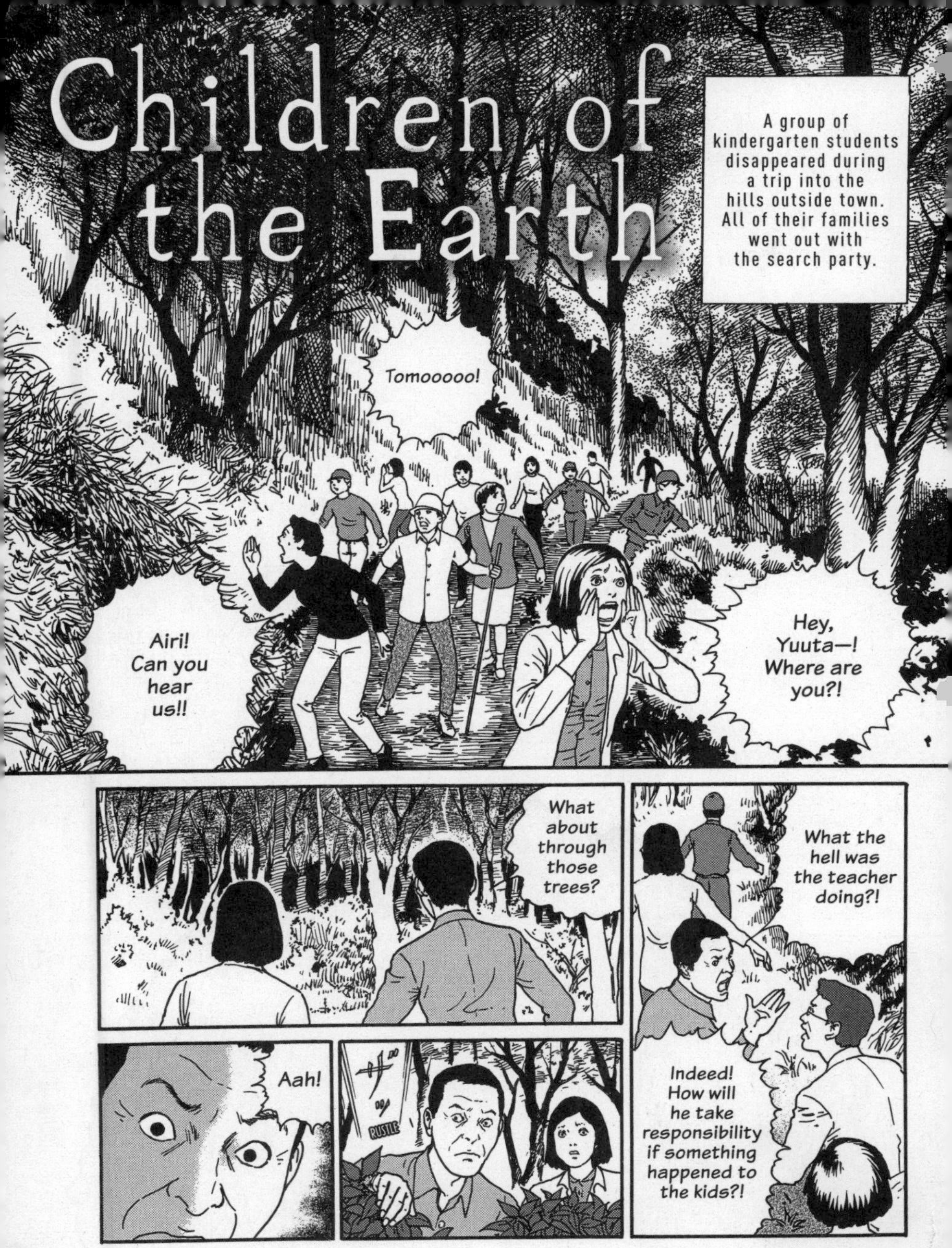
A group of kindergarten students disappeared during a trip into the hills outside town. All of their families went out with the search party.
Children of the Earth
Tomoooooo!
Hey, Yuuta—! Where are you?!
Airi! Can you hear us!!
What the hell was the teacher doing?!
Indeed! How will he take responsibility if something happened to the kids?!
What about through those trees?
RUSTLE
Aah!

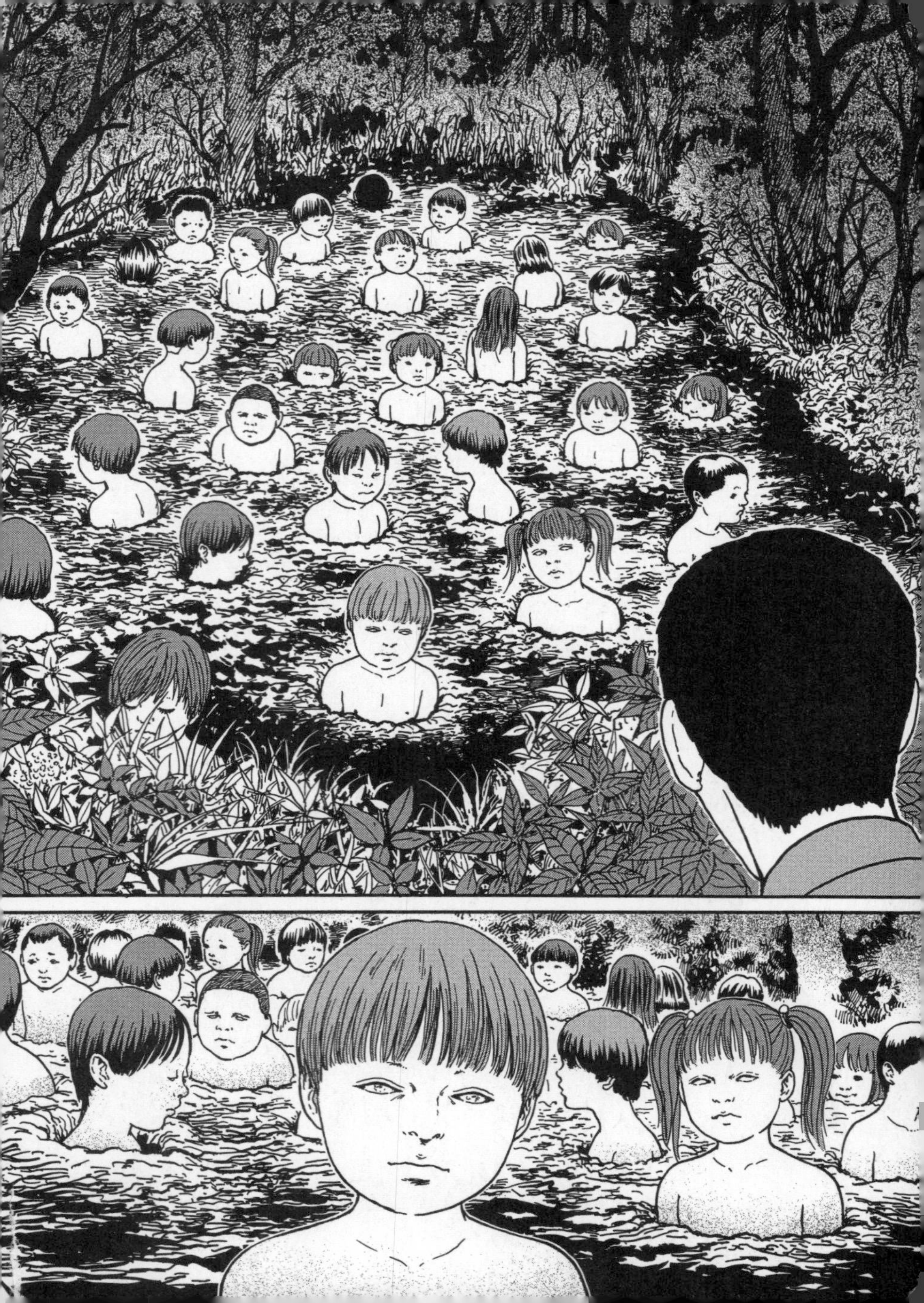

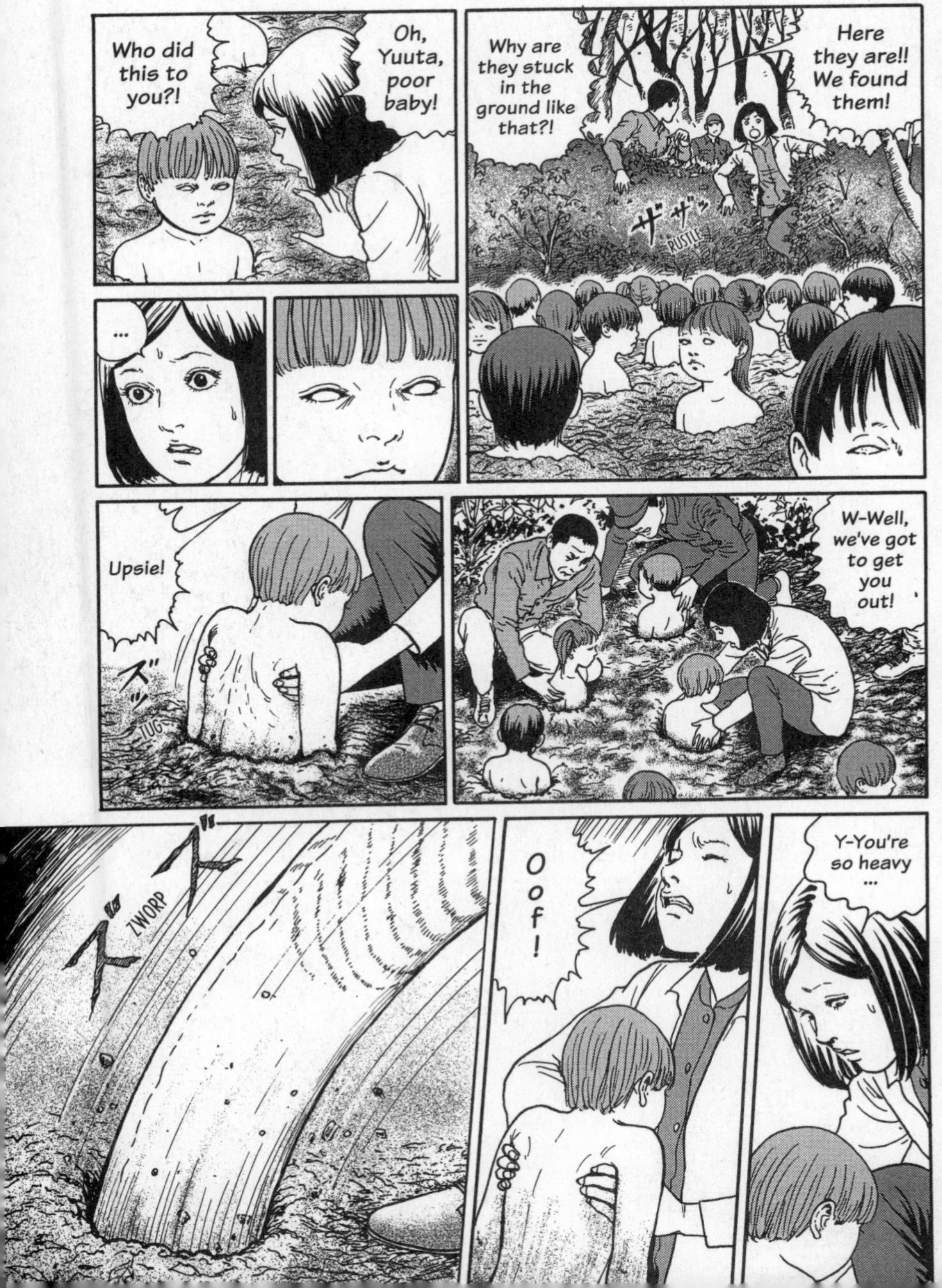
Here they are!! We found them!
Why are they stuck in the ground like that?!
ザザッ
RUSTLE
Oh, Yuuta, poor baby!
Who did this to you?!
...
W-Well, we've got to get you out!
Upsie!
ズッ
TUG
Y-You're so heavy ...
Oof!
ZWORP

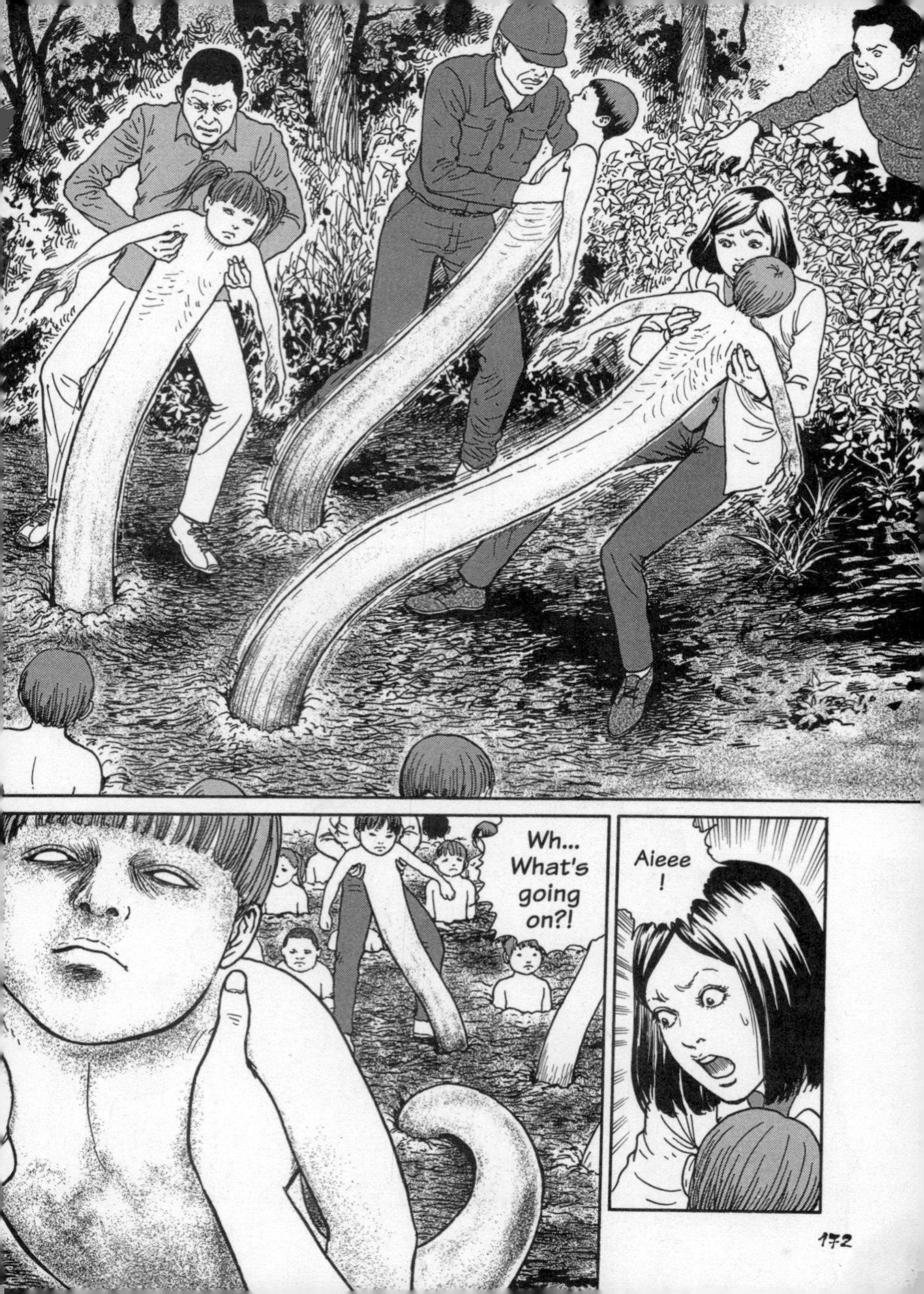
Aieee!
Wh... What's going on?!

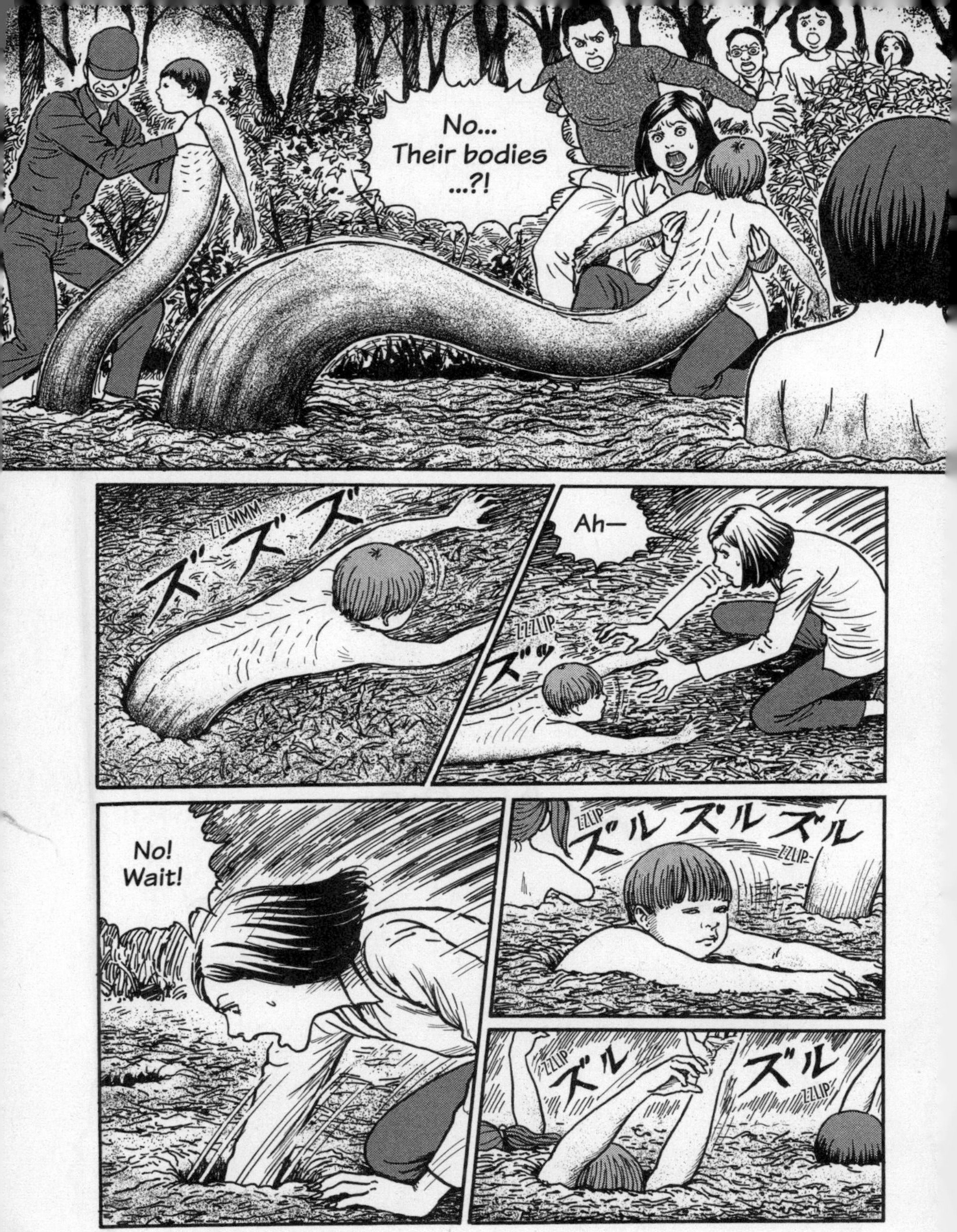
No... Their bodies ...?!
Ah—
ZZLIP
ズッ
ZZMMM
ズズズ
ZZLIP
ズルズルズル
ZZLIP
ZZLIP
ズル
ズル
ZZLIP
No! Wait!

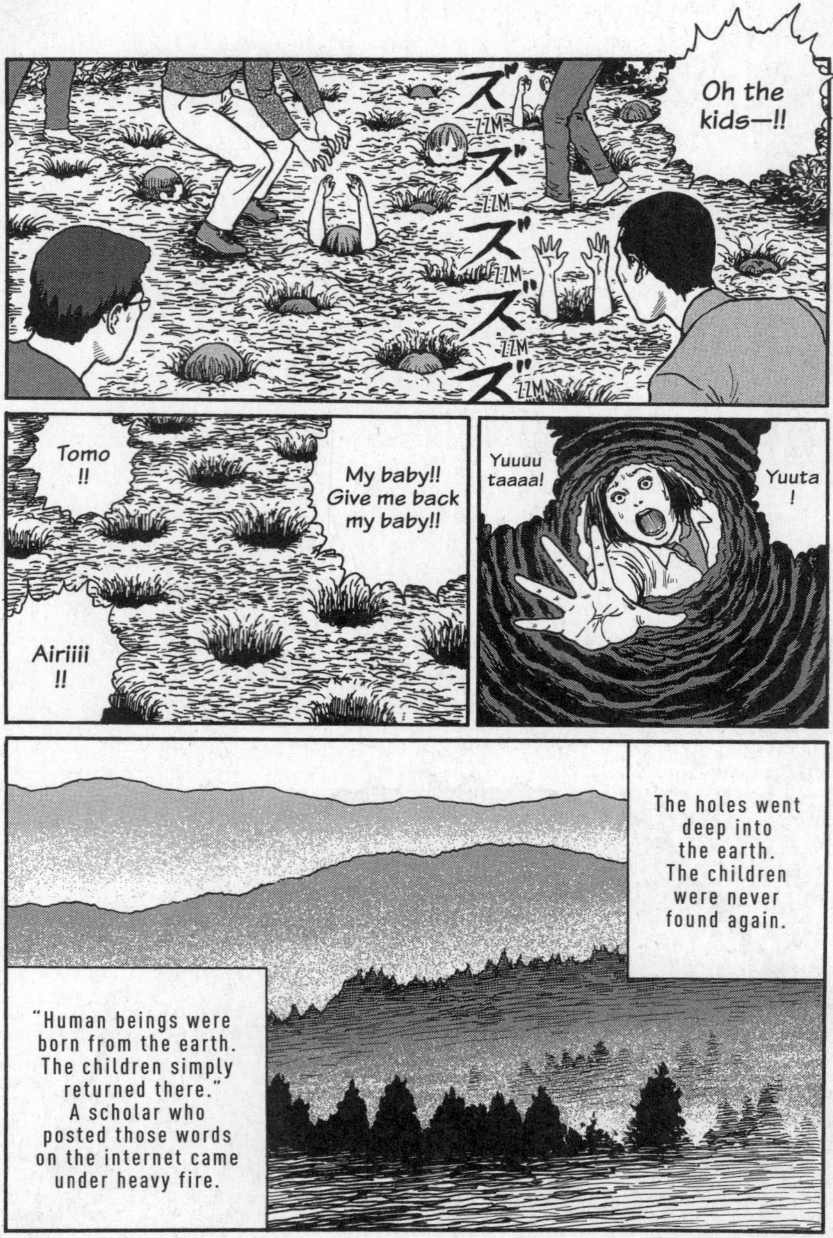
Oh the kids—!!
ズZZM
ズZZM
ズZZM
ズZZM
ズZZM
Yuuta !
Yuuuu taaaa!
My baby!! Give me back my baby!!
Tomo !!
Airiiii !!
The holes went deep into the earth. The children were never found again.
"Human beings were born from the earth. The children simply returned there." A scholar who posted those words on the internet came under heavy fire.

Children of the Earth: The End

Dissolving Classroom

The End

Afterword

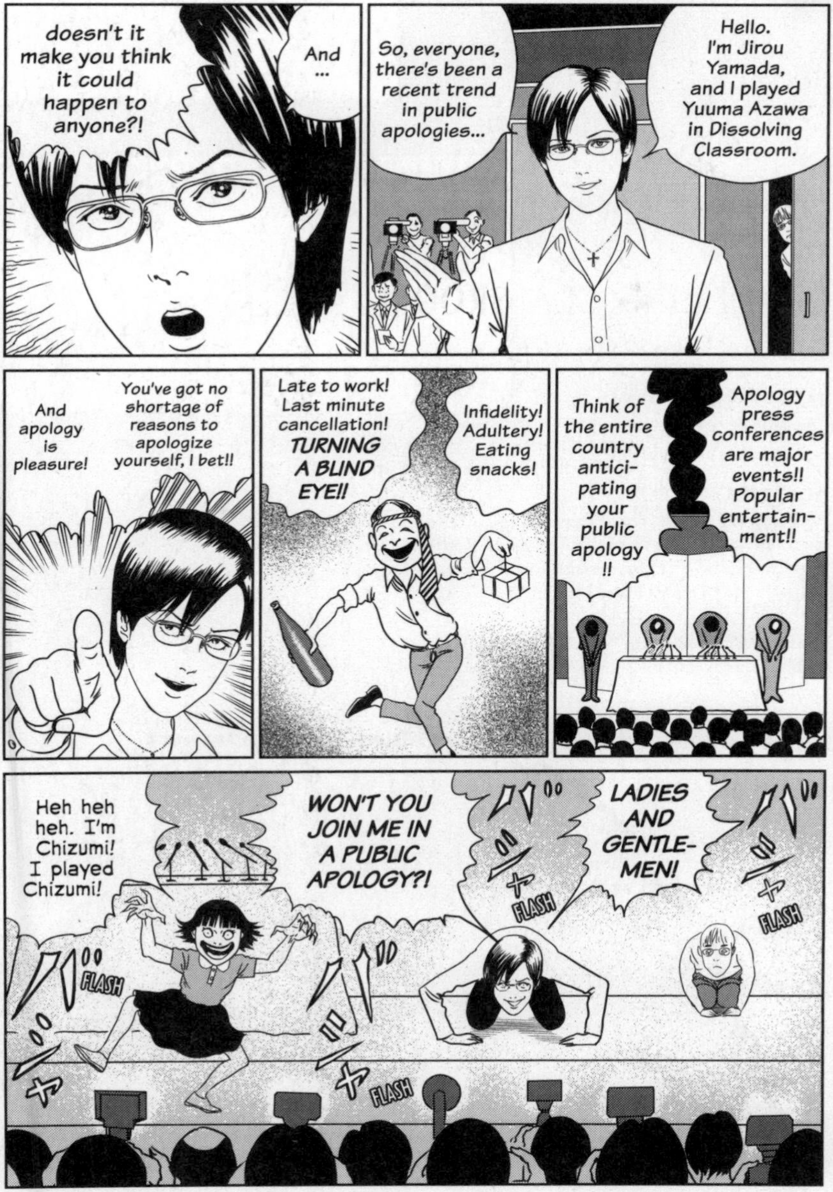
Hello. I'm Jirou Yamada, and I played Yuuma Azawa in Dissolving Classroom.
So, everyone, there's been a recent trend in public apologies...
And ...
doesn't it make you think it could happen to anyone?!
Apology press conferences are major events!! Popular entertain-ment!!
Think of the entire country antici-pating your public apology !!
Infidelity! Adultery! Eating snacks!
Late to work! Last minute cancellation! TURNING A BLIND EYE!!
You've got no shortage of reasons to apologize yourself, I bet!!
And apology is pleasure!
LADIES AND GENTLE-MEN!
FLASH
FLASH
WON'T YOU JOIN ME IN A PUBLIC APOLOGY?!
Heh heh heh. I'm Chizumi! I played Chizumi!
FLASH
FLASH

DISSOLVING CLAS

A Vertical Comics Edition

Translation: Melissa Tanaka
Production: Risa Cho
         Tomoe Tsutsumi

YOKAI KYOSHITSU
© 2015 Junji Ito. All rights reserved.
First published in Japan in 2015 by Akita Publishing Co., Ltd., Tokyo
English translation rights arranged with Akita Publishing Co., Ltd.
through TUTTLE-MORI AGENCY, INC., Tokyo.

Translation provided by Vertical Comics, 2017
Published by Vertical Comics, an imprint of Vertical, Inc., New York

Originally published in Japanese as *Yokai Kyoshitsu* by Akita Publishing Co., Ltd., 2015
Yokai Kyoshitsu first serialized in *motto!*, Akita Publishing Co., Ltd., 2013-2014

This is a work of fiction.

ISBN: 978-1-942993-85-8

Manufactured in the United States of America

First Edition

Second Printing

Vertical, Inc.
451 Park Avenue South
7th Floor
New York, NY 10016
www.vertical-comics.com

Vertical books are distributed through Penguin-Random House Publisher Services.